HOUGHTON MIFFLIN

Boston • Atlanta • Dallas • Geneva, Illinois • Princeton, New Jersey • Palo Alto

Authors

Kindergarten

Patsy F. Kanter
Consultant, Teacher, Author
Isidore Newman School
New Orleans, Louisiana

Janet G. Gillespie
Title 1 Specialist, Author
Woodlawn Elementary School
Portland, Oregon

Levels 1–6

Laurie A. Boswell
Profile Jr./Sr. High School
Bethlehem, New Hampshire

Mary Esther Reynosa
Elementary Mathematics Curriculum Specialist
Edgewood School District
San Antonio, Texas

Dr. Juanita Copley
Associate Professor of Education
University of Houston
Houston, Texas

Dr. Jean M. Shaw
Professor of Elementary Education
University of Mississippi
University, Mississippi

Audrey L. Jackson
Assistant Principal
Parkway School District
St. Louis County, Missouri

Dr. Lee Stiff
Associate Professor of Mathematics Education
North Carolina State University
Raleigh, North Carolina

Edward Manfre
Mathematics Education Consultant
Albuquerque, New Mexico

Dr. Charles Thompson
Professor of Mathematics Education
University of Louisville
Louisville, Kentucky

Consultants and Contributing Authors

Carole Basile
University of Houston
Houston, Texas

Cindy Chapman
Inez Science and Technology
Magnet School
Albuquerque, New Mexico

Dr. Deborah Ann Chessin
University of Mississippi
University, Mississippi

Dr. Richard Evans
Plymouth State College
Plymouth, New Hampshire

Dr. Robert Gyles
Community School District 4
New York, New York

Dr. Karen Karp
University of Louisville
Louisville, Kentucky

Casilda Pardo
Armijo Elementary School
Albuquerque, New Mexico

Caitlin Robinson
Mitchell Elementary School
Albuquerque, New Mexico

Acknowledgments See page 497.

Printed in the U.S.A.

ISBN: 0-395-84741-9

23456789-VH-03 02 01 00 99 98 97

Contents

CHAPTER 3 · Addition and Subtraction

page 84

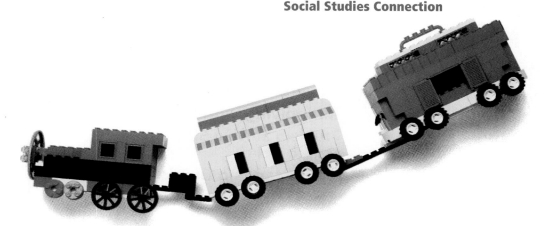

CHAPTER 6 — Multiplication and Division to 9

page 190

CHAPTER 7 — Geometry

page 226

8 Fractions

CHAPTER 9 Measurement and Time

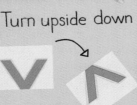

Turn upside down

V ^ X

5   10

x

CHAPTER
10

Decimals

page 346

Multiplying by 1-Digit Numbers

page 378

$7 \times 0 = 0$

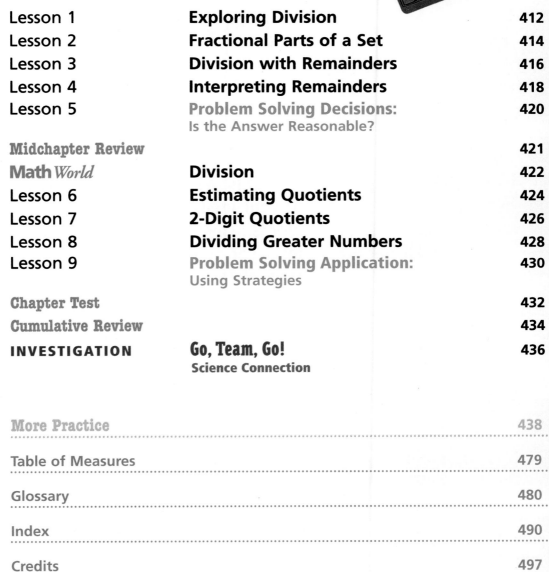

Use What You Know

2
+ 7
9

8
- 4
4

• how to add and subtract

20 21 22 23

• how to use number lines

Vocabulary
• plus +
• minus −
• greater than >
• less than <

• the words and symbols

Addition and Subtraction

Try This!

What is math all about? Show some of your ideas with a picture and words. Think about what you learned last year. You may use ideas about time, shapes, counting, or any other math you remember.

What You'll Need

crayons, pencil, paper

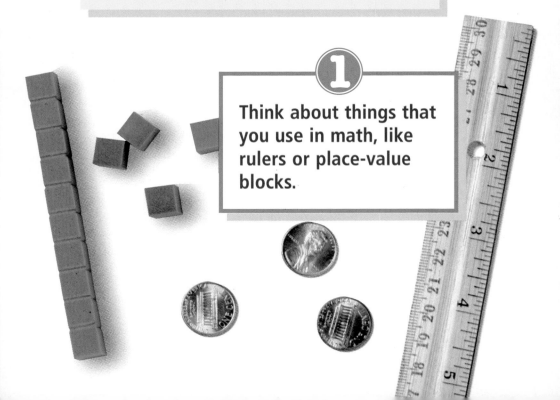

1

Think about things that you use in math, like rulers or place-value blocks.

2

Draw a picture of yourself doing math. Use "thought bubbles" to tell what you are working on.

 3

Write some ideas about what you might do in math this year on your drawing.

How did you decide what to put in your picture?

What one idea would you like to learn more about? Why?

Ready to Go!

LESSON 1

Using Numbers in Your Classroom

Cooperative Learning Checklist
☐ Work alone.
☑ Work with a partner.
☑ Work with a group.

Getting Started

What You'll Need:
► recording sheet

You do not have to go far away to hunt for numbers. Look around! You may be surprised by how many numbers you can find in your classroom.

Activity

1

Find numbers in your classroom. Record the numbers on your recording sheet.

2

Tell where you found them and how they are used. Share your findings with your classmates.

Look at the clock in the picture.

1. What time does it show?

2. Is it morning or night in the picture? How do you know?

Estimation Look at the book sale sign.

3. Suppose you want to buy 3 books. Will you need more than 2 quarters? Explain your answer.

4. Suppose your friend has $1.00. Will she be able to buy 2 books for herself and 1 book for you? Explain your answer.

 Copy the chart. Decide what the numbers mean. Fill in the third column.

Where to Find Numbers		
Numbers We Found	**Where We Found Them**	**What They Mean**
1 to 6	number cube	5. ?
1 to 12	clock	6. ?
1 to 31	calendar	7. ?

Estimation Look at the bookcase.

8. Are there fewer than 10 books? How can you tell if your answer is reasonable?

9. If 2 students each bought 2 books, are there any books left on the shelf? Explain your answer.

10. **Create Your Own** Write a question using a number from the classroom picture.

Counting and Ordering

Suppose you are waiting in line for a cable car ride. The cars are numbered in counting order. You will ride in car 36. Will your car come before or after the car numbered 37?

Here's A Way!   Use a number line.

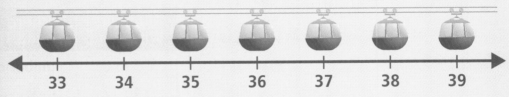

33   34   35   36   37   38   39

1 Look at the number line. Number 36 comes before 37.

So, you are in the car ahead of car 37.

2 Use the number line to find the number that comes between 34 and 36.

Number 35 comes between 34 and 36.

Talk About It!

- What happens to the numbers as you move from left to right on the number line?

- What happens to the numbers as you move from right to left on the number line?

Other Examples How is the number line above different from the number line on the right? How are the two number lines alike?

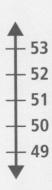

53
52
51
50
49

Show What You Know!

Write the missing numbers.

1.
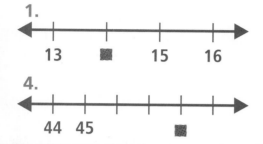
13 ▪ 15 16

2.

22 23 ▪ 25

3.
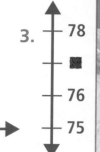
78
▪
76
75

4.

44 45 ▪

5.

▪ 58 59

Work It Out!

Write the missing number.

6.

80 81 ▪

7.

19 20 ▪

8.

▪ 33 34

9.
▪ 98 99

Write the missing numbers.

10. 18, 19, 20, ▪, ▪   11. 28, 29, ▪, 31   12. ▪, 10, 11, 12

13. 49, ▪, 51, 52   14. ▪, 79, 80, ▪, 82   15. ▪, ▪, 88, 89, 90

16. **Estimation** What number is shown by the gray box: 47, 53, or 55?
46   ▪   56

Mental Math Write the number that is 1 more. Then write the number that is 1 less.

17. 19   18. 700   19. 568   20. 23   21. 943   22. 37

23. 75   24. 99   25. 44   26. 201   27. 550   28. 29

29. **Number Sense** There are 25 students in the school cafeteria line. You are 11th. How many people are behind you? How many people are ahead of you? Explain.

More Practice Set 1.2, p. 438

Problem Solving
Act It Out

What You'll Need:
► paper squares
► scissors
► cubes or counters
► play money

What shapes do you see in this Native American bag? You can make another shape by cutting 2 corners off a square. How many sides does the new shape have?

Sometimes acting out or modeling a problem helps you to solve it.

Here's A Way! Use Act It Out to solve the problem.

1 Understand

- You can cut up a paper square to solve the problem.

2 Plan

- Decide which 2 corners to cut off from a paper square.

3 Try It

- Cut or tear off 2 corners from the paper square.

- Count the number of sides and record your answer.

4 Look Back

- The new shape has 6 sides. How did acting out the problem help you to solve it?

Show What You Know!

Use Act It Out to solve the problem.

1. You and 2 friends have 11 counters. One friend takes 4 counters. The other friend takes 5 counters. You take the rest. Who has the most?

2. **Critical Thinking** For problem 1, suppose you and 2 friends have 110 counters. One friend takes 40 counters. The other friend takes 50 counters. How would you solve the problem?

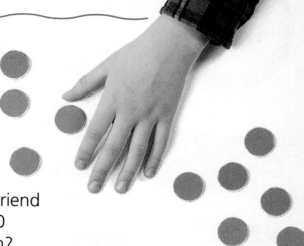

Work It Out!

Use Act It Out or any strategy to solve these problems.

3. You and your older brother are in line at the bakery. You take a ticket with the number 67 on it. Number 53 is being waited on. How many more people will be waited on before it is your turn?

4. Write the next two numbers in the pattern. Describe the pattern.

   a. 1, 3, 5, 7, ■, ■   b. 3, 6, 9, 12, ■, ■

5. Look at this triangle. How can you put four of these triangles together to make a square?

6. You have three coins that total 30 cents. What are the coins? Is there more than one answer?

7. You get to throw the bean bag three times. You win if the total is an odd number greater than 10. Show at least three ways you can win.

Share Your Thinking

8. Which problems did you solve by using Act It Out? How are those problems alike?

9. Explain how a different strategy could have been used to solve one of the problems.

Cooperative Learning
Checklist
☐ Work alone.
☑ Work with a partner.
☑ Work with a group.

Properties of Addition

What You'll Need:
▶ two colors of connecting cubes
▶ calculator
▶ recording sheet

Vocabulary:
addend
order property
zero property
Glossary p. 480

A pattern of steps makes a dance. A pattern of notes makes a song. There are patterns in addition, too. Here are two patterns and properties of addition that may help you add more quickly and easily.

Activity

Use What You Know

four plus three equals seven

$4 + 3 = 7$

In the number sentence, 4 and 3 are addends, 7 is the sum.

Order Property

1 Use cubes in two different colors to model the sum $6 + 3$. Write a number sentence.
$6 + 3 = $ ▦

2 Turn the cubes around. Write a new number sentence.
$3 + 6 = $ ▦

3 What do you notice about the addends? What about the sums?

4 Now model these.
a. $4 + 6$ and $6 + 4$
b. $5 + 7$ and $7 + 5$

An *addend* is a number that is added to another number. Changing the order of the addends does not change the sum. This is the *order property* of addition.

5 Use cubes to model. Complete the number sentences.

$0 + 5 = \blacksquare$ $9 + 0 = \blacksquare$

6 Draw your models. What do you notice about the sums?

7 Now try these.

$7 + 0$ and $5 + 0$

If you add zero to a number, the sum equals that number. This is the zero property of addition.

Show What You Know!

Mental Math Try these problems. Use mental math. Be ready to tell what property helps you know your answer is reasonable.

1. $3 + 8$	2. $7 + 0$	3. $9 + 5$	4. $0 + 13$	5. $6 + 5$
$8 + 3$	$0 + 6$	$5 + 9$	$4 + 0$	$5 + 6$

 Solve. Use a calculator if necessary.

6. $58 + 0$	7. $23 + 72$	8. $8 + 99$	9. $77 + 35$	10. $41 + 54$
$0 + 58$	$72 + 23$	$99 + 8$	$35 + 77$	$54 + 41$

11. **Critical Thinking** Look at the sums in exercises 6 - 9. Does the size of the addends change how the addition properties work? Explain.

12. How can the properties you learned help you add?

13. **Create Your Own** Use your recording sheet to make up rules for a game to play with a friend. Use addition and the properties you have learned in this game.

Patterns Find a pattern. Write the next problem.

14. $3 + 1 = \blacksquare$
$4 + 1 = \blacksquare$
$5 + 1 = \blacksquare$
$\blacksquare + \blacksquare = \blacksquare$

15. $2 + 5 = \blacksquare$
$3 + 5 = \blacksquare$
$4 + 5 = \blacksquare$
$\blacksquare + \blacksquare = \blacksquare$

16. $4 + 6 = \blacksquare$
$5 + 6 = \blacksquare$
$6 + 6 = \blacksquare$
$\blacksquare + \blacksquare = \blacksquare$

Using Doubles to Add

Nature shows us many doubles, or pairs. How many pairs can you find on these bugs?

African beetle

spider

ladybug

You can use doubles to help you add.

Here's A Way! **Find 5 + 6.**

Use doubles facts to find 5 + 6.

1 5 + 5 = 10

So, 5 + 6 is 1 more.

2 6 + 6 = 12

So, 5 + 6 is 1 less.

3 Both ways show that 5 + 6 = 11.

Talk About It!

Why do you need to subtract 1 from the sum of 6 and 6?

Write a double that helps. Then solve.

1. $8 + 9$
2. $8 + 7$
3. $6 + 7$
4. $5 + 4$
5. $6 + 5$
6. $10 + 9$

Find the sum.

7. $8 + 8$
8. $7 + 6$
9. $5 + 4$
10. $6 + 6$
11. $5 + 6$
12. $9 + 7$

13. $9 + 8$
14. $9 + 9$
15. $6 + 8$
16. $3 + 4$
17. $5 + 9$
18. $10 + 4$

Algebraic Reasoning Find the missing signs. Use < or >.

19. $11 + 10 \blacksquare 10 + 10$

20. $9 + 8 \blacksquare 9 + 9$

21. $8 + 7 \blacksquare 8 + 8$

22. $12 + 13 \blacksquare 12 + 12$

23. **Critical Thinking** What other sums can you find because you know $5 + 5$ and $6 + 6$?

Use a double to find the sum.

24. $9 + 9 = 18$
$8 + 9 = \blacksquare$

25. $10 + 10 = 20$
$10 + 9 = \blacksquare$

26. $14 + 14 = 28$
$14 + 15 = \blacksquare$

27. $6 + 6 = 12$
$7 + 6 = \blacksquare$

28. $4 + 4$
29. $7 + 8$
30. $3 + 4$
31. $5 + 4$
32. $5 + 6$

Write the missing number.

33. $4 + 3 = 6 + \blacksquare$

34. $8 + 9 = 7 + \blacksquare$

35. $5 + 6 = 3 + \blacksquare$

Problem Solving

36. There are 10 beetles in one sand pile on the beach and the same number of beetles in another. One beetle leaves. How many beetles are left?

37. There are 10 crickets in the shed and 1 more than that outside the shed. How many are there in all?

cricket

More Practice Set 1.5, p. 438

LESSON 6

Problem Solving
Is There Enough Information?

New Pretty Village.

Suppose this is 1900. A Pretty Village toy set costs only 50 cents. You have five coins. Do you have enough money to buy the set?

You Decide

- Can 5 coins make 50 cents or more? Explain.
- Can 5 coins make less than 50 cents? Explain.
- Do you have enough information to solve the problem? Explain.

Work It Out!

Read the problem. Is there enough information? If so, solve it and show your work. If not, tell what else you need to know.

1. Your game starts at 5:00. If you leave your house at 4:00, will you arrive before the game starts?

2. You have more pencils than your friend has. You give away some pencils. Now who has more pencils?

"Pacing Bob," 19 Cents.
Same as above, except one horse, and two-wheel instead of four-wheel wagon. Size, 13½ inches long, 6½ inches high. Shipping weight, 20 ounces. No. 49K1067 Price............19c

3. You have some dimes. Do you have enough money to buy the Pacing Bob horse? Will you get change?

4. You have some nickels. Do you have enough money to buy a toy for 29 cents? Will you get change?

5. **Create Your Own** Write a problem that does not have enough information. See if a friend can solve it.

Share Your Thinking

6. How can you tell if a problem has enough information? Too much information?

Midchapter Review

for Pages 1-12

Solve. Show your work. (page 6)

Problem Solving

1. Suppose you are making 3 sandwiches. You have 6 slices of bread, 3 pieces of cheese, and 9 pickle slices. How can you make all the sandwiches the same?

2. Your class is planting tulips. You plan to have 3 rows of 6 tulips. In each row, you want 2 purple tulips after each white tulip. How many of each color do you need?

Concepts

Write the number that belongs in the box. (page 4)

3.
   47 ■ 49 50

4. ■, ■, 61, 62, 63

5. 91 92 ■ 94

6.
   0 ■ ■ 6

7.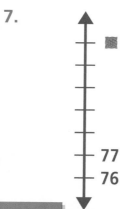
   ■
   77
   76

8.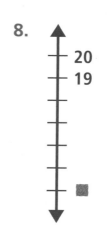
   20
   19
   ■

Skills

Find the sum. (page 10)

9. 3 + 3   10. 2 + 1   11. 7 + 6   12. 4 + 5   13. 3 + 4

14. 9 + 9   15. 5 + 6   16. 9 + 10   17. 8 + 7   18. 6 + 6

Math World

Throughout history, different groups of people have counted and written numbers in different ways.

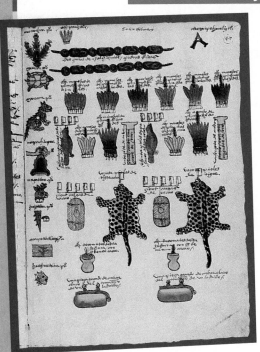

An Aztec Puzzle

The way we write numbers comes from India and is about 1500 years old. About 800 years ago, the Aztecs of Mexico used picture symbols to write numbers. This diagram shows some of the Aztec numbers. Can you find them?

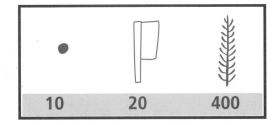

| 10 | 20 | 400 |

Ten by Any Other Name

The original language of the Fiji Islanders has no word for 10. But it does have a word for 10 boats, *bola* (boh LAH). In English, there are also words that mean "many" without telling a number. What does the word *team* mean? Can you think of other words for groups?

Try This!

The Fulani (ful LAH nee) people of western Africa are known for their singing and storytelling. Their language is called Fulfulde (ful FULD). Learn how Fulfulde number words are made.

1   Look at the Fulfulde words for the numbers 1 through 5.

2   The Fulfulde word for 6 is made of the words for 5 and 1. The Fulani think of 6 as 5 + 1.

3   Look at the Fulfulde word for 8. What two number words is it made of? Why does this make sense?

1	go'o
2	didi
3	tati
4	nayi
5	jowi
6	jowi e go'o
7	jowi e didi
8	jowi e tati
9	jowi e nayi
10	sappo

4   The Fulani people use the number 10 to make the words for 11 through 19. How do you think they write these numbers?

sappo   e   ?

Respond

Work with a partner to make . . . your own picture symbols for the numbers 1 to 5.

Internet:
Houghton Mifflin Education Place
Explore the Math Center. at
http://www.eduplace.com

15

Using Tens to Add

Your class is making a small aquarium. You choose eight blue fish and five yellow fish. How can you find how many fish you have in all?

You can use a ten frame and look for 10's when you add.

Use What You Know

You can use a ten frame and counters to show names for 10, such as 9 + 1 and 7 + 3.

9 + 1

7 + 3

Here's A Way! Find 8 + 5.

❶ Draw a ten frame. Use counters to show the first addend on the ten frame.

8 + 5

❷ Use counters of another color to show the second addend. Make a 10. Count on with the leftover counters.

8 + 2 + 3

❸ Write the sum.

Talk About It! How did names for 10 help you find the sum?

Find the missing number. You may use counters or make a drawing.

1. 9 + 5 = 10 + ■   2. 6 + 8 = 10 + ■   3. 9 + 3 = 10 + ■

Find the sum. Use mental math when you can.

4. 6 + 8   5. 9 + 7   6. 4 + 9   7. 8 + 7   8. 6 + 5

9. **Critical Thinking** How does knowing 8 + 2 = 10 help you find 8 + 6?

Work It Out!

Find the missing number. You may use counters or make a drawing.

10. 8 + 3 = 10 + ■   11. 9 + 6 = 10 + ■   12. 4 + 8 = 10 + ■

Write the sum.

13. 8
    + 3

14. 9
    + 9

15. 9
    + 8

16. 7
    + 8

17. 8
    + 4

18. 9 + 5   19. 8 + 6   20. 7 + 5   21. 9 + 3   22. 15 + 7

Problem Solving Using Data

Use the chart to answer the question.

23. How many yellow tangs and angelfish do you see?

24. If yellow tangs and tomato clownfish are the only fish swimming in the tank, how many fish are in that tank?

Tropical Fish at the Aquarium

Types of Fish	Yellow Tang	Emperor Angelfish	Tomato Clownfish	Spot-Tail Butterfly Fish
Number Seen	6	5	10	3

More Practice Set 1.7, p. 439

Three or More Addends

Vocabulary:
grouping
property
Glossary p. 480

At a party you break a piñata and win some favors. You have 7 stickers, 5 balloons, and 2 whistles. How many favors do you have in all? You need to add three numbers to find the answer.

Here's A Way!   Find 7 + 5 + 2.

You can add three numbers in different ways.

1 Add 7 and 5. Then add 2.

$$
\begin{array}{r}
7 \\
5 \\
+\ 2 \\
\hline
14
\end{array}
$$
$7 + 5 = 12$

2 Add 5 and 2. Then add 7.

$$
\begin{array}{r}
7 \\
5 \\
+\ 2 \\
\hline
14
\end{array}
$$
$5 + 2 = 7$

3 Add 7 and 2. Then add 5.

$$
\begin{array}{r}
7 \\
5 \\
+\ 2 \\
\hline
14
\end{array}
$$
$7 + 2 = 9$

You have 14 party favors.

Talk About It!   Does it matter which numbers you add first? Why or why not?

Other Examples Find 6 + 4 + 6.

Find a sum of 10 first.
$6 + 4 + 6 = \blacksquare$
$10 + 6 = 16$

Find a double first.
$6 + 4 + 6 = \blacksquare$
$12 + 4 = 16$

The grouping property says that no matter how you group the numbers to add, the sum is always the same.
$1 + 1 + 2 = 4$
$1 + 1 + 2 = 4$

Show What You Know!

Find the sums. Look for doubles or sums of 10.

1. 4
    6
  + 3

2. 2
    7
  + 6

3. 4
    6
    6
  + 1

4. 1
    9
    7
  + 3

5. 9
    9
  + 9

6. 3 + 3 + 9   7. 8 + 2 + 7   8. 9 + 3 + 2 + 1

9. **Number Sense** In exercise 8, which numbers did you add first? Did you use the order or the grouping property?

> **Use What You Know**
>
> The Order Property says that changing the order of the addends does not change the sum.
>
> 1 + 1 + 2 = 4
> 1 + 2 + 1 = 4

Work It Out!

Find the sums. Look for doubles and sums of 10.

10. 6
     1
   + 6

11. 3
     6
   + 2

12. 4
     4
     5
   + 5

13. 5
     4
     3
   + 1

14. 9
     5
   + 4

15. 3
     8
   + 7

16. 8 + 1 + 2   17. 1 + 8 + 8   18. 3 + 3 + 7   19. 2 + 5 + 6

Problem Solving

20. A girl got 7 games and 2 balloons from the piñata. So did her friend. How many party favors did the 2 children get?

21. A boy got 12 party favors. There were 5 balloons, 3 games, and some whistles. How many whistles did the boy get?

22. There were 4 badges, 5 horns, and 6 hats. Is that enough for 12 children to share? Explain.

23. You spent $5 on games, $2 on horns, and $1 on balls. How much change did you get from a $10.00 bill?

More Practice Set 1.8, p. 439

Math Journal

Teach some friends how to add three or more numbers. Tell them about the grouping property. What helpful hints could you give?

Counting Up or Back to Subtract

Suppose 15 students voted on whether to invite the mayor to give a speech. Eight students voted yes. How many students voted no? You can subtract to find the answer.

Here's A Way! Find 15 − 8.

Count Up

15 − 8 = ■

Count up to 10. Think 8. Count 9, 10. You counted up 2.

15 − 8 = ■

Think 10. 5 more is 15.

5 + 2 = 7
So, 15 − 8 = 7

Count Back

15 − 8 = ■

Think 10. 15 − 5 is 10.

10 − 8 = ■

Count back to 8. Count 9, 8. You counted back 2.

5 + 2 = 7
So, 15 − 8 = 7

Talk About It! How does thinking about 10 help you count up and count back?

Find the difference. Record whether you count up or count back.

1. 15
− 9

2. 16
− 8

3. 11
− 3

4. 11
− 0

5. 18
− 6

6. 20
− 1

7. 13
− 8

8. 14
− 3

9. 16
− 9

10. 15
− 2

11. 17
− 8

12. 19
− 3

Work It Out!

Find the difference.

13. 14
− 8

14. 13
− 9

15. 6
− 5

16. 12
− 7

17. 15
− 4

18. 8 − 5

19. 11 − 5

20. 10 − 8

21. 9 − 3

22. 18 − 6

23. 16 − 2

24. 6 − 3

25. 17 − 7

26. 12 − 4

27. 20 − 6

28. **Algebraic Reasoning** Copy and complete the table.

Number	3	?	?	?	7	8	9	?
Number + 4	7	8	9	10	?	?	13	14

29. **Patterns** What pattern do you see between the rows in the completed table? Explain.

Problem Solving

30. You are 9 years old. Your brother is 12 years old. How much older is your brother?

31. Suppose your class has 19 students. A boy and a girl are each running for class president. If the boy receives 8 votes, did he win the election? How do you know?

More Practice Set 1.9, p. 440

Math Journal

Which works best for you, counting up or counting back? Explain.

Missing Addends

CHICAGO

You have 6 snow globes, and your friend gives you some more. Now, you have 10 snow globes. How many snow globes did your friend give you? Make a part-part-whole mat to find the missing number.

Here's A Way!   Find 6 + ■ = 10.

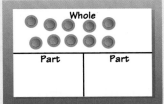

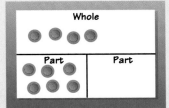

1 Place 10 counters on the whole section of the mat. This will show the total number of snow globes you now have.

2 Show the part of the whole that you began with. There were 6 snow globes to begin with. So move 6 counters to a part section.

3 Show the part of the whole that you were given by moving the rest of the counters to the other part section. How many counters are in this part?

4 Use the number you found to complete the addition sentence.

6 + 4 = 10 So, your friend gave you 4 snow globes.

Talk About It!

Explain how the counters on the mat in Step 3 show 6 + 4.

Show What You Know!

Use a mat to help solve each problem. Write a number sentence
to show your solution.

1. You have 15 pencils. Some of them are yellow. The other 8 are green. How many of your pencils are yellow?

2. By noon your friend's class has made 8 model snakes. At the end of the day, they have made 17 snakes. How many did they make in the afternoon?

Work It Out!

Copy and complete.

3.
$$\begin{array}{r} 6 \\ + \blacksquare \\ \hline 11 \end{array}$$

4.
$$\begin{array}{r} 9 \\ + \blacksquare \\ \hline 14 \end{array}$$

5.
$$\begin{array}{r} \blacksquare \\ + 9 \\ \hline 13 \end{array}$$

6.
$$\begin{array}{r} \blacksquare \\ + 5 \\ \hline 7 \end{array}$$

7.
$$\begin{array}{r} 7 \\ + \blacksquare \\ \hline 13 \end{array}$$

8. $12 = \blacksquare + 9$

9. $\blacksquare + 10 = 17$

10. $15 = 6 + \blacksquare$

11. $13 = 7 + \blacksquare$

12. $5 + \blacksquare = 9$

13. $\blacksquare + 8 = 11$

14. $8 + \blacksquare = 15$

15. $10 = 4 + \blacksquare$

16. $\blacksquare + 3 = 5$

17. **Critical Thinking** Tell how you used addition facts to find the missing numbers.

Mixed Review

Add or subtract.

18. $2 + 3$

19. $4 - 2$

20. $1 + 5$

21. $7 - 4$

22. $6 + 4$

23. $2 + 6$

24. $9 + 1$

25. $10 - 2$

More Practice Set 1.10, p. 440

Problem Solving
Using Act It Out and Other Strategies

LESSON **11**

Getting Started

What You'll Need:
▶ colored cubes

Problem Solving Process
✓ Understand
✓ Plan
✓ Try It
✓ Look Back

Choose a Strategy You Have Learned
✓ Act It Out
  Look for a Pattern
  Guess and Check
  Draw a Picture
  Make a Table
  Work Backward
  Make a List
  Work a Simpler Problem

At an Olympic Pin Trading Center, a trader shows his pins in an interesting design. He decides to change the design.

The trader's pins make a triangle pointing down. He wants to move only two pins. Can he form a triangle pointing up?

• What design are the pins in now?

• What design is he trying to make?

• How many pins can he move?

• Explain a strategy the trader can use to solve the problem. Then solve it.

Work It Out!

Use any strategy to solve the problem. Show your work.

1. Suppose you have 12 Olympic pins. You give half of them to a friend. If you get 2 more, how many will you have?

2. You have 1 more Olympic pin than your classmate has. If you give her 1 of yours, who will have more? How do you know?

3. How could you cut this rectangular sign so it has 6 sides instead of 4? Is there more than one way? Would your answer change if the sign were a square?

4. You and 2 friends have 17 pins. You give 3 of your pins to one friend. She gives 3 pins to the other friend, and he gives 3 pins back to you. How many pins do you and your 2 friends have now?

5. You have 9 pins. You trade 1 pin for 2 pins. If you then trade 3 pins for 1 pin, how many pins will you have?

6. Suppose your friend has 12 trading cards. You have 4 more than she has. How many of your cards can you give to her so that you both have the same number?

7. Your classmate has 1 more trading card than you. Suppose she gives you 1 of her cards. Will you have the same number? Explain.

Share Your Thinking

8. Which problems did you solve by using Act It Out? What objects did you use for models?

9. How did you solve problem 7?

Using Subtraction

You have a collection of 12 marbles. There are 5 large marbles. How many small marbles do you have? How many more small marbles do you have than large ones?

Here's A Way! Subtract.

Separate
How many small marbles are there?

> Separate the part you know from the whole to find the part you do not know.

$$12 - 5 = \blacksquare$$

There are 7 small marbles.

Compare
How many more small marbles than large are there?

> Find out how much more one amount is than another.

$$7 - 5 = \blacksquare$$

There are 2 more small marbles than large ones.

Talk About It!

In the comparing section, how did lining up the marbles help you find the difference?

Use subtraction to solve these problems. Write a number sentence. Share your thinking.

1. You had 13 marbles. You lost 9. How many marbles do you have left?

2. Five of your friends want jacks. There are only 4 jacks. How many more jacks are needed so everyone has one?

3. You saw 4 children on the slide and 2 on the swings. How many more children were on the slides than on the swings?

4. **Critical Thinking** How is finding a missing addend like subtracting? Hint: Think about the whole and parts.

Work It Out!

Find the differences.

5. 11 − 4	6. 15 − 6	7. 12 − 2	8. 17 − 1	9. 10 − 7
10. 14 − 5	11. 19 − 3	12. 18 − 9	13. 13 − 3	14. 17 − 8
15. 10 − 3	16. 12 − 7	17. 14 − 7	18. 15 − 8	19. 10 − 2
20. 6 − 4	21. 7 − 6	22. 12 − 3	23. 8 − 5	24. 9 − 6

Problem Solving

25. Your teacher made 14 snacks for the class. There were 8 left. How many snacks did the students eat?

26. There are 13 friends coming to your party. So far, 7 friends have arrived. How many more friends are to come?

27. You brought 20 pieces of melon to a picnic. After the picnic, no pieces were left. How many pieces were eaten?

28. You bought a soccer ball for $8 and a basketball for $9. Do you know how much money you have left? Explain.

More Practice Set 1.12, p. 441

LESSON 13

Adding and Subtracting 9

Your class is having a plant sale. You sold 5 plants on Monday. Later, you sold 9 more. How can you keep track of how many plants have been bought and sold?

Here's A Way! Add and subtract with 9.

Add

How many plants did you sell altogether?

1 When one addend is 9, you can use 10 to help you add.

$$5 + 9$$
$$5 + 10 = 15$$

2 Since 10 is 1 more than 9, you added 1 too many. Subtract 1 from the sum.

$$15 - 1 = 14$$
You sold 14 plants.

Subtract

If you began with 15 plants and sold 9, how many would you have left to sell?

1 When you are subtracting 9, use 10 to help you subtract.

$$15 - 9$$
$$15 - 10 = 5$$

2 Since 10 is 1 more than 9, you subtracted 1 too many. Add 1 to the sum.

$$5 + 1 = 6$$
You have 6 plants left.

Talk About It! Compare adding with 9 to subtracting with 9.

Show What You Know!

Use 10 to add or subtract 9.

1. 9
+ 4

2. 16
− 9

3. 7
+ 9

4. 14
− 9

5. 17
− 9

6. 23
− 9

7. 5 + 9 8. 8 + 9 9. 9 + 6 10. 13 − 9 11. 8 + 9

Work It Out!

Mental Math Find the answer. Use mental math when you can.

12. 12
− 9

13. 9
+ 7

14. 9
+ 9

15. 10
+ 10

16. 15
− 9

17. 5 + 9 18. 19 − 9 19. 2 + 9 20. 13 − 9 21. 16 + 9

Algebraic Reasoning Copy and complete the number sentence.

22. 17 − ■ = 9   23. ■ + 9 = 9   24. 5 + ■ = 14

25. ■ + 9 = 14   26. 13 − ■ = 4   27. 9 + ■ = 12

28. 10 − ■ = 1   29. 18 − ■ = 9   30. 15 − ■ = 6

Problem Solving

Use the seed packet to answer the questions.

31. The Flax have grown to 9 inches. How many more inches do they need to grow to full height?

32. If the Black-Eyed Susans and the Bachelor's Buttons are full grown, which is taller? How many inches taller?

Assorted
Wildflower Seeds

Types of Flowers	Height at Full Growth
Flax	18 inches
Black-Eyed Susan	24 inches
Bachelor's Button	30 inches
Baby's Breath	40 inches

More Practice Set 1.3, p. 441

Fact Families

Getting Started

What You'll Need:
▶ number cube
▶ counters of two
different colors

Vocabulary:
fact family
Glossary p. 480

A group of facts that are related is called a **fact family**. The facts below make up a fact family.

$3 + 5 = 8$ $8 - 5 = 3$
$5 + 3 = 8$ $8 - 3 = 5$

In this activity you will find some other fact families.

Activity

1
Roll the number cube. Put that number of counters in a part section of your mat. Roll the cube again. Put that number of counters of another color in the other part section.

2
Push all of your counters onto the whole section of your mat.

3
Write two addition number sentences to start the fact family.

$6 + 7 = 13$
$7 + 6 = 13$

Start again. Put the whole number of counters into the parts, one section at a time by color. Write two subtraction sentences to complete the fact family.

Repeat the steps 5 times. Write 5 sets of number sentences.

Show What You Know!

Write the number sentence that is missing from the fact family.

1. $6 + 9 = 15$
$15 - 9 = 6$
$15 - 6 = 9$

2. $6 + 7 = 13$
$7 + 6 = 13$
$13 - 6 = 7$

3. $9 + 3 = 12$
$3 + 9 = 12$
$12 - 3 = 9$

4. $8 + 9 = 17$
$17 - 8 = 9$
$9 + 8 = 17$

Write the rest of the number sentences in the fact family.

5. $16 - 7 = 9$ 6. $7 + 5 = 12$ 7. $18 - 9 = 9$ 8. $6 + 6 = 12$

9. **Critical Thinking** Why are there only 2 number sentences for exercise 7?

Write a fact family using the numbers.

10. 12, 8, 4   11. 6, 6, 12   12. 5, 12, 7   13. 13, 9, 4

14. 5, 4, 9   15. 7, 6, 13   16. 10, 20, 10   17. 13, 8, 5

Write a fact family using the numbers given in exercises 18 and 19.

18. 6 brown chairs, 4 black chairs, 10 chairs

19. 3 cats, 5 dogs, 8 animals

20. **Create Your Own** Write two story problems using both the numbers and items that are given in exercises 18 and 19. Write one addition story and one subtraction story.

More Practice Set 1.14, p. 442

Math Journal

How can knowing a fact family help you add and subtract?

Problem Solving
Using Strategies

Read more about beavers in the pages of the *Appalachian Mountain Club Outdoors.*

Beavers build their lodges out of branches and mud. A beaver lodge is about 4 feet wide and 2 feet high. Its walls are a foot thick. Fresh air comes in through a small hole in the roof. Most beaver lodges have two underwater openings.

Problem Solving Process
✓ Understand
✓ Plan
✓ Try It
✓ Look Back

Choose a Strategy You Have Learned
✓ Act It Out
  Look for a Pattern
  Guess and Check
  Draw a Picture
  Make a Table
  Work Backward
  Make a List
  Work a Simpler Problem

Each side in this twin lodge has two openings. How many different ways can a beaver go from one side of the lodge to the other?

- What is the question you have to answer?

- Through how many different openings can a beaver leave one of the lodges?

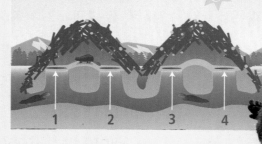

1   2   3   4

- How many openings are there in total in a twin lodge?

- How can you show one of the ways a beaver might go from one lodge to the other?

- Explain a strategy that can help you solve the problem. Then solve the problem.

Work It Out!

Use any strategy to solve the problem. Show your work.

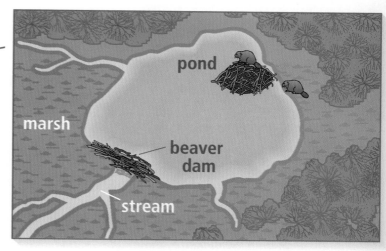

1. The beaver is going to swim to the dam. Should it swim straight across the pond or along the shore?

2. There are 4 beavers in the lodge and 2 beavers in the pond. If 1 beaver goes into the lodge, how many beavers will be in the lodge?

3. Is the beaver more than halfway done cutting down this tree? Explain.

4. The father beaver brings 3 branches to help build the lodge. The mother beaver brings 2 more than the father. How many branches do they bring in all?

5. If it takes one beaver 2 days to cut down a tree, how long will it take 2 beavers to cut down 4 trees?

6. Young beavers are called kits. There are 4 kits and 3 adult beavers in the pond. Two kits return to the lodge with an adult beaver. How many kits and adult beavers are left in the pond?

7. There are 9 kits and 4 adult beavers in the lodge. How many more kits than adults are there in the lodge?

8. **Create Your Own** Write a problem about beavers. See if a friend can solve it.

Share Your Thinking

9. How did you solve problem 6? Check with your classmates. What strategies did they use?

10. Did you use Act It Out to solve a problem? If you did, tell how the strategy helped you.

Chapter 1 Test

for Pages 1–33

Test-Taking Tips
Make notes or use models to help you find the answers.

Problem Solving

Solve. Show your work. (pages 6, 24)

1. Suppose you stack blocks in the shape of a triangle. You use 6 blocks for 3 rows. How many more blocks do you need if you want to make the triangle 6 rows in all?

2. You have 12 squares of paper, all the same size. You are arranging them to form a rectangle using all 12 squares. How many different rectangles can you make?

Concepts

Use the number line to find each missing number. (page 4)

3. What number is missing?

68 69 ▨ 71

4. What numbers are missing?

19 20 ▨ 22 ▨ 24

5. What numbers are missing?

82 83 ▨ ▨ ▨ 87

6. Which shows the lesser number, the red box or the blue box?

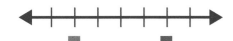

▨   ▨

Write the missing numbers. (page 4)

7. 39, 38, ▨ , ▨

8. ▨ , ▨ , 97, 98, ▨ , ▨

Find the sum. Look for doubles and sums of 10. (pages 16, 18)

9. 4 + 3 + 4   10. 2 + 6 + 8   11. 1 + 4 + 9   12. 3 + 3 + 3

13. 5 + 8 + 5   14. 7 + 6 + 6   15. 7 + 7 + 4   16. 5 + 9 + 2 + 1

Complete the number sentence. (page 22)

17. $8 + \blacksquare = 14$

18. $\blacksquare + 7 = 16$

19. $12 = 3 + \blacksquare$

20. $13 = 5 + \blacksquare$

Find the difference. (pages 20, 26)

21. $\begin{array}{r} 9 \\ -\ 6 \\ \hline \end{array}$

22. $\begin{array}{r} 17 \\ -\ 9 \\ \hline \end{array}$

23. $\begin{array}{r} 15 \\ -\ 7 \\ \hline \end{array}$

24. $\begin{array}{r} 16 \\ -\ 8 \\ \hline \end{array}$

25. $10 - 0$

26. $13 - 6$

27. $12 - 5$

28. $18 - 9$

Find the answer. (page 28)

29. $\begin{array}{r} 8 \\ +\ 5 \\ \hline \end{array}$

30. $\begin{array}{r} 14 \\ -\ 7 \\ \hline \end{array}$

31. $\begin{array}{r} 2 \\ +\ 9 \\ \hline \end{array}$

32. $\begin{array}{r} 15 \\ -\ 6 \\ \hline \end{array}$

Find the missing number. Write _a_, _b_, _c_, or _d_. (page 28)

33. $5 + \blacksquare = 11$ a. 6   b. 17   c. 5   d. 16

34. $\blacksquare + 8 = 8$ a. 16   b. 2   c. 9   d. 0

35. $16 - \blacksquare = 7$ a. 8   b. 9   c. 23   d. 22

Performance Task

(page 6, 12, 24)

You invited 14 guests to your swim party at the town pool. You want to give each guest an underwater whistle. Of course, you want one for yourself, too. You have a bag that has 7 whistles.

- How many more whistles will you need?

- Explain how you solved the problem.

- Then, write your own story problem about the pool party. Solve your new problem.

Keep In Mind . . .

Your work will be evaluated on the following:

☑ Strategy for solving

☑ New problem that uses the story

☑ Correct answers

☑ Method for checking

Cumulative Review

Properties of Addition (Chapter 1)
Use the properties of addition to find the sums: 3 + 4; 6 + 4 + 7; 8 + 0.

Here's A Way!

Order property:
4 + 3 = 3 + 4 = 7
Grouping property:
6 + 4 + 7 = 17
6 + 4 + 7 = 17
Zero property: 8 + 0 = 8

Find the sums. Name the property you used.

1. 8 + 4 = ▨   2. 5 + 6 = ▨
   4 + 8 = ▨   6 + 5 = ▨

3. 17 + 0   4.   9   5.   10
   0 + 17   4   3
                  + 2   + 5

6. How can understanding the properties of addition make it easier for you to add numbers?

Using Doubles to Add (Chapter 1)
Add 8 and 9.

Here's A Way!

   8 + 8 = 16
8 + 8 is 1 more.
So, 8 + 9 = 17.
   9 + 9 = 18
8 + 9 is 1 less.
So, 8 + 9 = 17.

Use doubles to find the sum.

7. 8 + 7   8. 6 + 5
9. 12 + 11   10. 5 + 4
11. 9 + 11   12. 9 + 8

13. How could you use subtracting 1 in any of these exercises?

Using Tens to Add (Chapter 1)
Add 6 and 7.

Here's A Way!

Look for sums of 10. Then, add the leftover ones.
   6 + 4 = 10
   10 + 3 = 13
So, 6 + 7 = 13.

Write the missing number.

14. 8 + 5 = 10 + ▨
15. 9 + 6 = 10 + ▨
16. 6 + 8 = 10 + ▨
17. 7 + 9 = 10 + ▨
18. 5 + 7 = ▨   19. 4 + 8 = ▨

20. How can you use 7 + 3, 6 + 4, 8 + 2, 5 + 5, and 1 + 9 to add?

Counting On to Subtract (Chapter 1)

Subtract 9 from 16.

Here's A Way!

Think of 9. Count up 1 to 10.
6 more is 16.

$1 + 6 = 7$ So, $16 - 9 = 7$.

Think of 16. 6 less is 10.
Count back 1 to 9.

$6 + 1 = 7$ So, $16 - 9 = 7$.

Count up or back to solve.

21. $12 - 5$
22. $13 - 9$
23. $17 - 6$
24. $11 - 6$
25. $10 - 3$
26. $15 - 10$

27. How could you use a number line to count up or back?

Fact Families (Chapter 1)

Write the rest of the fact family for $8 + 9 = 17$.

Here's A Way!

■ + ■ = 17 $9 + 8 = 17$

$17 - ■ = ■$ $17 - 8 = 9$

$17 - ■ = ■$ $17 - 9 = 8$

Write the rest of the fact family.

28. $8 + 6 = 14$
29. $7 - 4 = 3$
30. $8 + 5 = 13$
31. $7 + 9 = 16$

32. How many number sentences are in the fact family for $5 + 5$? Explain how you know.

Problem Solving

Problem Solving Process
✓ Understand
✓ Plan
✓ Try It
✓ Look Back

Choose a Strategy You Have Learned
✓ Act It Out
  Look for a Pattern
  Guess and Check
  Draw a Picture
  Make a Table
  Work Backward
  Make a List
  Work a Simpler Problem

Solve. Show your work.

33. Suppose you and 2 friends have 16 stickers. One friend takes 6. The other friend takes 5. You take the rest. Who has the most stickers?

34. There are 14 books about dinosaurs on the shelf in your library. Suppose you check out 3 of them and your friend checks out 2. How many books about dinosaurs will be left?

35. On your way to school, you count 7 white cars, 3 blue cars, 4 red cars, and 3 bicycles. How many cars do you count in all?

INVESTIGATION

Don't Go Thirsty!

Science Connection   **With Your Group**

Keep In Mind . . .

Your work will be evaluated on the following:

☑ How you find the total amounts of juice

☑ How you decide which size bottles of juice to buy

☑ How clear and complete your chart is

☑ How well you group works together

Your class is going on a nature walk. You need to have plenty of juice to drink. How much juice should you buy for your class? Experiment and use the charts to find out. You need to find out what size drink containers your classmates have and what kind of juice each person wants. Then you can decide how much juice you need.

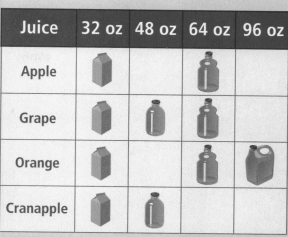

Juice	32 oz	48 oz	64 oz	96 oz
Apple				
Grape				
Orange				
Cranapple				

1

Plan It

- What kinds of containers could your group bring in? They should be unbreakable. Everyone chooses one container to bring to class.

- Fill your container with water. Pour the water into a measuring cup to find the capacity. Record the number of ounces.
- Remember, there are 8 ounces in a cup. You can write ounces as oz.

2

Put It Together

- Look at the chart below. Make your own chart to show the kind of juice you and your classmates want.

With a calculator add numbers in a column. Record. Add another column.

3

Wrap It Up

- The table above shows the different sizes of bottles each juice comes in. Use the table to decide how many and what size bottles of juice to buy.
- Make a shopping list.

4

Discuss Your Results

- Did you meet all of the goals in Keep In Mind?
- What were the other groups' results? How much juice will you have left over? Do you want to make any changes to your list?

Juice Choices:

Apple	Cranapple	Orange	Grape
8 oz	10 oz	12 oz	12 oz
12 oz	8 oz		12 oz
12 oz	10 o		12 oz
12 oz	+ 6 o		12 oz
12 oz	34 oz		36 oz

Shopping list:
1 64 oz apple
1 32 oz cran-
   apple
2 32 oz orange
1 48 oz grape

Internet

> Visit the **Math Center** at **Houghton Mifflin Education Place.** http://www.eduplace.com

Use What You Know

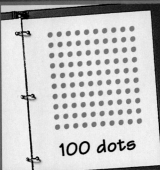

100 dots

- how to count to 100 and beyond

- how to tell time

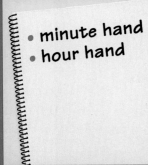

- minute hand
- hour hand

- the vocabulary

CHAPTER 2

Place Value, Money, and Time

Try This!

A minute may seem like a long or short time, depending on what you are doing. Ask a friend to keep track of time as you try these things.

What You'll Need

pennies, watch, pencil, paper

1

How many pennies do you think you can count in 1 minute? How many smiley faces do you think you can draw in 1 minute?

Counting for 1 Minute

	Guess	Actual	Close or Not Close
Coin Count			
Smiley Faces			
Marbles			

2

Make a prediction (or guess) about each activity. Then, do the activities to find out how long they really take.

3

Show your results on a chart. Tell whether your prediction was close or not close.

What did you think about to make each prediction?

How can you use counting to tell time?

Ready to Go!

Cooperative Learning
Checklist

☐ Work alone.
☑ Work with a partner.
☑ Work with a group.

LESSON 1

Tens and Ones

What You'll Need
- 2 number cubes, each labeled 0–5
- tens blocks
- ones blocks

You can show tens and ones with place-value blocks. You can write 2-digit numbers using the digits 0, 1, 2, 3, 4, 5, 6, 7, 8, 9.

Activity

1
Roll the number cubes. Use the numbers to write a 2-digit number.

2
- Copy the chart.
- Use tens and ones blocks. See how many different ways you can show your number.

For each way, record the number of tens and ones blocks you used.

3
Show your number with the least number of blocks you can use. Complete this number sentence to show what you did.

■ = ■ tens + ■ ones

35

Tens	Ones
0	35
1	25
2	15
3	5

35 = 3 tens + 5 ones

4
Repeat steps 1–3 two more times.

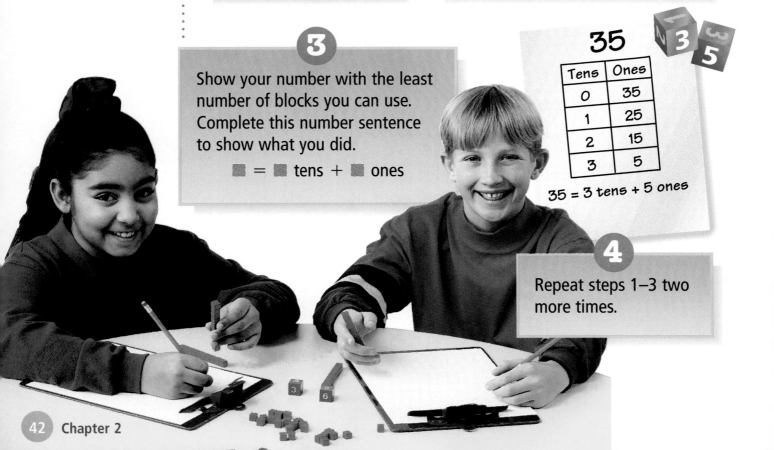

1. **Number Sense** How can you show the number 63 with the least number of blocks?

2. **Number Sense** How can you show the number 63 with the greatest number of blocks?

Write the number of tens and ones. Then write the number.

3.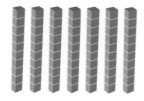

4.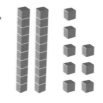

5.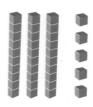

6.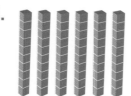

7.

8.

Complete the number sentences. Then draw pictures to show the numbers.

9. 52 = ▇ tens + ▇ ones

10. 91 = ▇ tens + ▇ one

11. 60 = ▇ tens + ▇ ones

12. 33 = ▇ tens + ▇ ones

13. 24 = ▇ tens + ▇ ones

14. 49 = ▇ tens + ▇ ones

15. 11 = ▇ ten + ▇ one

16. 36 = ▇ tens + ▇ ones

17. 73 = ▇ tens + ▇ ones

18. 15 = ▇ ten + ▇ ones

19. **Critical Thinking** If you rolled 0 and 3, how many 2-digit numbers could you make? Explain.

20. Write six pairs of digits that would only make one number.

More Practice Set 2.1, p. 442

Math Journal

Why is the digit 0 needed for writing some numbers?

Hundreds, Tens, and Ones

What You'll Need:
▶ centimeter squared paper
▶ hundreds, tens, and ones blocks

Our counting system is based on groups of ten.

10 ones = 1 ten

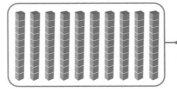

10 tens   =   1 hundred

You can use hundreds, tens, and ones blocks to show 3-digit numbers.

Activity

• Copy the place-value chart below.

1

Cover all of the squares on your paper with place-value blocks. Record how many of each kind of block you used.

• Take turns. Try to cover it with different numbers of hundreds, tens, and ones blocks.

• After each turn, record the blocks you used.

2

Cover the paper with the least number of place-value blocks you can use. Record your results.

Hundreds	Tens	Ones
1	26	14

Name

3

Use the blocks in step 2 to count the squares on the paper.

- Skip-count the hundreds and the tens blocks. Count the ones.
- Write the number of squares.

4

Complete the number sentence to show the total number of squares you counted.

■ **hundreds** + ■ **tens** + ■ **ones** = ■

Show What You Know!

Write the number of hundreds, tens, and ones. Then, write the number.

1.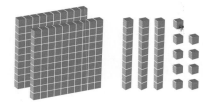

2.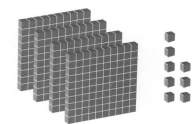

3.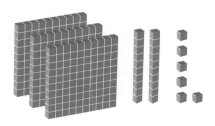

4.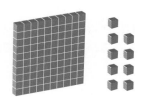

5. **Critical Thinking** Why are there no tens blocks used to show 109?

Draw a picture showing each number with hundreds, tens, and ones blocks.

6. 362   7. 41   8. 237   9. 100   10. 531   11. 485

12. 206   13. 89   14. 399   15. 642   16. 12   17. 501

18. **Number Sense** Draw a picture of how you would show 120 if you had only tens and ones blocks.

More Practice Set 2.2, p. 443

Place Value

Vocabulary:
value
Glossary, p. 480

You and your friends have bought 235 beads to make friendship necklaces. You can show a number in the hundreds in different ways.

Here's A Way! Show 235 in different ways.

1. Show the number with place-value blocks.

   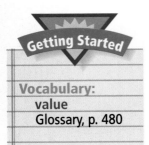

2. Use the blocks to help you write the expanded form of the number.

   200 + 30 + 5

3. Use the expanded form to help you write the number in a place-value chart.

Hundreds	Tens	Ones
2	**3**	**5**
A **2** is in the hundreds place. Its value is 200.	A **3** is in the tens place. Its value is 30.	A **5** is in the ones place. Its value is 5.

4. Write the number in standard form. Then, write it in words.

   235
   two hundred thirty-five

Talk About It! What is the value of the digit 5 in 235?

Show What You Know!

Write the number in standard form and in expanded form.

1.

2.
Hundreds	Tens	Ones
5	8	0

3.
Hundreds	Tens	Ones
4	0	9

4. seven hundred forty-four

5. eight hundred twenty

6. Draw a picture of place-value blocks to show 300 + 20 + 6.

7. **Critical Thinking** For the expanded form 300 + 7, you write the standard form 307. Why do you need a zero in the tens place?

Work It Out!

Write the number in standard form.

8. 100 + 10 + 4   9. 40 + 9   10. 800 + 60 + 3   11. 600 + 7

12. three hundred five   13. nine hundred twenty   14. fifty-eight

Write the value of the digit 4.

15. 342   16. 804   17. 45   18. 492   19. 465

Write the value of the digit 9.

20. 922   21. 519   22. 693   23. 279   24. 190

25. **Algebraic Reasoning** Copy and complete the table. Make up your own problem for the last two boxes.

In	239	589	409	499	?
Out	240	590	?	?	?

More Practice Set 2.3, p. 443

Math Journal

What happens to the tens digit when you add 1 to 19?

Problem Solving
Look for a Pattern

What plays have you seen?

You have a ticket to see a play. The ticket tells you where you will sit. How will you find your seat in the theater?

You can look for a pattern in the way the seats are numbered.

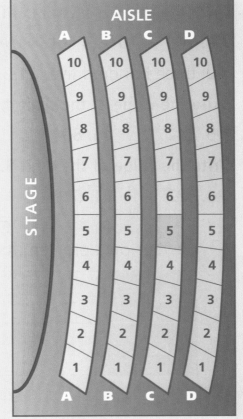

ROW **C** SEAT **5**

The Davis School Presents:

The King's Wish

Here's A Way! Look for a Pattern to solve.

1 Understand

- Study the ticket. What do the letter and the number mean?

2 Plan

- Look at the seating plan.
- Can you see a pattern? Describe it.

3 Try It

- What is your row?
- What is your seat number?
- Use the pattern to find your seat.

4 Look Back

- Did you find your seat? It's the one in a darker color. How did the seat pattern help?

Look for a pattern to solve the problem.

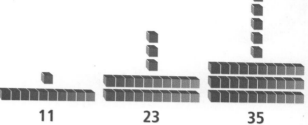

11   23   35

1. Draw the next set of blocks. Describe the pattern.

2. Write the fourth number in the pattern. Describe the pattern in the numbers.

3. **Critical Thinking** How did the blocks help you to see the number pattern?

Work It Out!

Use Look for a Pattern or another strategy to solve the problem.

4. Look at this Native American design. Name the color of the next snake.

5. On Monday 1 student is absent from your class. On Tuesday 2 students are absent. On Wednesday 3 are absent. Does that mean 4 will be absent on Thursday? Explain.

6. Copy and extend the number pattern. You may use place-value blocks.

5, 8, 11, 14, 17, 20, ▨, ▨, ▨, ▨

7. The musical pattern will continue. Describe the pattern. Show what the next two notes will be.

8. **Create Your Own** Make up your own art, music, or number pattern. See if a friend can continue the pattern.

9. A number cube has the numbers 1–6. You can roll the cube three times. On your first roll, you get 2. To get a sum of 10, what can your next two numbers be?

Share Your Thinking

10. How did you solve problem 9?

LESSON 5 Thousands

You are at the big game! There are 1230 people sitting in your section.

You can show a number in the thousands in different ways.

Which do you like better, baseball or football?

Here's A Way! Show 1230 in different ways.

1 Show the number with place-value blocks.

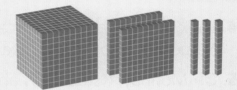

2 Use the blocks to help you write the expanded form of the number.

$$1000 + 200 + 30$$

3 Use the expanded form to help you write the number in a place-value chart.

Thousands	Hundreds	Tens	Ones
1	2	3	0

4 Write the number in standard form. Then, write it in words.

1230

one thousand two hundred thirty

Talk About It!

How could you show 1230 with place-value blocks if you didn't have thousands blocks?

one thousand → 10 hundreds
→ 100 tens
→ 1000 ones

Write the number in expanded form and in standard form.

1.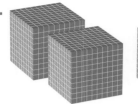

2.
Thousands	Hundreds	Tens	Ones
5	8	4	0

3. three thousand two hundred one   4. three thousand twelve

5. Draw a picture of place-value blocks for the number 2306. Then, write the number in expanded form.

6. **Critical Thinking** In the number 1111, how does the value of the digit 1 change in each place?

Work It Out!

Write the number in standard form.

7. two thousand twenty-four   8. 4000 + 600 + 30 + 2

9. six thousand fourteen   10. 1000 + 900 + 5

Write the value of the digit 7.

11. 4976   12. 6027   13. 3742   14. 7152   15. 8579

Write the value of the digit 2.

16. 2438   17. 9926   18. 5208   19. 4612   20. 3250

21. Draw a picture of place-value blocks for the number 3024. Then, write the number in expanded form.

Number Sense Complete the chart. Add or subtract only once for each row. Write your own numbers for the last row.

Start	Add or Subtract	Finish
327	− 20	307
684	22. ?	9684
1726	23. ?	1720
24. ?	25. ?	26. ?

More Practice Set 2.5, p. 444

51

Problem Solving
Logical Reasoning

Logical Reasoning

Ask Yourself:

Can I eliminate any possibilities?

Can I sort the information?

Suppose you and a friend share a garden. You have room for one more kind of flower. Your friend likes pansies, bluebells, tulips, and lilies. You like tulips, daisies, pansies, and violets. What should you plant?

A Venn diagram can help you sort the information.

You Decide

- Which flowers does your friend like?

- Which flowers do you like?

- Which flowers do you both like?

- Decide what you will plant.

My Friend | Both of Us | Me

bluebells   pansies   daisies

lilies   tulips   violets

Work It Out!

Use a Venn diagram to sort the information.

1. Here is a list of gardening tools. Some are used for dirt. Some are used for water. One is used for both dirt and water. Make a Venn diagram to show how each tool is used.

   Gardening Tools

   hose
   pail
   sprinkler
   shovel
   rake

2. Your friend can play after school on Tuesday, Wednesday, or Thursday. You can play on Monday, Tuesday, or Friday. When can you play together?

Share Your Thinking

3. How can a Venn diagram help you and your friend decide what to do when you play together?

Midchapter Review

for Pages 40–52

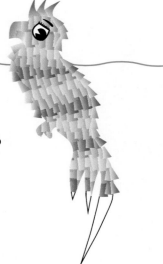

Problem Solving

Solve the problem. Show your work. (page 48)

1. Suppose you are asked to paint the rest this piñata one color. What color should you paint it?

2. Model the number pattern with place-value blocks. Find the next three numbers.
15, 10, 17, 12, 19, ▤ ▤ ▤

Concepts

Write the number of hundreds, tens, and ones. Then write the number. (pages 44, 46, 50)

3.   4.    5.   6.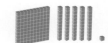

7.

Hundreds	Tens	Ones
4	7	0

8.

Hundreds	Tens	Ones
0	9	2

9. two hundred thirty-five

10. four hundred ten

Skills

Write the number in expanded form. (page 50)

11. 3241

12. 6067

13. nine thousand four hundred twenty-eight

14. 5688

Write the number in standard form. (page 50)

15. 3000 + 900 + 50 + 8

16. six thousand three hundred ten

17. 5000 + 200 + 40 + 9

18. seven thousand seventy-one

Math World

**Explore different ways of measuring
and telling time throughout history.**

about 365 days

about 29 days

Comparing Calendars

When some early calendar-makers needed
to keep track of time, they used the moon
and sun. Lunar calendars are based on the
time it takes the moon to go around Earth
once — about 29 days. Solar calendars are
based on the time it takes Earth to circle the
sun once — about 365 days. The Egyptians used
solar calendars. They discovered that the Nile
River flooded at the same time every year.

Taking the Leap

Our calendar has 365 days in a year. This is how
long it takes Earth to circle the sun — almost. To
keep in time with it, we add an extra day to
February in leap years. People born on February 29
don't have a birthday every year. Band leader
Jimmy Dorsey died when he was 53, but he had
only 13 birthdays.

Try This!

TELL TIME USING ARUSHA MAASAI HAND SIGNALS

The Arusha Maasai (ah ROO shah MAH say) of northern Tanzania (tan ZAN ee ah) use hand signals when they talk about numbers.

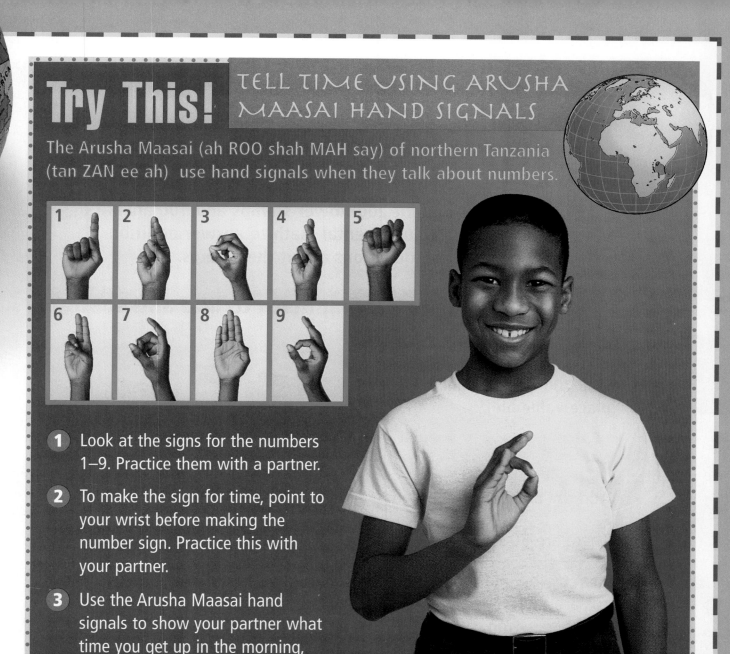

1 2 3 4 5
6 7 8 9

1. Look at the signs for the numbers 1–9. Practice them with a partner.

2. To make the sign for time, point to your wrist before making the number sign. Practice this with your partner.

3. Use the Arusha Maasai hand signals to show your partner what time you get up in the morning, what time you eat dinner, and what time you go to bed.

More Hand Signals

American Sign Language also uses hand signals. It is a language that many hearing-impaired people use in the United States and Canada. The hand signals are based on ideas, not words. So, the signal for "used up" can mean "used up time" or "used up money."

Respond

Work with a partner. . .
to make your own hand signal for 10.

 Internet: Houghton Mifflin Education Place
Explore the Math Center at
http://www.eduplace.com

Mental Math: Addition and Subtraction

Your class bought 200 flower stamps and 100 animal stamps. You can use mental math to answer addition and subtraction questions about the stamps.

Here's A Way! Use mental math to add and subtract.

Add What is the total number of stamps?

1 Find 200 + 100. Think of place-value blocks.

 +

2 hundreds + 1 hundred

2 Add the number of hundreds.

Think: **2 + 1 = 3**

There are 300 stamps altogether.

$200 + 100 = 300$

Subtract How many more flower stamps than animal stamps are there?

1 Find 200 − 100. Think of place-value blocks.

2 hundreds − 1 hundred

2 Subtract the number of hundreds.

Think: **2 − 1 = 1**

There are 100 more flower stamps.

$200 - 100 = 100$

Talk About It! How did basic facts help you do mental math?

Other Examples What basic fact can help you find each answer?

a.	b.	c.	d.
8000	4000	1200	$40 + 20 + 10 = 70$
− 3000	+ 2000	− 700	
5000	6000	500	

Complete the number sentences.

1. 2 + 5 = ▓
   20 + 50 = ▓
   200 + 500 = ▓
   2000 + 5000 = ▓

2. 9 − 4 = ▓
   90 − 40 = ▓
   900 − 400 = ▓
   9000 − 4000 = ▓

3. **Patterns** Explain how you found 9000 − 4000.

Work It Out!

Mental Math Write the answer. Use mental math.

4. 80 + 50   5. 800 − 200   6. 90 − 30   7. 40 + 30   8. 700 + 400

9. 200 − 100   10. 900 − 700   11. 500 + 200   12. 5000 + 4000

13. 6000 + 4000   14. 2000 + 3000   15. 900 − 600   16. 700 − 300

17. 60
   + 30

18. 700
   − 500

19. 600
   − 200

20. 30
     20
   + 30

21. 700
   − 600

22. 50
     20
   + 40

23. 200
     200
   + 100

24. 300
     500
   + 100

25. 900
   + 400

26. 40
     40
   + 30

27. **Algebraic Reasoning** Copy and complete the table. Use mental math.

Number	100	?	300	400	?	600
Number + 300	400	500	600	?	800	?

28. **Patterns** Describe a pattern you see in the chart.

29. **Create Your Own** Write an addition problem and a subtraction problem that both have the answer 6000. Use basic facts with 6 to help you.

More Practice Set 2.7, p. 444

Cooperative Learning
Checklist
☐ Work alone.
☑ Work with a partner.
☑ Work with a group.

Rounding

LESSON 8

Sometimes you can use a number that tells about how much or about how many. When you don't need an exact number, you can use a rounded number.

Find out how to round a number.

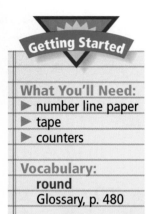

Getting Started

What You'll Need:
▶ number line paper
▶ tape
▶ counters

Vocabulary:
round
Glossary, p. 480

To round a number, you can say the nearest ten.

Activity

Round to the Nearest Ten

1 Cut out four number lines. Tape them together. Write 0–40 by ones in the boxes.

2 Put a counter on 24. It is between 20 and 30.

3 Decide which ten 24 is nearer to. It is nearer to 20. So, 24 rounds down to 20.

4 Put a counter on 15. It is halfway between 10 and 20.

5 When a number is halfway between two tens, round up to the next ten. So, 15 rounds up to 20.

6 Round to the nearest ten.
  a. 6   b. 38   c. 25

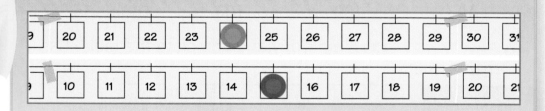

Round to the Nearest Hundred

1 Cut out four more number lines. Tape them together. Write 100–500 by tens in the boxes.

2 Put a counter on 280. It is between 200 and 300.

3 Decide which hundred 280 is nearer to. It is nearer to 300. So, 280 rounds up to 300.

4 Put a counter on 350. It is halfway between 300 and 400.

5 When a number is halfway between two hundreds, round up to the next hundred. So, 350 rounds up to 400.

6 Round to the nearest hundred.
  a. 170   **b.** 210   **c.** 150

To round a number, you can say the nearest hundred.

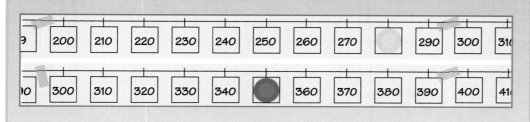

| | 200 | 210 | 220 | 230 | 240 | 250 | 260 | 270 | | 290 | 300 | 310 |
| | 300 | 310 | 320 | 330 | 340 | ⬤ | 360 | 370 | 380 | 390 | 400 | 410 |

Show What You Know!

Round to the nearest ten. Use your 0–40 number line to help you.

1. 35   2. 16   3. 24   4. 7   5. 32   6. 29

7. 12   8. 36   9. 18   10. 21   11. 11   12. 15

13. How are the numbers halfway between tens alike?

Round to the nearest hundred. Use your 100–500 number line.

14. 120   15. 260   16. 150   17. 430   18. 370   19. 240

20. How are the numbers halfway between hundreds alike?

21. **Critical Thinking** How are the halfway numbers on your 100–500 line like the halfway numbers on your 0–40 line? How are they different?

22. **Critical Thinking** You know that 25 is halfway between 20 and 30. How can this help you round 26 to the nearest 10 without a number line?

Comparing and Ordering

Season's High Scores

Team	Score
Comets	140
Hoopers	145
Flying Fish	137

The Junior Basketball League had a great season!

You can compare these high scores to put them in order from greatest to least.

Here's A Way! Order 140, 145, and 137.

Stack the scores. Line up the hundreds, tens, and ones.

1 Compare the hundreds.

```
140
145
137
```

The hundreds are the same. So, compare the next place.

2 Compare the tens.

```
140
145
137
```

4 tens is greater than 3 tens. So, 140 and 145 are greater than 137.

140 and 145 > 137

3 Compare the ones.

```
140
145
```

5 ones is greater than 0 ones. So, 145 is greater than 140.

145 > 140

4 Write the scores in order from greatest to least. **145, 140, 137**

< means "is less than"
> means "is greater than"

Talk About It! Why did you start comparing at the left?

Other Examples Put the numbers in order from least to greatest.

The thousands are the same.

```
5671        5671        5439
5439        5439        5428
5428        5428
```

5428, 5439, 5671

5439 and 5428 < 5671   5428 < 5439

Show What You Know!

1. **Critical Thinking** How could you use place-value blocks to compare numbers?

Copy and complete the number sentence. Write < or >.

2. 224 ■ 118   3. 158 ■ 185   4. 74 ■ 61   5. 103 ■ 49

6. 452 ■ 439   7. 74 ■ 68   8. 269 ■ 281   9. 309 ■ 310

Write a digit to make a true number sentence.

10. ■6 > 79   11. ■17 > 548   12. 6■5 > 687   13. ■465 > 8121

Order from greatest to least.

14. 92, 42, 113   15. 5027, 4898, 5632   16. 2246, 2230, 2237

Work It Out!

Copy and complete. Write < or >. Use blocks if you like.

17. 162 ■ 262   18. 98 ■ 89   19. 389 ■ 308

20. 1077 ■ 1007   21. 865 ■ 1865   22. 1243 ■ 1187

23. 436 ■ 398   24. 104 ■ 79   25. 958 ■ 1002

Order from least to greatest.

26. 163, 98, 89   27. 45, 13, 29   28. 8442, 7109, 7019

29. 352, 523, 235   30. 6138, 5259, 8135   31. 4617, 4716, 4167

32. Write the greatest 3-digit number. Write the least 3-digit number. Tell how you know.

33. Write all the odd numbers that are greater than 178 and less than 192. How many numbers could you write?

34. **Logical Reasoning** During a basketball tournament, your team scores more points than the Comets. The Comets score more points than the Hoopers. Which team scores the greater number of points, your team or the Hoopers? How can you tell?

More Practice Set 2.9, p. 445

Problem Solving
Using Look for a Pattern and Other Strategies

Problem Solving Process
✓ Understand
✓ Plan
✓ Try It
✓ Look Back

Choose a Strategy You Have Learned
✓ Act It Out
✓ Look for a Pattern
  Guess and Check
  Draw a Picture
  Make a Table
  Work Backward
  Make a List
  Work a Simpler Problem

You are helping a scientist dig up an ancient Mayan (MAH yuhn) city in Mexico. Suddenly you discover a large flat stone. It has markings on it! The markings seem to be Mayan numerals.

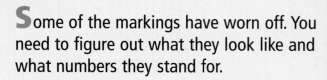

Some of the markings have worn off. You need to figure out what they look like and what numbers they stand for.

- How can you tell that the marks on the stone stand for numbers?

- What do the lines and dots mean? Are they like anything you have seen before?

- What patterns do you see?

- Do you think the Mayan numerals are in order? Why?

- Explain how you will solve the problem. Then solve it.

Use any strategy to solve the problem. Show your work.

1. At 12:00 you find the stone. By 3:00 you have dug up half of it. If you keep digging at the same pace, when will the whole stone be uncovered?

2. You find 7 pieces of pottery. They come from 3 different pots. What is the greatest number of pieces that could come from the same pot?

3. Suppose you dig up this piece of a blanket. How many diamond shapes were in the blanket when it was new? Explain.

4. A string of beads hangs from an ancient earring. The pattern of the beads is 2 green, 1 blue, 2 green, 1 blue, and so on. There once were 18 beads, but half of them dropped off. How many of each color are missing?

5. You put 4 pieces of pottery into a box. One of the pieces breaks into 2 pieces. Now how many pieces are there?

6. You dig up a folded cloth. If you unfold the cloth, it will crumble. What was the shape of the cloth before it was folded?

7. These are seven numerals from ancient Egypt. Put them in order from the least to the greatest value. Then write the next two numerals.

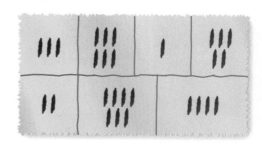

8. What strategy helped you to solve problem 7? How is this strategy useful in learning about the past?

Coin Patterns

Suppose you and two friends want to buy tickets for a 50¢ carnival ride. You each have some money. But is it enough? How can you check?

Here's A Way! | Count coins.

Use the chart. Skip-count to find the value of the coins.

| 50¢ | 25¢ | 10¢ | 5¢ | 1¢ |

You have:

25¢ ➔ 50¢

One friend has:

25¢ ➔ 35¢ ➔ 45¢ ➔ 50¢

Your other friend has:

10¢ ➔ 20¢ ➔ 30¢ ➔ 40¢ ➔ 45¢ ➔ 50¢

Each of you has 50¢. Everyone has enough.

Talk About It!

What counting patterns do you use when you count the coins? How do the patterns make counting the coins easier?

Show What You Know!

Write these amounts. Point to each coin as you skip-count.

1.

2.

3.

4.

5. **Patterns** What skip-counting pattern do you use with nickels?

Work It Out!

Write the money amount.

6.

7.

8.

9.

10.

11.

12.

13.

14. Draw a picture of the money amount in exercise 13 using only two coins.

15. **Number Sense** Name some amounts of money you can make using only dimes. How are the amounts alike? Why does this make sense?

16. **Patterns** Suppose you have 8 quarters. Show how you would use a skip-counting pattern to find their value.

More Practice Set 2.11, p. 445

Dollars and Cents

Your neighborhood held a sidewalk sale. You sold some of your old toys. How could you count the bills and coins you collected?

Here's A Way! Count bills and coins.

1 Put the bills and coins in order from the greatest value to the least value.

2 Point to each bill or coin as you count. Use mental math to find the total.

$10.00 ➤ $15.00 ➤ $16.00 ➤ $16.25 ➤ $16.35 ➤ $16.40 ➤ $16.41

You collected $16.41 or sixteen dollars and forty-one cents.

Talk About It!

• Why do people usually count money from the greatest to the least value?

• Look at the money below. What are the different ways to write the same money amounts?

ten dollars	five dollars	one dollar
$10.00	$5.00	$1.00

twenty-five cents	ten cents	five cents	one cent
quarter	dime	nickel	penny
$.25	$.10	$.05	$.01
25¢	10¢	5¢	1¢

Show What You Know!

Write the money amount below. Use a dollar sign and decimal point.

1.

2.

3.

4.

5. thirty-six cents

6. six dollars and eight cents

7. seven cents

8. What does the zero mean in $4.05?

9. **Algebraic Reasoning** Use *dollar, dime,* or *penny* to complete this sentence: A ten-dollar bill is to a one-dollar bill as a dime is to a _____.

Work It Out!

Which is more?

10. $8.93 or 980 pennies

11. 6 dollars or 20 quarters

12. 20 nickels or $1.05

13. 9 dimes or 2 dollars

Complete the chart.

Garage Sale Cashbox

Numbers	Pictures	Words	Compare to $3.50
$3.75	🪙25 25 25	three dollars and seventy-five cents	$3.75 > $3.50
$2.09	14. ?	15. ?	16. ?
17. ?	25 25 ●	18. ?	19. ?
20. ?	21. ?	two dollars and twenty-three cents	22. ?
$3.25	23. ?	24. ?	25. ?

More Practice Set 2.12, p. 446

13

Making Change

You bought a box of chalk for $2.49. You gave the clerk $3.00 and received 51¢ as change.

You can check if the clerk gave you the correct change by counting on.

What do you like to draw with chalk?

Here's A Way! Check your change.

1 Start with the price of the chalk. $2.49

2 Count on from the price.
Begin with the coins that have the least value.

$2.50 $2.55 $2.65 $2.75 $3.00

Is $3.00 the amount you gave the clerk?
Yes! $.51 is the correct change.

Talk About It!

• Why does counting on work?
• How could you have counted on in a different order?

Other Examples

You paid 75¢.   Your change is 18¢.

58¢   59¢   60¢   65¢   75¢

Is your change correct? How do you you know?

Draw the correct change.

1. You paid $2.75.

2. You paid 50¢.

3. You paid $4.00.

4. Critical Thinking Why might the clerk give you different change than the pictures you drew?

Work It Out!

Has the store clerk given you the correct change? Explain.

5. A toothbrush costs $1.97.
You paid $2.00.
Your change:

6. A box of soap cost 69¢.
You paid 75¢.
Your change:

Draw the correct change.

7. A magazine costs $2.35.
You paid $3.00.

8. A postcard costs 46¢.
You paid $1.00.

9. A beach ball costs $3.27.
You paid $5.00.

10. A cap costs $4.48.
You paid $5.00.

11. A puzzle costs $2.99.
You paid $10.00.

12. A pencil costs 29¢.
You paid $1.00.

13. Create Your Own Write a story problem about making change. Ask a classmate to solve it.

Mixed Review

Look for a pattern. Write the missing numbers.

14. 23, 33, ▪, ▪, 63

15. 320, 420, ▪, 620, ▪

16. ▪, ▪, 66, ▪, 88, 99

17. 1, 4, ▪, 10, ▪, ▪, 19

More Practice Set 2.13, p. 446

LESSON 14

Problem Solving
Using Strategies

You can read more about coins in the pages of *Zillions*.

The first Lincoln penny was made in 1909. Since then, more than 338 billion pennies have been made. If all those pennies were stacked on top of each other, they would reach higher than the moon!

Problem Solving Process

✓ Understand
✓ Plan
✓ Try It
✓ Look Back

Choose a Strategy You Have Learned

✓ Act It Out
✓ Look for a Pattern
   Guess and Check
   Draw a Picture
   Make a Table
   Work Backward
   Make a List
   Work a Simpler Problem

Suppose you have $1.00 in pennies. If you stack them, will the stack be taller than a drinking cup? (Most cups are 4 inches high. About 12 pennies make a 1–inch stack)

- How many pennies make $1.00?

- About how many pennies make a stack 1 inch high?

- About how many pennies make a stack 2 inches high?

- Explain a strategy that could help you to solve this problem. Then solve the problem.

Use any strategy to solve the problem. Show your work.

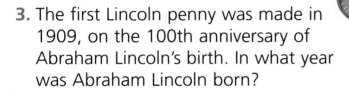

1. Suppose you have the coins shown. Describe how you would share the coins equally with a friend.

2. Which is worth more, 10 dimes or twice as many pennies?

3. The first Lincoln penny was made in 1909, on the 100th anniversary of Abraham Lincoln's birth. In what year was Abraham Lincoln born?

4. Which is worth more, all the pennies it would take to cover this book or all the dimes it would take?

5. How many pennies will fit around one penny? How many dimes will fit around one dime?

6. Put these five coins in order from least value to greatest value in only four moves. On each move, you can switch any two of the coins.

7. **Create Your Own** Write a problem about coins. See if a friend can solve it.

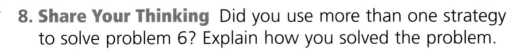

Share Your Thinking

8. **Share Your Thinking** Did you use more than one strategy to solve problem 6? Explain how you solved the problem.

Telling Time: Patterns of Five

There are 60 minutes in 1 hour. It takes the minute hand 60 minutes to go once around the clock.

What time is it? You can count by 5's to tell time.

Here's A Way! Skip-count to tell time.

1 The minute hand takes 5 minutes to move from one number to the next. Point to each number as you skip-count by 5's.

2 The first clock shows 2 o'clock. To read the rest, skip-count by 5's.

| 2:00 | 2:05 or 5 minutes after 2:00 | 2:10 or 10 minutes after 2:00 | 2:15 or 15 minutes after 2:00 |

Talk About It!

- How does skip-counting by 5's help you to tell time?
- How many minutes are there between 2:00 and 2:15?

Other Examples

5:55 or 5 minutes until 6:00

8:45 or 15 minutes until 9:00

1. Write the numbers missing around the clock.

2. **Critical Thinking** What happens to the hour hand while the minute hand moves 60 minutes?

3. **Patterns** How long does it take the minute hand to move from 12 to each odd number on the clock? What pattern do you see?

Write the time in more than one way.

6:15
15 minutes
after 6:00

4.

5.

6.

Work It Out!

Match the clocks that show the same time. Write a, b, c, or d.

7. 8:20   8. 7:25   9. 12:10   10. 11:35

a.   b.   c.   d.

Write the time.

11.   12.   13.   14.   15.

Mixed Review

Write the answer.

16. 17
   − 8

17.   4
      4
    + 3

18. 14
   − 7

19.   3
      6
    + 7

20.   9
      2
    + 9

21. 16
   − 9

More Practice Set 2.15, p. 447

73

LESSON 16

Using A.M. and P.M.

There are 24 hours in a day. The hours from 12:00 midnight to 12:00 noon are labeled A.M. The hours from 12:00 noon until 12:00 midnight are labeled P.M.

A.M. and P.M.

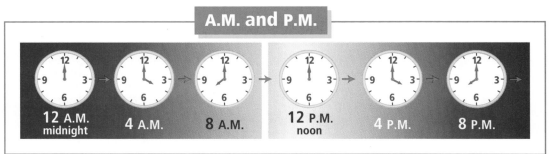

| 12 A.M. midnight | 4 A.M. | 8 A.M. | 12 P.M. noon | 4 P.M. | 8 P.M. |

You can show the times you do things each day.

Activity

1 Spin the 1–12 spinner to get the hour. Spin the 00–55 spinner to get the minutes. Record the time.

2 Write something you do at this time of day. Write A.M. or P.M. to show which part of the day you mean.

3 Do steps 1–2 six times. Then, rewrite your list to show the order in which you do the activities.

Look at the pictures or read the words. Tell whether it is A.M. or P.M.

1.

2.

3.

4. when you eat supper

5. when you go to school

6. when you get home from school

7. when you eat lunch

8. when you go to bed

9. when you get up

10. It is 3:00. The stars are out. Is it A.M. or P.M.?

11. It is 10:00. The sun is out. Is it A.M. or P.M.?

12. How many hours are there from 12:00 noon to 12:00 midnight? From 12:00 midnight to 12:00 noon?

13. How many times does the hour hand go all the way around the clock in one day? Explain.

14. **Critical Thinking** Are you awake during more hours labeled A.M. or more hours labeled P.M.? Explain.

Problem Solving

Be sure to write A.M. or P.M.

15. You are going to a puppet show. The show starts at 3:30 P.M. It lasts for one hour What time will it end?

16. You are going on a hike with your family. You will start hiking at 11:00 A.M. If you hike for 2 hours, what time will you finish?

17. The town library opens at 9:00 A.M. It stays open for 8 hours. What time does it close?

More Practice Set 2.16, p. 447

LESSON 17

Problem Solving
Choose a Computation Method

An estimate is a number that is close to an exact amount. An estimate tells *about* how much or how many.

This park sign tells how long it takes to hike each trail. Do you think the times are exact, or are they estimates?

Choose a Computation Method

Ask Yourself:

Do I need an exact answer or an estimate?

Should I use a model, paper and pencil, mental math, or a calculator?

What operation should I use?

HIKING TRAILS

Meadow Trail   30 minutes

Lake Trail   1 hour

Cliff Trail   2 hours

You Decide

- Does everyone hike at the same speed?
- Can the weather change how fast you hike?
- Are there things to stop and look at along a trail?
- Decide if the times are exact or estimates. Explain your thinking.

Decide if the number is exact or an estimate.
Explain your decision.

1. The park receives 5000 visitors a year.

2. The barbell weighs 25 pounds.

3. The lake is 150 feet deep.

4. The carton contains 12 eggs.

5. The sun is 93 million miles from Earth.

6. The building is 96 stories high.

7. The computer costs $1054.

8. The rock is 1000 years old.

9. The rabbit can run 35 miles in an hour.

10. **Critical Thinking** You joined a scout troop last year. Your friend asks you how long you have been a scout. Do you give an exact number of months or an estimate? Why?

Share Your Thinking

11. Tell about a time when you needed to give an exact number. Tell about another time when you only needed to give an estimate.

Chapter 2 Test

for Pages 40–77

Test-Taking Tips

As you read the problem slowly, make sure you understand what you are asked to do.

Problem Solving

Solve. Show your work.

1. Suppose your family wants to take a bus tour. The first bus leaves at 7:30 A.M. Then there is a bus every 2 hours after that. The last bus is at 3:30 P.M. How many times in a day does a bus leave?

2. Suppose you save 5¢ one week, 10¢ the next week, and 15¢ the third week. If you continue saving in this same way, how much money will you have saved after 6 more weeks?

Concepts

Answer the question. (page 58)

3. Does 86 round to 80 or 90?   4. Does 443 round to 400 or 500?

5. Is 513 closer to 500 or 600?   6. Is 159 closer to 100 or 200?

Find the value shown. Write *a*, *b*, *c*, or *d*. (pages 64, 66)

7.
   | a. 57¢ | b. 47¢ |
   | c. 62¢ | d. 42¢ |

8.
   | a. 56¢ | b. 81¢ |
   | c. 86¢ | d. 85¢ |

9.
   | a. $0.30 | b. $3.05 |
   | c. $3.10 | d. $3.01 |

10.
   | a. $5.05 | b. $5.30 |
   | c. $5.15 | d. $5.20 |

Write the coins for the correct change. (page 68)

11. You paid 75¢.

12. You paid $3.00.

Write the number in standard form. (page 50)

13. 2000 + 100 + 60 + 4

14. five thousand sixteen

Write the number in expanded form. (page 50)

15. three thousand nine hundred ninety

16. 8123

Find the missing sign. Write >, <, or =. (page 60)

17. 56 ● 45

18. 403 ● 430

19. 1518 ● 1802

20. 1649 ● 1614

Order from least to greatest. (page 60)

21. 22, 49, 37

22. 240, 158, 215

23. 5631, 9036, 8725

24. 7925, 7011, 7592

Write the time. (page 72)

25.   **26.**   **27.**   **28.**

Performance Task

(pages 64, 66, 68)

You bought a book that cost $1.63. You gave the clerk $2.00. How much change should you get?

- Draw pictures of the different coins you could get.

- For each picture, write how you would count out the change.

Keep In Mind . . .

Your work will be evaluated on the following:

☑ Neat, clear drawings

☑ Correct solutions that show counting up

☑ Method for checking

☑ Labels for all parts

Cumulative Review

Missing Addends (Chapter 1)
Find the missing addend.
5 + ■ = 7

Think of part-part-whole.

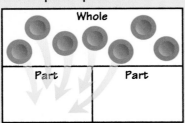

5+ another part = 7
    5 + 2 = 7

Complete the number sentence.

1. 10 + ■ = 15   2. ■ + 3 = 11

3. ■ + 7 = 12   4. 9 + ■ = 16

5. 8 + ■ = 14   6. 11 + ■ = 17

7. In an addition sentence, can an addend ever be larger than the sum? Why or why not?

Counting and Ordering (Chapter 1)
Find the missing numbers.
45, ■, ■, 48

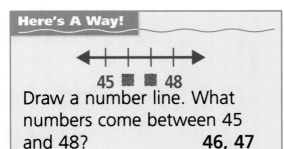

45 ■ ■ 48
Draw a number line. What numbers come between 45 and 48?   **46, 47**

Write the missing numbers.

8. 31, ■, 33, ■   9. 86, 87, ■, ■

10. ■, 77, ■, 79   11. ■, ■, 65, 66

12. 48, ■, ■, 51   13. 25, ■, ■, 22

14. How is problem 13 different from problems 8–12?

Using Doubles to Add (Chapter 1)
Add 7 and 6.

7 + 7 = 14   7 + 6 is 1 less.
So, 7 + 6 = 13.

6 + 6 = 12   7 + 6 is 1 more.
So, 7 + 6 = 13.

Use doubles to find the sum.

15. 9 + 8   16. 7 + 8   17. 5 + 6

18. 4 + 5   19. 4 + 3   20. 6 + 7

21. How did using doubles help you solve problems 19 and 20?

Addition (Chapter 1)
Find 9 + 1 + 9.

Look for sums of 10. Look for doubles.
Add 9 and 1. Then add 9.
9 + 1 + 9 = 19
Or, add 9 and 9. Then add 1.
9 + 9 + 1 = 19

Look for sums of 10 or doubles. Find the answer.

22. 3 + 8 + 8   **23.** 2 + 8 + 4

24. 7 + 3 + 7   **25.** 6 + 7 + 4

26. 2 + 5 + 2 + 5   **27.** 3 + 2 + 7 + 3

28. What numbers did you add first in problem 27? Why?

On to Subtract (Chapter 1)
Find 11 − 8.

Think of 8. Count up 2 to 10
One more is 11.
2 + 1 = 3 So, 11 − 8 = 3
Think of 11. 1 less is 10.
Count back 2 to 8.
1 + 2 = 3 So, 11 − 8 = 3

Count up or back to find the answer.

29. 17 − 4   **30.** 12 − 6

31. 15 − 3   **32.** 16 − 6

33. 18 − 3   **34.** 14 − 0

35. How does thinking of 10 help you subtract?

Problem Solving

Problem Solving Process
✓ Understand
✓ Plan
✓ Try It
✓ Look Back

Choose a Strategy You Have Learned
✓ Act It Out
✓ Look for a Pattern
  Guess and Check
  Draw a Picture
  Make a Table
  Work Backward
  Make a List
  Work a Simpler Problem

Choose a strategy you know to solve the problem. Show your work.

36. Suppose there are 18 students in your class. Half of the students ride a bus to school. Six students walk to school and the rest come by car. How many students in the class come by car?

37. Order the numbers from least to greatest. Then write the next 3 numbers in the pattern.

22, 1, 13, 7, 19, 4, 10, 16

Snack Attack!

Nutrition Connection   **With Your Group**

Your group is in charge of planning snacks for a
kindergarten class of 20 students. You need to plan
healthful foods for five days of school.

You will have to think about what kinds of food
would make good snacks. You can use a grocery
flyer to make your choices. Then, write your menu
and your shopping list.

1

Plan It

- Look at a grocery store flyer for good snack ideas for a kindergarten class. Discuss your ideas.
- List some snack choices. Plan a different food for each day.
- What else will you need to serve the snacks?
- How many students are in the kindergarten class? How much food do you need for each student? How much to drink?

2

Put It Together

- Choose five snacks and drinks. Start writing a shopping list.
- List the things you need to buy for serving.
- Tell how much of each item you need. List the prices from the flyer.

Figure out how much the groceries will cost.

Shopping List

20 cups	$1.00
20 napkins	$1.00
1 box of crackers	$3.00
20 slices of cheese	$2.50
1 bag of popcorn	$2.50
1 bottle of grape juice	$2.00
1 bag of pretzels	$1.50
1 bottle of fruit punch	$2.00
1 bag of carrot and celery sticks	$2.50
1 bottle of apple juice	$2.00
1 package of cookies	$2.00
1 carton of milk	$2.00
TOTAL:	**$24.00**

3

Wrap It Up

- Make a menu and describe your decisions. Draw a picture of the snacks for the kindergarten class.

4

Discuss Your Results

- Did you meet all of the goals in Keep In Mind?
- Share your menu with other groups. What kinds of foods appear most often?
- Suppose *your* class could have snacks every day for a week. How would you change the menu?

Monday

Tuesday

Internet

> Visit the **Math Center** at **Houghton Mifflin Education Place.**
http://www.eduplace.com

Addition and Subtraction

Use What You Know

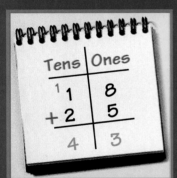

hundreds	tens	ones
1	8	2

The value of the 8 in 182 is 8 tens, or 80.

- place-value ideas

Tens	Ones
¹1	8
+ 2	5
4	3

- how to regroup in addition and subtraction

- sum
- difference
- plus
- minus

- the vocabulary

Try This!

Use place value, addition, and subtraction to create number puzzles.

What You'll Need

index cards, marker

1

Make a card for the digits 1, 2, 3, 4 and a card for the symbol +.

2

Arrange the cards to make and record addition puzzles. Find the sums. What is the greatest sum you can make? The least sum?

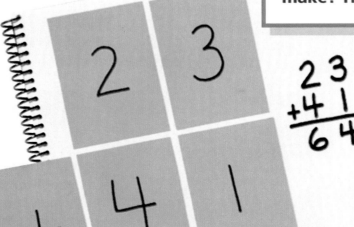

$$\begin{array}{r} 2\ 3 \\ +4\ 1 \\ \hline 6\ 4 \end{array}$$

Now make cards for 6, 7, 8, 9, and a card for the symbol −. What is the greatest difference you can make? The least difference?

How did you find each?

How many different addition puzzles can you make? Subtraction?

What place-value ideas helped you decide where to put the digit cards?

Ready to Go!

☐ Work alone.
☑ Work with a partner.
☐ Work with a group.

LESSON 1

Regrouping and Addition

Use what you know about regrouping to play this addition game.

Getting Started

What You'll Need:
▶ two number cubes
▶ place-value blocks
▶ place-value mat
▶ recording sheet

Adding to 300!

Activity

● **Keep track of how many turns you and your partner take. Can you reach 300 if you each take 6 turns or fewer?**

How to Play!

1 One partner tosses the number cubes. Put them side by side to make a 2-digit number.

2 Show the number on the place-value mat using the fewest place-value blocks. Write the number on the recording sheet.

3 The other partner tosses the cubes again. Show the new number with blocks. Write the new number on the recording sheet. Use the blocks to add the 2 numbers. Regroup if you need to. Record the sum.

4 Take turns using blocks on the mat to add more numbers. Regroup whenever you need to. Make sure you record the sums as you go along. Did you reach 300 in 6 turns or fewer? Try the game again.

Use What You Know

You know you can regroup 10 ones for 1 ten and regroup 10 tens for 1 hundred.

Show What You Know!

1. **Critical Thinking** When did you need to regroup your blocks?

2. **Critical Thinking** Would you get the wrong answer if you did not regroup your blocks at all?

Use your place-value blocks. Be sure to regroup when you can. Write the sum.

3. 15
   + 9

4. 19
   + 81

5. 64
   + 28

6. 20
   + 10

7. 39
   + 72

8. 34 + 62

9. 18 + 82

10. 31 + 25

11. 75 + 23

Adding 2-Digit Numbers

You have used place-value blocks to add. Sometimes you had to regroup ones and tens.

What is another way to add 2-digit numbers?

Here's A Way! Find 38 + 24.

1 Add the ones.

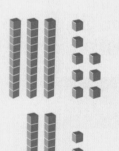

$$38$$
$$+ 24$$

8 + 4 = 12

2 Regroup the ones if you need to.

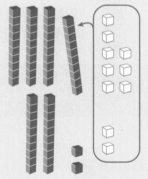

$$\overset{1}{3}8$$
$$+ 24$$
$$\overline{2}$$

12 ones = 1 ten, 2 ones

3 Add the tens.

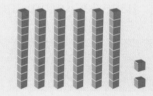

$$\overset{1}{3}8$$
$$+ 24$$
$$\overline{62}$$

1 ten
3 tens
+ 2 tens
6 tens

Talk About It! What does the 1 over the 3 stand for?

Other Examples You may need to regroup more than once.

$$59$$
$$+ 42$$

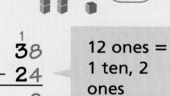

$$\overset{1}{5}9$$
$$+ 42$$
$$\overline{1}$$

11 ones = 1 ten, 1 one

$$\overset{1}{5}9$$
$$+ 42$$
$$\overline{101}$$

10 tens = 1 hundred, 0 tens

Use your blocks to complete these problems.

1.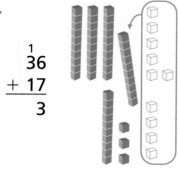

$$\begin{array}{r} {}^{1} \\ 36 \\ +\ 17 \\ \hline 3 \end{array}$$

2.

$$\begin{array}{r} 25 \\ +\ 18 \\ \hline \end{array}$$

Will you need to regroup? Write *yes* or *no*. Then add.

3. 26 + 59   4. 90 + 38   5. 53 + 48   6. 75 + 15

7. **Critical Thinking** How did you know whether you needed to regroup in exercises 3 – 6?

Work It Out!

Write the sum. You may use place-value blocks if you want.

8. $\begin{array}{r} 60 \\ +\ 35 \\ \hline \end{array}$
9. $\begin{array}{r} 88 \\ +\ 41 \\ \hline \end{array}$
10. $\begin{array}{r} 76 \\ +\ 72 \\ \hline \end{array}$
11. $\begin{array}{r} 58 \\ +\ 32 \\ \hline \end{array}$
12. $\begin{array}{r} 72 \\ +\ 47 \\ \hline \end{array}$

13. $\begin{array}{r} 64 \\ +\ 71 \\ \hline \end{array}$
14. $\begin{array}{r} 55 \\ +\ 68 \\ \hline \end{array}$
15. $\begin{array}{r} 32 \\ +\ 65 \\ \hline \end{array}$
16. $\begin{array}{r} 75 \\ +\ 13 \\ \hline \end{array}$
17. $\begin{array}{r} 66 \\ +\ 81 \\ \hline \end{array}$

18. 64 + 32   19. 17 + 92   20. 83 + 25   21. 35 + 19

22. **Create Your Own** Write two problems for a friend. One should need regrouping and the other should not.

23. **Problem Solving** A bag has 25 stickers. Another has 31 stickers. A third has 29 stickers. What is the most stickers you could get in 2 bags?

Mixed Review

Round to the nearest ten or hundred.

24. 43   25. 69   26. 7   27. 315   28. 567

More Practice Set 3.2, p. 448

Adding 3-Digit Numbers

The Park Row Building, at 386 feet, was once the tallest building in New York City. In 1907 the Citibank building was built. It is 355 feet taller. How tall is it?

You can add to find out.

The Park Row Building, New York City

Here's A Way! Find 355 + 386.

1 Add the ones. Will you have to regroup?

$$
\begin{array}{r}
\overset{1}{3}55 \\
+\ 386 \\
\hline
1
\end{array}
$$

2 Add the tens. Will you have to regroup?

$$
\begin{array}{r}
\overset{1\ 1}{3}55 \\
+\ 386 \\
\hline
41
\end{array}
$$

3 Add the hundreds.

$$
\begin{array}{r}
\overset{1\ 1}{3}55 \\
+\ 386 \\
\hline
741
\end{array}
$$

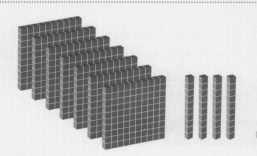

The Citibank building is 741 feet tall.

Talk About It! How is adding 3-digit numbers like adding 2-digit numbers?

Show What You Know!

Write the sum. Use mental math when you can.

1. 174 + 115	2. 456 + 387	3. 271 + 419	4. 321 + 188	5. 470 + 364

6. 477 + 31   7. 300 + 36   8. 832 + 129   9. $500 + $150

10. **Mental Math** Explain how you could use mental math to do one of the exercises above.

Work It Out!

Write the sum.

11. 732 + 159	12. $358 + 57	13. 116 + 133	14. 726 + 434	15. 300 + 500

16. 395 + 278	17. 350 + 150	18. 115 + 93	19. 229 + 456	20. $425 + 236

21. 236 + 425   22. 440 + 332   23. 662 + 115   24. 439 + 501

25. 675 + 225   26. 375 + 225   27. 345 + 445   28. $117 + $225

29. **Copy and complete this table. Write new examples in the last two boxes.**

Start	200	250	300	?	400	?	?	?
End	385	?	485	?	?	635	?	?

30. **Algebraic Reasoning** Write a rule that connects the Start and End numbers.

31. **Problem Solving** The part of the Empire State Building that people use is 381 meters tall. There is a tower on top that is 68 meters tall. How tall is the building with the tower?

More Practice Set 3.3, p. 448

Estimating Sums

Vocabulary:
front-end
estimation
Glossary, p. 480

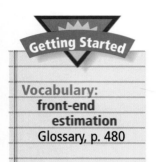

Suppose you and a friend want to collect 700 stamps. You have 378 stamps. Your friend has 438 stamps. Do you have enough stamps in your collection?

Here are two ways to estimate the sum.

| **Here's A Way!** | **Estimate 378 + 438.** |

Front-end Estimation
Add the front-end digits.

$$378 \qquad 3 \text{ hundreds} \qquad 300$$
$$+ 438 \qquad + 4 \text{ hundreds} \qquad + 400$$
$$\qquad\qquad 7 \text{ hundreds} \qquad 700$$

A front-end estimate is 700.

Rounding
Round the numbers and add.

$$378 \qquad 400$$
$$+ 438 \qquad + 400$$
$$\qquad\qquad 800$$

378 rounds up to 400

438 rounds down to 400

The rounded estimate is 800.

Both estimates show that you have more than 700 stamps.

Talk About It!

• Why is the actual sum greater than the front-end estimate?

• Why is estimating the number of stamps in the collection enough to answer the question?

Show What You Know!

Estimate the sum. How did you get your estimate?

1. 391 + 277
2. 183 + 488
3. $178 + $324
4. 493 + 238
5. 665 + 112
6. 289 + 543
7. 715 + 235
8. 391 + 512

Which sum is greater? Choose a or b.

9. a. 306 + 349
   b. 463 + 189
10. a. $392 + $204
    b. $528 + $169
11. a. 486 + 432
    b. 245 + 601

12. **Critical Thinking** Is estimating money amounts different than estimating whole numbers? Explain.

Work It Out!

Estimate each sum. Tell how you estimated.

13.   164
    + 234

14. $521
    + 234

15.   432
    + 275

16. $197
    + 256

17.   346
    + 259

18. 654 + 248
19. 134 + 284
20. 732 + 198
21. 522 + 420

Estimate. Which two numbers on the stamps have a sum of:

22. about 900?
23. about 700?
24. about 600?

Is the sum more or less than 1000?

25. 789 + 352
26. 588 + 298
27. 812 + 143

28. **Write About It** Write another problem about a stamp album. Can it be solved by finding an estimate? Explain.

Problem Solving

29. Suppose one page of a stamp album holds 55 stamps. You have filled one page. Another page has 38 stamps on it. Do you have more than 90 stamps? Explain.

30. Some rare stamps are very expensive. Suppose you see a stamp worth $580 and another one worth $320. If you have $1000, could you buy them? Explain.

More Practice Set 3.4, p. 449

Three or More Addends

207 feet

191 feet

143 feet

156 feet

Start/ Finish

Your class is having a bike race. How long will the race course be?

Estimate first. Then find the exact answer. Add the length of each side of the path.

Here's A Way! Find 207 + 191 + 156 + 143.

1 Estimate by rounding.

```
  207        200
  191        200
  156        200
+ 143      + 100
            700
```

The race course will be about 700 feet long.

2 Add the ones. Regroup.

```
    1
  207
  191
  156
+ 143
    7
```

> Look for numbers that make 10.
> 7 + 3 = 10

3 Add the tens. Regroup. Then add the hundreds.

```
  1 1
  207
  191
  156
+ 143
  697
```

The race course will be exactly 697 feet long.

Talk About It!

Compare the answer to the estimate. Is the answer reasonable?

Estimate the sum. Record the estimate. Then add. Use your estimate to check if your answer is reasonable.

1.	2.	3.	4.	5.
33	133	189	12	395
11	211	216	34	125
+ 182	+ 182	+ 545	11	105
			+ 21	+ 75

6. **Critical Thinking** How did you estimate in exercise 5?

Work It Out!

First write an estimate. Then add.

7.	8.	9.	10.	11.
39	61	19	84	47 miles
19	131	219	28	82 miles
+ 42	23	+ 176	+ 47	+ 99 miles
	+ 14			

12.	13.	14.	15.	16.
28	15	$150	23	48
16	36	139	16	59
+ 227	+ 63	+ 627	+ 59	+ 54

17. 14 + 64 + 20

18. 66 + 121 + 118

19. 201 + 389 + 225

20. $36 + $48 + $13

21. 214 + 163 + 412

22. 52 + 123 + 481

Problem Solving

23. How long is a race course if the sides of the path are 215 feet, 301 feet, and 115 feet?

24. **Number Sense** Choose three digits. Make a 3-digit number. Add it to 467. Try to come as close to 1000 as you can.

More Practice Set 3.5, p. 449

Math Journal

Explain how you chose your 3-digit number in exercise 24.

Problem Solving
Number Sense

Is a 12-egg carton with 10 eggs almost full or almost empty? What about a large mixing bowl with 10 raisins in it?

You can use your number sense to answer questions like these.

Number Sense

Ask Yourself:

How can the number be shown in different ways with models?

How does the number compare to other numbers?

What will happen to the numbers when I add, subtract, multiply, or divide them?

Is the number or measurement reasonable in this situation?

You Decide

- Does the number 10 mean the same thing for the egg carton and the bowl? Explain.

- Does your answer make sense? Explain.

Work It Out!

Write *true* or *false*. Explain your answer. The number 83:

1. is more than 50 but less than 100.

2. is closer to 67 than to 830.

3. is the number of people in your house.

4. could be the age of someone's grandfather.

5. is about the number of hours you sleep every night.

6. is less than the number of people who live in your state.

7. Create Your Own Write a problem like the one in the introduction, where 5 is a big number.

Share Your Thinking

8. How did you use number sense to answer questions 5 and 6?

Midchapter Review

for Pages 84–96

for Pages 84–96

Problem Solving

Solve using any strategy. Show your work. (page 96)

1. Suppose you pick up 19 shells on the beach. You have 4 pink shells, 7 white shells, and 2 orange shells. The rest are brown. Do you have more white shells or brown shells?

2. This month Iris, Peter, and Lani — in that order — will take turns writing the date on the board. Which child will be the tenth to write the date?

Concepts

Estimate each sum. Tell how you estimated. (page 92)

3. $\begin{array}{r} 332 \\ + 437 \\ \hline \end{array}$
4. $\begin{array}{r} 589 \\ + 103 \\ \hline \end{array}$

5. Which two numbers have a sum closest to 400?
214 321 278 191

6. Is the sum of 436 + 399 more than or less than 800? Explain.

Skills

Write the sum. (pages 88, 90, 94)

7. $\begin{array}{r} 73 \\ + 18 \\ \hline \end{array}$
8. $\begin{array}{r} 49 \\ + 25 \\ \hline \end{array}$
9. $\begin{array}{r} 666 \\ + 38 \\ \hline \end{array}$
10. $\begin{array}{r} 351 \\ + 269 \\ \hline \end{array}$

11. 26 + 27
12. 19 + 52
13. 513 + 390
14. 754 + 528

15. $\begin{array}{r} 45 \\ 13 \\ + 270 \\ \hline \end{array}$
16. $\begin{array}{r} 462 \\ 108 \\ + 229 \\ \hline \end{array}$
17. $\begin{array}{r} 17 \\ 37 \\ 11 \\ + 22 \\ \hline \end{array}$
18. $\begin{array}{r} 115 \\ 193 \\ 225 \\ + 401 \\ \hline \end{array}$

Math World

Addition and Subtraction

Around the World

Find out more about some of the symbols and machines people have used for addition and subtraction throughout history.

Fancy Footwork

In ancient Egypt, a symbol that looked like a pair of human legs walking to the left meant to add. A pair of legs facing the other way was the symbol for subtraction. The symbols appear on the Rhind papyrus, an ancient scroll filled with math problems.

Adding Machines

Throughout history, people have used different tools to help them add. Here are some of them on the time line.

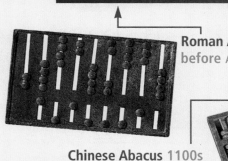

A.D. 1   A.D. 500   A.D. 1000

Roman Abacus
before A.D. 100

Chinese Abacus 1100s

Pascal's calculating machine 1642

Try This!

The Chinese invented this very old game. Today, Nim is a popular game on the Internet. You don't need a computer for this version, though. You do need a partner and 21 counters.

1 Spread the counters out in front of you. Decide who will go first.

2 Take turns removing 1, 2, or 3 counters.

3 Play until all the counters are gone. The player who removes the last counter loses.

Hint: Add the number of counters you and your partner remove each round. Try removing a total of 4 counters every time.

A.D. 1500   A.D. 2000

modern pocket calculator 1960s

Monroe's calculating machine 1900s

Respond

Work with a partner. . .

to make and solve math problems using the Egyptian walking feet.

Internet:
Houghton Mifflin Education Place
Explore the Math Center. at
http://www.eduplace.com

LESSON 7

Regrouping and Subtraction

Getting Started

What You'll Need:
▶ two number cubes
▶ place-value blocks
▶ place-value mat
▶ recording sheet

Use What You Know

You know you can regroup 1 ten as 10 ones and 1 hundred as 10 tens.

You have used place-value blocks and regrouping to add. Now try this subtraction game.

Subtraction 200!

Activity

• Use place-value blocks to show 200 on the mat. Write 200 on the recording sheet.

• See how many rounds you can play without running out of blocks!

1

• One partner tosses the number cubes. Decide which cube is the ones and which is the tens.

2

• Put the cubes side by side to make a 2-digit number.

• Record the 2-digit number.

3
- Remove that number of blocks. Regroup if you need to.
- Subtract and record the difference.

4
- The next player follows steps 1 through 3. A round is over when each person has had a turn.

5
- Play four rounds. See if you can do it without running out of blocks!

Show What You Know!

1. When did you need to regroup?

2. **Logical Reasoning** How can you make a 2-digit number with the cubes so that the difference is as large as possible? Explain your reasoning.

3. **Critical Thinking** What is the greatest number of blocks a player could have left after the first turn?

4. **Number Sense** Is it possible to run out of blocks in 3 turns? Explain your answer.

Use your place-value blocks to find the difference. Record your answer.

5.	6.	7.	8.	9.
20 − 3	70 − 30	63 − 9	58 − 8	52 − 12

10.	11.	12.	13.	14.
100 − 25	45 − 17	153 − 76	125 − 89	285 − 48

15. 36 − 24   16. 42 − 15   17. 60 − 34   18. 92 − 76

19. 200 − 10   20. 245 − 23   21. 407 − 25   22. 231 − 47

Math Journal

Describe how to subtract a 3-digit number from a 3-digit number using place-value blocks.

Subtracting from 2-Digit Numbers

What You'll Need:
► place-value blocks

If a cheetah ran at top speed for an hour, it would go 62 miles. An ostrich would go 45 miles in an hour. How much farther would the cheetah run?

You can subtract to find the answer.

Here's A Way! **Find 62 − 45.**

1 Look at the ones. Do you need to regroup?

$$\begin{array}{r} 62 \\ -\ 45 \\ \hline \end{array}$$

5 ones > 2 ones

2 Regroup 1 ten as 10 ones.

$$\begin{array}{r} {\scriptstyle 5\ 12} \\ \cancel{6}2 \\ -\ 45 \\ \hline \end{array}$$

Another name for 6 tens, 2 ones is 5 tens, 12 ones

3 Subtract the ones. Then, subtract the tens.

$$\begin{array}{r} {\scriptstyle 5\ 12} \\ \cancel{6}2 \\ -\ 45 \\ \hline 17 \end{array}$$

4 Check the answer by adding.

$$17 + 45 = 62$$

5 Explain what the answer means.

The cheetah would run 17 miles farther than the ostrich.

Talk About It! Why can you add to check the answer?

Find the difference. Use place-value blocks or mental math.

1. 32
    − 15

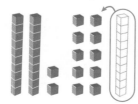

2. 44
    − 25

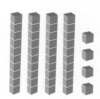

3. 85
    − 23

4. 41
    − 18

5. 45
    − 39

6. 64
    − 5

7. **Critical Thinking** How do you decide whether you need to regroup the ones? Explain.

Work It Out!

Write the difference. You may use place-value blocks.

8. 28
    − 19

9. 83
    − 52

10. 43
    − 23

11. 26
    − 8

12. 65
    − 28

13. 50
    − 25

14. 71
    − 43

15. 55
    − 40

16. 36
    − 28

17. 46
    − 29

18. 72 − 8   19. 86 − 49   20. 87 − 50   21. 50 − 49

22. 58 − 37   23. 58 − 38   24. 58 − 39   25. 58 − 40

26. **Patterns** Describe a pattern you see in exercises 22 – 25. Explain how the pattern helps you find 58 – 41.

Problem Solving

27. At top speed, a giraffe could run 32 miles in an hour. A gazelle could run 50 miles. A pronghorn antelope could run 61 miles. Which animal is fastest? How much farther would it go than each of the other two?

28. If a pronghorn antelope and an ostrich ran at top speed for an hour, which would go farther?

More Practice Set 3.8, p. 450

Subtracting from 3-Digit Numbers

In 1996 Shannon Lucid was in space for 188 days. In 1987 Yuri Romanenko was in space for 326 days. How many fewer days was Lucid in space than Romanenko?
Subtract to find out.

Here's A Way! Find 326 − 188.

1 Subtract the ones. Regroup if you need to.

$$\begin{array}{r} {}^{1}3\overset{16}{\cancel{2}}\cancel{6} \\ -\ 188 \\ \hline 8 \end{array}$$

2 Subtract the tens. Then subtract the hundreds. Regroup if you need to.

$$\begin{array}{r} {}^{2}\overset{11}{\cancel{3}}\overset{1}{\cancel{2}}\overset{16}{\cancel{6}} \\ -\ 188 \\ \hline 138 \end{array}$$

3 Check your answer by adding 138 and 188.

$$\begin{array}{r} {}^{1}\ {}^{1}\ \\ 138 \\ +\ 188 \\ \hline 326 \end{array}$$

4 Explain what the answer means.

Lucid was in space 138 days fewer than Romanenko.

Talk About It! Why do you regroup the tens twice?

Other Examples Subtract. Describe when you need to regroup.

$$\begin{array}{r} 674 \\ -\ 291 \\ \hline 383 \end{array} \qquad \begin{array}{r} \$324 \\ -\ 187 \\ \hline \$137 \end{array} \qquad \begin{array}{r} 795 \\ -\ 342 \\ \hline 453 \end{array}$$

Show What You Know!

Find the difference. Use mental math when you can.

1. $\begin{array}{r} 249 \\ -\ 57 \\ \hline \end{array}$
2. $\begin{array}{r} 388 \\ -163 \\ \hline \end{array}$
3. $\begin{array}{r} 543 \\ -345 \\ \hline \end{array}$
4. $\begin{array}{r} 100 \\ -\ 98 \\ \hline \end{array}$
5. $\begin{array}{r} 654 \\ -456 \\ \hline \end{array}$

6. 764 − 127   7. 160 − 60   8. 371 − 91   9. 217 − 139

10. **Critical Thinking** How is subtracting 3-digit numbers like subtracting 2-digit numbers? How is it different?

Work It Out!

Find the difference.

11. $\begin{array}{r} 777 \\ -369 \\ \hline \end{array}$
12. $\begin{array}{r} 542 \\ -\ 21 \\ \hline \end{array}$
13. $\begin{array}{r} 919 \\ -\ 86 \\ \hline \end{array}$
14. $\begin{array}{r} \$847 \\ -258 \\ \hline \end{array}$
15. $\begin{array}{r} 432 \\ -174 \\ \hline \end{array}$

16. $\begin{array}{r} 140 \\ -\ 70 \\ \hline \end{array}$
17. $\begin{array}{r} 637 \\ -365 \\ \hline \end{array}$
18. $\begin{array}{r} \$321 \\ -198 \\ \hline \end{array}$
19. $\begin{array}{r} 432 \\ -198 \\ \hline \end{array}$
20. $\begin{array}{r} 472 \\ -187 \\ \hline \end{array}$

21. 178 − 169   22. $600 − $200   23. 248 − 58

24. 821 − 93   25. $561 − $440   26. 621 − 20

27. 525 − 275   28. 768 − 496   29. 435 − 189

Problem Solving   Using Data

Use the chart to solve these problems.

30. Which astronaut made the longest space flight? How much longer was his flight than the second-longest flight?

31. A year has 365 days. How many more days in space would Kizim, Solovyov, and Atkou have needed for their flight to last a year?

Longest Space Flights

Astronaut	Days
Polyakov	438
Titov	366
Romanenko	326
Kizim, Solovyov, and Atkou	237
Berezovoi and Lebedev	211
Lucid	188

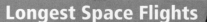

More Practice Set 3.9, p. 450

Problem Solving
Guess and Check

Getting Started

What You'll Need:
▶ calculator

A museum displays 16 masks from around the world on two walls. Six more masks fit on the left wall than on the right wall. How many masks fit on each wall?

You can solve some problems by using Guess and Check.

Here's A Way! Use Guess and Check.

1 Understand

• What do you know about the masks on each wall?

• How many masks are there in all?

2 Plan

• Start with a guess that is easy to check.

3 Try It

• Try a guess that 12 masks fit on the left.

• Check your guess. Will your next guess be higher or lower? Why?

• Use each guess to help you plan the next one.

> First guess:
> 12 masks on the left
> Check:
> $12 - 6 = 6$ masks on the right
> $12 + 6 = 18$
> 12 is too high

4 Look Back

• There are 11 masks on the left and 5 masks on the right. How did checking each guess help you solve the problem?

Show What You Know!

Use Guess and Check to finish the problem.

1. What 3 toys can you buy for exactly 95¢?

2. **Critical Thinking** What can you learn from guesses that are not right?

First guess:
25¢
30¢
+ 35¢
90¢

Which toys should I choose next?

Work It Out!

Use Guess and Check or any strategy to solve the problem.

3. **Calculator** How can you put these six weights on a scale so that the two sides balance? You may use a calculator.

15 25 10 5 45 30
POUNDS

4. How can you fold a square piece of paper 3 times so that when you unfold it, the folds will make 8 triangles?

5. If you double a mystery number and subtract 10, you get 6. What is the mystery number?

6. A classroom has 6 rows of seats with 5 seats in each row. Three seats are empty. How many seats are full?

7. The sum of 2 numbers is 30. Their difference is 8. What are the numbers?

8. There are 4 third-grade classes at a school. Each class has 25 students. Five students in each class do not buy lunch at school. The rest do. How many students buy lunch at school?

Share Your Thinking

9. Can you ever use Guess and Check with another strategy? Explain.

10. What was your first guess in problem 7? Why did you choose it?

Estimating Differences

Suppose you have directions for a model that needs 987 blocks. You know you have about 465 blocks. About how many more blocks do you need?

You can estimate to answer the question.

Here's A Way! Estimate 987 − 465.

Front-end Estimation
Use the digit in the hundreds place to estimate.

$$
\begin{array}{lll}
987 & 9 \text{ hundreds} & 900 \\
-\,465 & -\,4 \text{ hundreds} & -\,400 \\
\hline
& 5 \text{ hundreds} & 500
\end{array}
$$

The front-end estimate is 500.

Rounding
Round both numbers to the nearest hundred to estimate.

$$
\begin{array}{ll}
987 & 1000 \\
-\,465 & -\,500 \\
\hline
& 500
\end{array}
$$

987 rounds up to 1000

465 rounds up to 500

The rounded estimate is 500.

Both methods give the same estimate. You need about 500 more blocks.

Talk About It!

- Find the exact answer. How close is the estimate?

- Would the two methods ever give different estimates? Explain.

Show What You Know!

Estimate which difference is greater. How can you tell?

1. 346 − 128 or 885 − 346
2. 610 − 333 or 451 − 346
3. 492 − 227 or 578 − 219
4. 212 − 145 or 534 − 309

Estimate. Which two numbers have a difference of:

5. about 100?
6. about 200?
7. about 300?
8. about 500?

9. **Number Sense** Use only the digits 4 through 9. Write two 3-digit odd numbers whose difference is about 300.

236 123 770 442

Work It Out!

Estimate the difference. Write the name of the method you used.

10.	62	11.	626	12.	313	13.	86	14.	951
	− 21		− 204		− 196		− 28		− 312

15. 729 − 311
16. 629 − 492
17. 462 − 193
18. 296 − 189

19. 71 − 29
20. 812 − 561
21. 63 − 22
22. 421 − 198

23. 716 − 299
24. 198 − 105
25. 511 − 296
26. 225 − 131

Estimate. Is the answer on the calculator reasonable?

27. 436
    − 182   254

28. 771
    − 362   621

Problem Solving

29. One package has 425 blocks. Another has 195 blocks. About how many more blocks are in the larger package?

30. If you buy both packages, about how many more blocks will you need to make a 900-block model?

More Practice Set 3.11, p. 451

Subtracting With Zeros

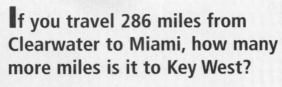

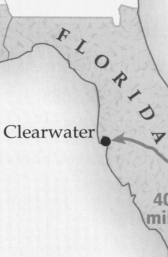

If you travel 286 miles from Clearwater to Miami, how many more miles is it to Key West?

You can subtract to find out.

Clearwater

403 miles

Miami

Key West

Gulf of Mexico

MEXICO

Here's A Way! **Find 403 − 286.**

1 Estimate by rounding.

$$403 \implies 400$$
$$-\,286 \qquad -\,300$$
$$\qquad\qquad 100$$

It is about 100 miles to Key West.

2 There are not enough ones. There are no tens to regroup. Regroup the hundreds.

$$\overset{3\,10}{4\cancel{0}3}$$
$$-\,286$$

3 Then, regroup the tens. Subtract the ones.

$$\overset{\quad 9}{\underset{3\,10\,13}{4\cancel{0}\cancel{3}}}$$
$$-\,28\cancel{6}$$
$$\qquad\quad 7$$

4 Subtract the tens. Then, subtract the hundreds.

$$\overset{\quad 9}{\underset{3\,10\,13}{4\cancel{0}\cancel{3}}}$$
$$-\,286$$
$$\;\;117$$

It is 117 miles to Key West.

5 Check by adding.

$$\overset{1\ 1}{117}$$
$$+\,286$$
$$\;\;403$$

Talk About It! How does the estimate help you know the answer is reasonable?

Other Examples Subtract. Did you need to regroup?

$$304 \qquad\qquad \$500 \qquad\qquad 208$$
$$-\ \ 84 \qquad\qquad -\ 245 \qquad\qquad -\ 198$$

Write the difference. Use mental math when you can.

1. 400
    − 350

2. 704
    − 32

3. $920
    − 20

4. 804
    − 603

5. 500
    − 499

6. **Critical Thinking** When do you not have to regroup a zero in the tens place?

Work It Out!

Write the difference. Use mental math when you can.

7. 320
    − 119

8. 706
    − 545

9. 900
    − 417

10. 403
    − 94

11. $200
    − 50

12. 601
    − 287

13. 807
    − 706

14. $505
    − 25

15. 309
    − 115

16. 807
    − 602

17. 608 − 29   18. 320 − 20   19. 489 − 145   20. 600 − 599

Problem Solving Using Data

Use the table.

21. How much farther is it from Key West to Lakeland than from Clearwater to Miami?

22. **Estimation** You are going from Lakeland to Daytona Beach. You have driven 50 miles. Do you have more than 50 miles still to go?

Mixed Review

Write the answer.

23. 9
    + 3

24. 15
    − 7

25. 6
    + 5

26. 8
    + 9

27. 16
    − 9

Driving Distances

From	To		
	Daytona Beach	Key West	Lakeland
Daytona Beach	—	419 miles	110 miles
Key West	419 miles	—	400 miles
Lakeland	110 miles	400 miles	—

More Practice Set 3.12, p. 451

Problem Solving
Using Guess and Check and Other Strategies

Getting Started

What You'll Need:
▶ calculator

Welcome to the amusement park! There are all kinds of rides, games, and prizes.

Problem Solving Process
✓ Understand
✓ Plan
✓ Try It
✓ Look Back

Choose a Strategy You Have Learned
✓ Act It Out
✓ Look for a Pattern
✓ Guess and Check
 Draw a Picture
 Make a Table
 Work Backward
 Make a List
 Work a Simpler Problem

You and a friend won all these prizes. How can you share them so each of you has prizes worth the same amount of money?

- What problem do you need to solve?

- Do you each have to have the same number of prizes?

- Explain a strategy you can use to solve the problem. Then solve it.

$2.20 $2.25

$1.85

$.95

$2.75

Work It Out!

Use any strategy to solve each problem. Show your work.

1. How can 7 tickets cost $50?

2. Every hour, a booth gives a prize to 1 person. They have 5 prizes to give away. They give the first prize at 9 A.M. When will they give the last prize?

3. **Calculator** Can you visit all the rides by walking less than 1800 yards? Start and end at the entrance.

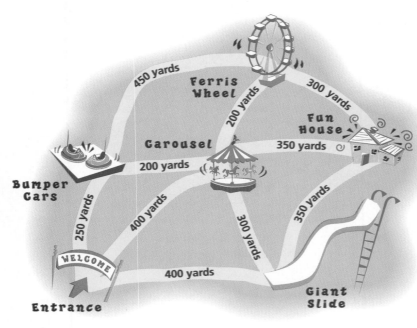

4. The amusement park is having a 1000-yard bicycle race for children. The race will start and end at the carousel. What path will the race follow?

5. The fun house costs 75¢. The other rides each cost 50¢. Can you go on each ride once if you have $3?

6. A puppet show and a concert each last 2 hours. The puppet show is at 10 A.M., 1 P.M., and 3 P.M. The concert is at 11:30 A.M and 2 P.M. How can you see both shows?

7. The fun house ride takes longer than the slide and shorter than the carousel. The Ferris wheel takes longer than the carousel. Which is the shortest ride?

Share Your Thinking

8. What strategy did you use for problem 7? Why?

9. Could you have used a different strategy for problem 7? Explain.

LESSON 14

Problem Solving
Using Strategies

You can read more about animals in the pages of *Ranger Rick.*

Tom Jager, one of the fastest swimmers ever, can swim about 150 yards in a minute. Dolphins can swim about 600 yards in a minute.

Problem Solving Process
✓ Understand
✓ Plan
✓ Try It
✓ Look Back

Choose a Strategy You Have Learned
✓ Act It Out
✓ Look for a Pattern
✓ Guess and Check
  Draw a Picture
  Make a Table
  Work Backward
  Make a List
  Work a Simpler Problem

What would happen if Tom Jager and a dolphin had a race? Suppose Jager gets a 1000 yard head start. About how long would it take the dolphin to pass Jager?

- How much of a head start does Tom Jager get?

- What other information do you have?

- Explain a strategy that can help you solve the problem. Then solve it.

Work It Out!

Use any strategy to solve the problem. Show your work.

1. Suppose each animal dove as deep as it could. Which animal would be closest to the surface? Explain.

Animal	Depth of Dive
Leatherback Sea Turtle	4000 ft
Elephant Seal	5000 ft
Sperm Whale	6000 ft

2. Which animals dive below 4500 ft?

3. Southern Gentoo (jehn TOO) penguins live on the icy-cold Antarctic Peninsula. When they are fully grown, they can be about 30 inches tall. Would a fully grown Gentoo penguin be shorter or taller than you? Explain your answer.

4. Gentoo penguins swim faster than any other penguins. They can swim as far as 40 feet in a second. At that speed, how long would it take a Gentoo to swim 240 feet?

5. Gentoos can stay underwater for 2 minutes before coming up to breathe. How many times does a Gentoo need to come up in 1 hour?

6. A zoo has 5 more adult penguins than baby penguins. There are 15 penguins in all. How many adults are there?

7. **Create Your Own** Write a problem about animals. Use data found in problems 1–5, or look up some new information. See if a classmate can solve your problem.

Share Your Thinking

8. What strategy did you use to solve problem 6? Explain how you could have used a different strategy.

9. Did you use Guess and Check for any of the problems? Explain how you used it if you did.

Chapter 3 Test

for Pages 84–115

Test-Taking Tips
Sometimes it helps to estimate an answer before looking at the answer choices.

Problem Solving

Solve. Show your work. (pages 106, 112)

1. Suppose you and your friend collect cans for recycling. Together you collect 124 cans. You give 10 cans to your friend so that you each have the same number. How many cans did your friend collect to start with?

2. You and your friends played a beanbag game. The winner tossed 5 beanbags to hit the target and scored 60 points. How did the winner get this score?

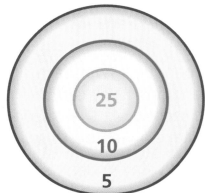

Concepts

Estimate the sum or difference two ways. First use front-end estimation, and then rounding. (pages 92, 108)

3.	4.	5.	6.
418	239	505	722
+ 392	+ 116	− 336	− 191

7. Which two numbers have a sum closest to 500?

325	140
292	368

8. Which two numbers have a difference closest to 400?

125	231
660	316

9. Estimate which sum is greater.

123	333
+ 345	+ 211

10. Estimate which difference is less.

721	562
− 440	− 457

Find the correct sum. Write *a, b, c,* or *d.* (pages 88, 90, 94)

11. 53 + 19	a. 54	b. 72	c. 92	d. 120
12. 268 + 450	a. 718	b. 698	c. 618	d. 598
13. 194 + 565	a. 459	b. 559	c. 669	d. 759
14. 11 + 42 + 18 + 20	a. 51	b. 71	c. 91	d. 910

Find the difference. (pages 102, 104)

15.	16.	17.	18.
73 − 49	92 − 36	835 − 288	216 feet − 124 feet

Find the difference. Circle the difference if you used mental math to solve. (page 110)

19.	20.	21.	22.
600 − 595	480 − 80	300 − 275	150 − 149

 Performance Task

(page 112)

Your school has a bake sale. On Wednesday and Thursday together, 50 cookies were sold. On Thursday and Friday together, 60 cookies were sold. The total for Wednesday, Thursday, and Friday was 90 cookies.

- Copy and complete the chart.

- Explain how you found the correct numbers.

- Write an addition or subtraction problem using the data in your chart.

Keep In Mind . . .
Your work will be evaluated on the following:
- ☑ Strategy for solving
- ☑ Written explanation
- ☑ Clear chart with labels
- ☑ Correct numbers and a method for checking

Cookie Sales

Day	Number of Cookies Sold
Wed.	?
Thurs.	?
Fri.	?

Cumulative Review

Adding and Subtracting 9
(Chapter 1)
Find 9 + 7 and 12 − 9.

> **Here's A Way!**
>
> Use 10. Then, subtract 1 or add 1.
>
> 10 + 7 = 17   12 − 10 = 2
> 17 − 1 = 16   2 + 1 = 3
> 9 + 7 = 16   12 − 9 = 3

Find the sum or difference.

1. 8 + 9   2. 18 − 9   3. 13 − 9
4. 5 + 9   5. 16 − 9   6. 4 + 9
7. 20 − 9   8. 3 + 9   9. 15 − 9

10. How can you use what you know about adding with 9 to help you add with 8?

Thousands (Chapter 2)
What number do the blocks show?

> **Here's A Way!**
>
>
>
> 2000 + 400 + 20 + 6
> 2426 (standard form)
> two thousand four hundred twenty-six

Write the number in standard form.

11.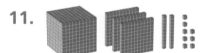

12. five thousand seven hundred sixty

13. nine thousand two hundred eleven

14. eight thousand ninety-nine

15. 7000 + 900 + 30 + 6

16. 6000 + 200 + 40 + 5

17. Write the greatest and least possible numbers using digits 4, 8, 6, and 3.

Place Value (Chapter 2)
Name the value of each digit in 342.

> **Here's A Way!**
>
> Model the number.
>
>
>
> 3 hundreds, 4 tens, 2 ones

Name the value of each digit in the number.

18. 399   19. 993
20. 704   21. 470

22. Make as many different numbers as possible with the digits 3, 7, and 5. Order the numbers from least to greatest.

Telling Time (Chapter 2)

What time is shown on the clock?

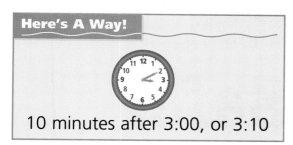

10 minutes after 3:00, or 3:10

Write the time.

23.   24.   25.

26.   27.   28.

29. How many minutes are in 1 hour?

Coin Patterns (Chapter 2)

Find the money amount.

You can use skip-counting.
Say: 50¢, 75¢, 85¢, 95¢.

Write: 95¢

Count the coins. Write the amount.

30.

31.

32.

33. What patterns help you count money? Why?

Problem Solving

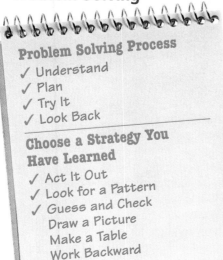

Problem Solving Process
✓ Understand
✓ Plan
✓ Try It
✓ Look Back

Choose a Strategy You Have Learned
✓ Act It Out
✓ Look for a Pattern
✓ Guess and Check
   Draw a Picture
   Make a Table
   Work Backward
   Make a List
   Work a Simpler Problem

Solve. Show your work.

34. Two numbers have a sum of 28 and a difference of 6. What are the numbers?

35. Suppose there are 28 students in your class. The students take turns counting off from 1 to 3 in order, starting with 1. Will more students say the number 2 or the number 3? Explain.

Make It Safe!

Social Studies Connection   **With Your Group**

Bad weather can happen anywhere. When storms do strike, people must often leave their homes to go to a safer place. Imagine that your school will be used as a shelter in an emergency. Your group is in charge of planning the supplies for the shelter. You will need to make a list of supplies that might be needed. Then you will decide how many of each item you should get. Finally, you will write a plan using a $900 budget.

1 Plan It

Pick one kind of storm to prepare an emergency shelter for.

- Why would a shelter be helpful?
- What needs would people have?
- Look at the chart below. It lists the cost of emergency supplies for one person. Which are useful?

2 Put It Together

- Decide how many people you will be able to help. How many people will fit in the school gym?
- Make a list of the most important supplies and how many to buy.
- Figure out how much the supplies will cost. Is it less than $900?

Plan

Budget

Our Shelter

3 Wrap It Up

- Draw a picture of what the shelter will look like.
- Write a paragraph explaining your plan. Include your budget.

4 Discuss Your Results

- Did you meet all of the goals in Keep In Mind?
- How is your plan different from other groups' plans? Discuss any changes you would make in your plan.

Emergency Supplies

Blanket $5.00	Cot $20.00
First aid kit ..$3.00	Pillow...........$9.00
Food.............$5.00	Flashlight $2.00
Batteries.......$3.00	Water $1.00

 Internet

> Visit the **Math Center** at **Houghton Mifflin Education Place.** http://www.eduplace.com

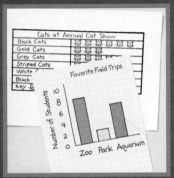

CHAPTER 4

Collecting and Organizing Data

Try This!

Find out fun facts about your classmates. Show the data in a graph.

What You'll Need

crayons, paper

1

Take a survey. Ask ten people these questions. If you start to fold your hands, which thumb is on top? If you cross your legs, which leg is on top? What hand do you write with?

If you start to fold your hands, which thumb is on top?

If you cross your legs, which leg is on top?

What hand do you write with?

2

Keep a tally of the data you gather.

Activity	Right	Left
Folding Hands	IIII	II
Crossing Legs		
Writing		

right hand

left hand

3

Use your data to make a graph. What does your graph show about left-handed people and right-handed people?

How could you add data about crossing your arms?

What different ways do you know to show data?

Ready to Go!

Cooperative Learning
Checklist

☐ Work alone.
☑ Work with a partner.
☑ Work with a group.

LESSON 1

Collecting and Recording Data

Getting Started

What You'll Need:
► recording sheet

Do you like to play soccer? Swim? Dance? What sports or ways to exercise do people your age like? You might want to do a survey of your classmates to find out.

Activity

● **Make a chart or use the chart on your recording sheet.**

1

Label the first column *Activity*. Ask each classmate to name a favorite sport or way to exercise.

②

Record their choices with your tally marks.

Baseball	|||	

③

Finally, count the tally marks. Record the number.

Baseball	|||	3

Show What You Know!

Karate

Use the chart at the right to answer exercises 1–4.

1. What is the most popular activity? How many students said it was their favorite?

2. Which is the least popular activity? How many students named it?

3. How many more students enjoy soccer than baseball?

4. How many students took part in the survey? How can you tell?

Use the survey you completed to answer exercises 5–9.

5. How is the Tally column different from the Number column? How is it the same?

6. **Critical Thinking** As you are collecting data, is it easier to use tallies or numbers to keep track of the results?

7. What is the most popular activity in your class? How many students said it was their favorite?

8. **Critical Thinking** Suppose some classmates did not have a favorite sport or exercise. How could you show that data on your tally sheet?

Our Favorite Ways to Exercise

Activity	Tally	Number
Bicycling	HHT IIII	9
Soccer	HHT I	6
Dance	II	2
Karate	III	3
Baseball	HHT	5

Problem Solving
Draw a Picture

You are buying a toy train. The engine is 8 inches long. Each of the 3 cars is 6 inches long. The space between the cars or car and engine is 1 inch. How many inches long is the train? You can solve problems like this by drawing a picture.

Here's A Way! Draw a Picture to solve the problem.

1 Understand

- What information do you need in order to find the length of the whole train?

2 Plan

- How many engines and train cars should you draw?

- How many spaces should you draw?
  Explain how you know.

3 Try It

- Draw a picture of the engine and the train cars.

- Add the numbers. What is your answer?

4 Look Back

- The train is 29 inches long. How did drawing a picture help you to solve the problem?

Show What You Know!

Copy and finish drawing the picture to help you solve this problem.

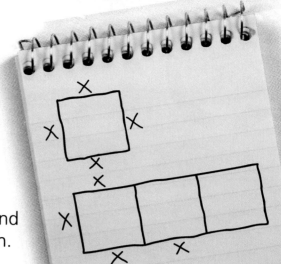

1. Four people can sit around 1 square table. If 3 square tables are pushed together, how many people can be seated?

2. **Critical Thinking** Can more people sit around 3 tables or 3 tables pushed together? Explain.

Work It Out!

Look at the chart. Then use Draw a Picture or any other strategy to solve the problem.

School Library

Type of Material	Space Allowed
Dictionary	4 inches
Video	2 inches
Telephone Book	3 inches

3. Your school librarian leaves 2 inches of shelf space between different kinds of materials. How much space will be needed for 5 dictionaries, 3 videos, and 2 telephone books?

4. If the librarian gets double the number of videos, will one 60-inch shelf be long enough for the materials in problem 3?

5. You can check out up to 3 books each time you visit the school library. Suppose you check out as many books as you can on Tuesday, Thursday, and Friday. How many books have you checked out?

6. You return the books two at a time. How many visits do you make to return the books?

Share Your Thinking

7. Which problems did you solve by drawing a picture?

8. Explain how you solved problem 5.

Problem Solving
Using Draw a Picture and Other Strategies

You decide to take part in a school arts and crafts show. Look at Native American beadwork for ideas.

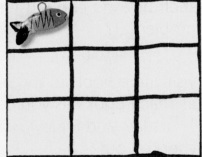

Traditional Native American dress

Problem Solving Process
✓ Understand
✓ Plan
✓ Try It
✓ Look Back

Choose a Strategy You Have Learned
✓ Act It Out
✓ Look for a Pattern
✓ Guess and Check
✓ Draw a Picture
　Make a Table
　Work Backward
　Make a List
　Work a Simpler Problem

To make a beaded badge, you can start with 3 rows of 3 beads. Get 9 beads with 3 different shapes. Every bead in each row and column will have a different shape. How can you arrange the beads?

- What problem needs to be solved?

- How many beads do you have? What kinds of shapes?

- How can you arrange your beads so that all the beads in every row and column are different shapes?

- Explain a strategy that you can use to solve the problem. Then solve it.

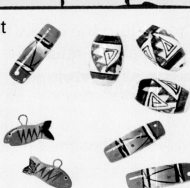

Work It Out!

Use any strategy to solve each problem. Show your work.

1. How much will 5 packages of beads cost?

2. How many packages of beads can you buy with 45¢?

3. **Critical Thinking** The first four beads in a classmate's bracelet are white, red, green, and blue. If he repeats the colors in the same order, what color will the ninth bead be?

Packages of Beads	Price
1	5¢
2	10¢
3	15¢

Look at the chart to answer these questions.

My Bead Collection

Color	Number
Blue	5
Red	3
Orange	0
White	2

4. You trade 3 of your blue beads for 2 white ones. You trade all of your red beads for 2 orange ones. You give away 1 of your white beads. How many beads of each color do you have now?

5. **Patterns** How would you put these beads together to make a bracelet with a pattern? Describe the pattern.

6. You want to make 5 new bracelets. It takes 10 beads to make each one. If there are 20 beads in a pack, how many packs should you buy?

7. **Create Your Own** Design your own bracelet. Use 10 beads with three different colors.

Share Your Thinking

8. Did you need to draw a picture to answer problem 5? Why or why not?

9. Which problem did you solve by using a strategy that is different from drawing a picture? What strategy did you use?

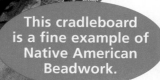

This cradleboard is a fine example of Native American Beadwork.

Pictographs

Vocabulary:
pictograph
Glossary, p. 480

This tally sheet shows some shells you might find at the beach. How can you show the data in a different way?

My Seashell Collection		
Seashell	**Tally**	**Number**
Clam	ЖЖ ЖЖ ЖЖ	15
Bay Scallop	ЖЖ ЖЖ	10
Periwinkle	ЖЖ ЖЖ ЖЖ ЖЖ	20
Mussel	ЖЖ	5

Here's A Way! Make a pictograph.

1 Draw a rectangle.

Make sections for the title, the shell names, the number of shells, and the key. Write the title and names for the kinds of shells.

2 Decide on a key.

Each pail stands for 5 shells.

3 Draw symbols to show the number.

There were 15 clam shells collected. Draw 3 pails next to the clam label. Complete the pictograph.

My Seashell Collection	
Clam	🪣 🪣 🪣
Bay Scallop	🪣 🪣
Periwinkle	🪣 🪣 🪣 🪣
Mussel	🪣

Key: 🪣 = 5 shells

Talk About It! How might skip-counting help you read the pictograph?

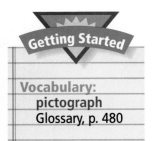

mussel

scallop

periwinkle

clam

Show What You Know!

Use the information in the tally chart below to make a pictograph. The pictograph has been started for you. Remember to write a title. Add a key telling what your symbol stands for.

1. Which bird was seen the least? Explain.

2. Which bird was seen most often?

Water Birds We Saw

Water Bird	Tally	Number
Kingfisher	ЍЍTT ЍЍTT	10
Great Blue Heron	ЍЍTT	5
Ring-Billed Gull	ЍЍTT ЍЍTT ЍЍTT	15
Sandpiper	ЍЍTT ЍЍTT ЍЍTT ЍЍTT	20

Kingfisher	
Great Blue Heron	
Ring-Billed Gull	
Sandpiper	
Key:	

Work It Out!

Use the pictograph to answer the question.

3. How many pieces of driftwood were found?

4. How many more horseshoe crabs than jellyfish were found?

5. How many items were found in all?

6. **Algebraic Reasoning** Would more or fewer pictures be needed if each picture stood for 6 items?

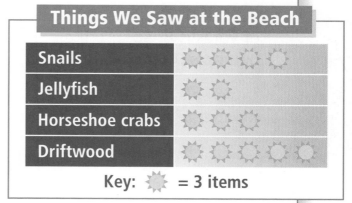

Things We Saw at the Beach

Snails	☀ ☀ ☀ ☀
Jellyfish	☀ ☀
Horseshoe crabs	☀ ☀ ☀
Driftwood	☀ ☀ ☀ ☀ ☀

Key: ☀ = 3 items

More Practice Set 4.4, p. 452

Math Journal

When do you think a pictograph should be used to show data?

Bar Graphs

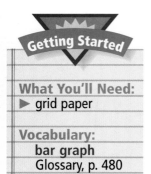

Getting Started

What You'll Need:
▶ grid paper

Vocabulary:
bar graph
Glossary, p. 480

How and when do you do homework? One class voted on these choices. Which idea was the most popular? You can organize the votes in a **bar graph** to make it easier to compare the data.

Here's A Way! Make a bar graph.

1 Write a title at the top.

2 Put on the ideas and label.

3 Put on the numbers and label.

Start at 0. The greatest number of votes is 8. So, use the numbers 0 to 8.

4 Draw bars to show the total number of votes for each idea.

Talk About It!

• Which idea was most popular?

• Do the bars in the graph show the number of ideas or the number of votes? Explain your answer.

votes for each idea

title

ideas

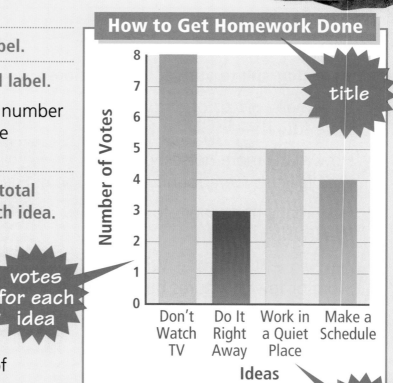

How to Get Homework Done

Show What You Know!

Here is another way you can make a bar graph. Use grid paper. Use the tally sheet to complete the graph.

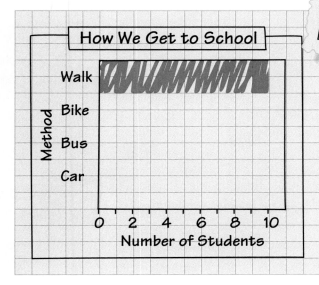

How We Get to School

Method	Number of Students
Walk	⊦⊦⊦⊦ ⊦⊦⊦⊦
Bike	❘ ❘ ❘ ❘
Bus	⊦⊦⊦⊦ ❘
Car	⊦⊦⊦⊦ ❘ ❘ ❘

1. How did you know how long to make each bar in the graph?

2. Did it help you draw the graph to have the information organized in the tally chart? Why or why not?

3. About how many people voted in this survey?

Work It Out!

Use the bar graph to do each exercise.

4. Which activity is the most popular?

5. How many of the students asked to play soccer?

6. **Critical Thinking** How is a bar graph like a pictograph? How is it different? Explain.

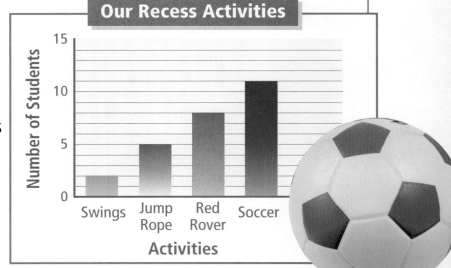

Our Recess Activities

7. **Critical Thinking** Look at the two bar graphs on this page. How are they alike? How are they different? Do they give different information? Explain.

8. **Create Your Own** Write a question about the data on this graph.

More Practice Set 4.5, p. 452

Line Graphs

Rainforests get a lot of rain. A **line graph** shows how something changes over time. This line graph shows rainfall amounts for January through June. How much rain fell in April?

Here's A Way! Read a line graph.

1 Read the title.

Where is this rainforest?

2 Read the labels.

What do the labels at the bottom and the side of the graph show?

3 Use the labels to answer the question.

Find April on the bottom of the graph. Go up to the point. Then go across to the left side of the graph to find the amount of rainfall.

About 13 inches of rain fell in April.

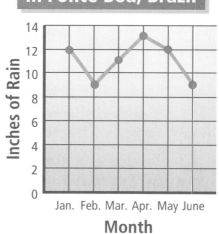

Monthly Rainfall in Fonte Boa, Brazil

Talk About It!

How did connecting the points on the line graph make it easier to see how the rainfall changed?

Use the rainfall graph on page 134 to answer the questions.

1. In what month did the least amount of rain fall? How many inches fell?

2. Which two months had about the same amount of rainfall?

3. Which four months had 9 inches or more of rainfall?

4. Did more rain fall in March or in May? How much more?

5. How did the amount of rainfall change between March and April? Explain.

Work It Out!

Use the line graph to answer the questions.

6. Which month had the greatest amount of rainfall?

7. Which two months had about the same amount of rainfall?

8. Which month had the least amount of rainfall?

9. **Critical Thinking** What happened to the amount of rainfall each month from October to December? How do you know?

10. **Create Your Own** Write a question to compare this data with the data on rainfall in Brazil. Exchange your question with a partner. Answer each other's questions.

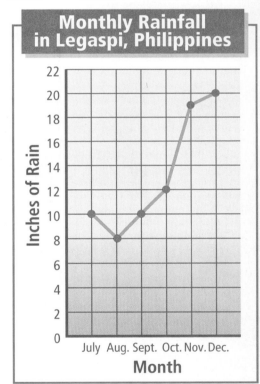

Monthly Rainfall in Legaspi, Philippines

Inches of Rain

July Aug. Sept. Oct. Nov. Dec.

Month

More Practice Set 4.6, p. 453

Math Journal

You can record data in more than one way. List some ways. When would you use each method? Explain.

LESSON 7

Using Temperature Data

Use What You Know

The temperature 31°F is read, "thirty one degrees Fahrenheit."

You can use computers to find out about the weather all over the world. Look at a temperature table to find out the weather in Chicago. *High* means the highest temperature that day. *Low* means the lowest temperature that day.

Here's A Way! Read a temperature table.

Daily Temperatures for the Week of November 11

CHICAGO	Mon.	Tues.	Wed.	Thurs.	Fri.	Sat.	Sun.
High	31°F	37°F	34°F	37°F	38°F	39°F	48°F
Low	18°F	18°F	20°F	27°F	32°F	34°F	29°F

1 Look at the title. It tells you what the table is about.

- What information is shown in this table?

2 Look at the labels on the side. They tell you what data is in each row.

- What do the labels High and Low mean?
- For what season does this table show information?

3 Look at the labels across the top. They tell you what data is in each column.

- Which day had the highest temperature? The lowest temperature?

Talk About It! Was the temperature ever 20 degrees on Wednesday? On Friday? How can you tell?

Use the table on page 136 to answer the questions.

1. Which day had the greatest difference in temperatures?

2. On which day was the difference between the high and low temperature 10 degrees?

3. Write the difference between the high and low temperatures for Friday. For Saturday. For Sunday.

4. **Critical Thinking** Could you show the data in a different way? How?

Work It Out!

The table below shows the high temperatures for Dallas and Chicago during one week. Use the table to answer the questions.

High Temperatures: Week of November 11							
	Mon.	Tues.	Wed.	Thurs.	Fri.	Sat.	Sun
Chicago	31°F	37°F	34°F	37°F	38°F	39°F	48°F
Dallas	75°F	68°F	74°F	67°F	61°F	74°F	78°F

5. What was the highest temperature in Chicago?

6. Was it warmer in Dallas or in Chicago? Explain.

7. In which of these cities would you go swimming outdoors? On which days? Explain.

8. Would you wear a coat outdoors in Chicago that week?

Problem Solving

9. **Algebraic Reasoning** The difference between the high and low temperatures one day was 16 degrees. If the low was 21 degrees, what was the high temperature?

10. **Create Your Own** Make up your own problem from the table.

More Practice Set 4.7, p. 454

Problem Solving
Is the Answer Reasonable?

Your class decides to collect newspapers for recycling for one week. On Thursday, you make a bar graph to show how much you have collected so far. What reasonable statements can you make about the recycling drive?

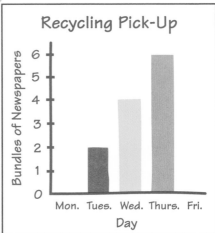

Recycling Pick-Up

You Decide

- Describe the pattern you see in the bar graph.
- Does the pattern have to continue? Explain.
- Can you tell what Friday's amount will be? Explain.

Work It Out!

Is each statement reasonable? Tell why or why not.

1. Your class will collect its largest number of newspapers on Friday.

2. Your class will collect more than 10 packs of newspapers in one week.

3. If the class collects cans it will get the same pattern as on the graph.

4. On Wednesday, your class collected twice as many packs as on Tuesday.

5. **Create Your Own** Suppose the recycling drive went on for three more weeks. Make a graph that would show the amount of newspapers collected in those weeks.

Share Your Thinking

6. How can you decide whether a pattern for collecting newspapers will continue? Explain your answer.

Midchapter Review
for Pages 122–138

Problem Solving

Solve. Show your work. (pages 124, 126, 128, 138)

1. You stack a tower of blocks with the following color pattern: 2 red, 1 blue, 2 red, 1 yellow. When the tower has 5 yellow blocks, how many red blocks will it have?

2. You invite 6 friends to a pizza party. There are 2 pizzas cut into 8 slices each. How many slices can you and your friends each have, if you all have the same number of slices?

Concepts

Read the table. Then, answer the question. (page 134, 136)

3. What kind of data is shown in the table?

4. How does the data change from Tuesday to Friday?

5. How does the data change between Friday and Saturday?

6. How would you find this type of data for your own neighborhood?

Denver Temperatures

Day	High
Tues.	65°F
Wed.	60°F
Thurs.	50°F
Fri.	35°F
Sat.	55°F

Skills

Use the bar graph to answer the question.
(pages 130, 132)

7. Which is the favorite activity? Which is the least favorite?

8. Which activity is about twice as popular as cooking?

9. Each student chose 1 activity. How many students voted?

10. How would you show an activity that no students liked?

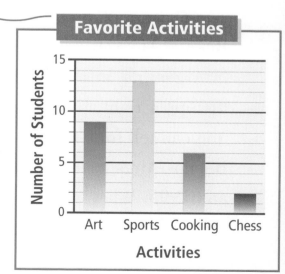

Favorite Activities

Math World

Explore different ways of recording and organizing data throughout history.

1925 1995

A Picture Record

The photograph on the upper left shows Buenos Aires (BWAY nohs EYE rays), a city in Argentina, in 1925. The photograph on the upper right shows Buenos Aires in 1995. You can tell from the photographs that Buenos Aires changed a lot between 1925 and 1995. What information can you collect from the photographs?

Try This! CHINESE TALLY STICK

About 2000 years ago, people in China would tally information on long wooden sticks called Han Sticks. Some sticks found on the Great Wall of China tell how much work the builders did each day. Follow these steps to make a tally stick that is similar to a Chinese Han Stick.

1 Cut a piece of paper in half the long way.

2 Write numbers and draw pictures to tell how many people did something. Write in columns.

3 Share your tally stick with a friend. Can your friend read your tally stick?

Chinese Writing

The Chinese write in long columns today because they used to write in columns on tally sticks.

Respond

Work with a partner . . .
to think of other ways to record data.

Internet:
Houghton Mifflin Education Place
Explore the Math Center at
http://www.eduplace.com

Experimenting with Chance

Cooperative Learning Checklist

- ☐ Work alone.
- ☑ Work with a partner.
- ☑ Work with a group.

Getting Started

What You'll Need:
- ▶ 5 red cubes
- ▶ 5 blue cubes
- ▶ recording sheet
- ▶ paper bag
- ▶ 10 blank cards

Put 5 red cubes and 5 blue cubes in a bag. What color cube do you think you will pick more often? Why? Experimenting with colored cubes can show you how you can make a good guess.

Activity

- Take turns picking 1 cube out of the bag.
- Use the recording sheet or another piece of paper. Make a tally for the color you pick.

1

- Pick one cube from the bag without looking.
- Mark the color of the cube on the recording sheet. Use a tally mark.
- Put the cube back in the bag.

2
- Take turns until you have chosen a cube 24 times.
- Each time you choose a cube, use a tally mark to record the result on your recording sheet.

3
- Now put 5 red cubes and 1 blue cube into the bag.
- Repeat Step 2 with this bag of cubes.

Show What You Know!

1. How often did you pick a red cube in Step 2? In Step 3?

2. How often did you pick a blue cube in Step 2? In Step 3?

3. Which color cube did you pick more often in Step 3? Why?

4. **Algebraic Reasoning** How many cubes of each color would you put in a bag so that you would be certain to pick blue cubes more often than red ones?

5. **Number Sense** If you had 4 red cubes and 4 blue cubes, which color would be picked more often? Why?

6. **Write About It** Compare your recording sheet with those of your classmates. What do you notice?

Problem Solving Using Data

The bar graph shows the results of picking a card many times from a deck of 10 cards.

7. How can you tell which color was picked the most even though there are no numbers on the graph?

8. Did the deck have more green cards or blue cards? Why do you think so?

9. **Create Your Own** Make a deck of 10 cards. Color one side of each card red, green, or blue. How would you create your deck so you will get results like those in the bar graph? Try it to check.

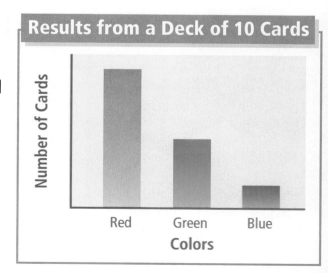

Results from a Deck of 10 Cards

Probability

You have used cubes to do an experiment with chance. Now do some experiments with spinners.

Activity

• **Take turns using the spinner.**
• **Record the results on a recording sheet.**

1 Make a spinner with 4 equal parts. Color 2 parts white, 1 part blue, and 1 part red.

2 Spin once. On what color does the spinner stop?

• Make a tally mark for that color on your recording sheet.

3 Take turns so that each of you spins the spinner 10 times.

• Use tally marks to record the colors.

4

Make a spinner with 6 equal parts. Color 1 part blue, 2 red, 1 yellow, 1 green, and 1 white.

- Suppose you spin 20 times. Which color will you spin most often? Why?

5

Spin the spinner 20 times. Use a tally to record your data.

- Did you get the results you thought you would?

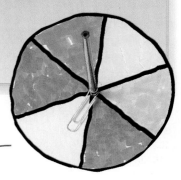

Show What You Know!

Use the spinners to answer the questions.

1. **Patterns** Think about the first spinner. Is the spinner more likely to stop on white than on red? Explain.

2. **Patterns** Think about the second spinner. Is the spinner less likely to stop on green than on blue? Explain.

Look at the three spinners below. Write a, b, or c to answer the question.

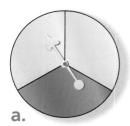   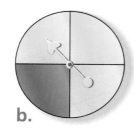   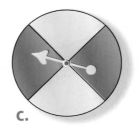

a.   b.   c.

3. **Estimation** Suppose you can win a game by spinning yellow the most often. Which spinner would you like to play with?

4. **Estimation** Suppose you can win a game by spinning green most often. Which spinner would you like to play with?

 Create Your Own Draw a spinner that would be

5. more likely to stop on green than on red.

6. impossible to stop on yellow.

7. equally likely to stop on blue or white.

8. **Critical Thinking** Describe how you chose to color your spinners.

LESSON 11

Make Predictions

Cooperative Learning
Checklist
☐ Work alone.
☑ Work with a partner.
☑ Work with a group.

When you say what you think will happen, you make a **prediction**. You made predictions with spinners. Now use cubes.

Getting Started

What You'll Need:
▶ recording sheet
▶ 2 number cubes

Vocabulary:
prediction
Glossary, p. 480

Activity

Sum	Tally	Total
1		
2		
3		
4		
5		
6		
7		
8		
9		
10		
11		
12		

1

Make a tally chart. Use the chart in the picture as a model.

• Roll two number cubes. Find their sum.

• Use a tally mark to record their sum in the Tally column.

2

Predict the sum you will roll most often with the two number cubes.

• Record your prediction on a separate piece of paper.

3

Take turns. Roll the cubes 30 times.
- Find the sums.
- Record the sums in the Tally column.

4

Find the number of times you rolled each sum.

Sum	Tally	Total
2	IIII	4
3	II	2

Show What You Know!

Compare how often you rolled each sum. Then answer the questions.

1. **Critical Thinking** Which sum did you roll most often? How does the sum compare to your prediction?

2. **Critical Thinking** Which sum did you roll least often? Why do you think that sum was rolled least often?

Choose one paragraph of a favorite book in your classroom. Use that paragraph to make predictions about how often letters of the alphabet appear in words.

3. Which letter do you think will appear most often? Explain.

4. Which letter do you think will not appear at all? Explain.

5. Use one table on your recording sheet to tally the number of letters. Add to complete the table.

6. Compare your predictions to the actual totals.

7. Use the other table to count the letters in another paragraph. Compare the results. Were the results about the same?

8. **Write About It** Why do you think some letters appear more often than other letters?

Ladybug, ladybug,

Fly away, do!

Fly to the mountain

To feed upon dew.

Feed upon dew

And when you are

through

Ladybug, ladybug,

Fly home again, do!

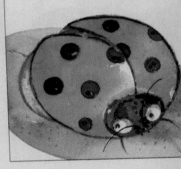

| **Mixed Review** | Find the answer. |

9.
$$\begin{array}{r} 9 \\ 5 \\ +1 \\ \hline \end{array}$$

10.
$$\begin{array}{r} 3 \\ 6 \\ +7 \\ \hline \end{array}$$

11.
$$\begin{array}{r} 500 \\ -\ \ 1 \\ \hline \end{array}$$

12.
$$\begin{array}{r} 9 \\ 2 \\ +9 \\ \hline \end{array}$$

13.
$$\begin{array}{r} 703 \\ -549 \\ \hline \end{array}$$

14.
$$\begin{array}{r} 8 \\ 8 \\ +2 \\ \hline \end{array}$$

147

Problem Solving
Using Strategies

Read more about the speed of birds from the pages of *Flight*.

Birds fly by flapping their wings up and down or by gliding. While gliding, birds hold their wings almost still.

Problem Solving Process
- ✓ Understand
- ✓ Plan
- ✓ Try It
- ✓ Look Back

Choose a Strategy You Have Learned
- ✓ Act It Out
- ✓ Look for a Pattern
- ✓ Guess and Check
- ✓ Draw a Picture
- ✓ Make a Table
- ✓ Work Backward
- ✓ Make a List
- ✓ Work a Simpler Problem

•**L**ook at the list telling how fast some birds fly. How can you put the facts on a bulletin board display for your class?

- What problem needs to be solved?

- What information do you have?

- Explain a strategy that can help you to solve the problem. Then solve it.

How Fast Does a Bird Fly?

Bird	Speed
Carrion Crow	31 miles in an hour
Common Crane	42 miles in an hour
Hummingbird	27 miles in an hour
Kestrel	20 miles in an hour
White Stork	42 miles in an hour

Work It Out!

Use any strategy to solve the problem. Show your work.

How High Does a Bird Fly?

Bird	Height in Feet
Bearded Vulture	25,000
Evening Grosbeak	12,000
Mallard Duck	21,000
Whistling Swan	4000

1. Which of the birds flies at the highest altitude? At the lowest altitude?

2. How could you rearrange these facts to make another kind of graph?

3. Which bird flies about twice as high as the Evening Grosbeak?

4. How much higher does the duck fly than the swan?

5. You want to pin two postcards on a sheet of paper that is 9 inches wide and 12 inches long. Can you leave a 1-inch space between the cards?

Scarlet Ibis 3 in. 5 in.

6. Sixteen students each wants to buy 1 postcard. Four other students each wants to buy 2 postcards. A store has 14 duck cards, 2 blue bird cards, and 5 owl cards. Are there enough cards for the 20 students?

7. A flock of 20 birds uses a birdbath, always four birds at a time. How many groups of four birds would be using the birdbath so that all the birds use it once?

Snowy Egret

8. A full birdbath has 12 cups of water. Each day it loses 3 cups of water. Once each day you add 1 more cup. In how many days will the birdbath be empty?

Share Your Thinking

9. Choose one of the problems you solved. What strategy did you use? How did it help you to solve the problem?

10. Did you combine two strategies in any of the problems? Explain.

Chapter 4 Test

for Pages 122-149

Test-Taking Tips
Remember that pictographs show amounts with pictures.

Problem Solving

Solve. Show your work. (pages 126, 128)

1. You are making a wooden sign that says WELCOME. You want each letter to be 6 inches wide. You will have to leave an inch of space between the letters. You also need 3 inches between the word and each edge of the sign. How wide will your sign need to be?

2. Suppose your school has $30 to spend on new paint sets. Each set costs $4. How many sets can the school buy?

Concepts

Answer the question. Use connecting cubes to help. (pages 144, 146)

3. You put 6 red cubes and 3 blue cubes in a bag. Which color are you more likely to pick from the bag? Why?

4. In another bag you put 5 green cubes and 5 yellow cubes. Which color would you be more likely to pick from this bag? Why?

5. Suppose you put all the red, blue, green, and yellow cubes into one bag. Which color would you be most likely to pick?

Choose the best answer. Write a, b, or c. (page 144)

6. On which color is the spinner most likely to stop?
   a. yellow   b. blue   c. red

7. On which color is the spinner least likely to stop?
   a. equally likely on   b. red   c. yellow
   blue and yellow

Use the pictograph to answer the question. (page 130)

8. How many plants were bought by parents?

9. Were more plants sold to teachers or to parents?

10. What was the total number of plants sold?

11. Could you show the same information in a bar graph? Explain.

Who Bought Plants?	
Students	🌱🌱🌱🌱🌱🌱
Teachers	🌱🌱🌱🌱🌱🌱🌱🌱🌱🌱🌱
Parents	🌱🌱🌱🌱🌱🌱🌱🌱🌱
Others	🌱🌱
Key: 🌱 = 1 plant	

 Performance Task

(page 130)

Suppose a class was asked what chores they do most often.

10 students said taking out the trash.

4 students said washing dishes.

8 students said feeding pets.

2 students said sweeping.

Create a pictograph using the data.

• Include a title and a key for your pictograph.

• Use the graph to write 3 true number sentences with >, <, or =.

Keep In Mind . . .

Your work will be evaluated on the following:

☑ Clear, correct pictograph

☑ Labels for all parts

☑ True number sentences

☑ Good title, key, and picture symbols

Cumulative Review

Ordering, Comparing (Chapter 1)
Order the numbers from greatest to least: 32, 36, 94, 17.

Here's A Way!

Compare the tens digits. If two numbers have the same tens digit, look at the ones digit.
94, 36, 32, 17

Order from least to greatest.

1. 64, 60, 88, 75   2. 16, 34, 15, 43

Compare the numbers. Write >, <, or =.

3. 56 ● 86   4. 93 ● 96   5. 67 ● 76

6. 10 ● 20   7. 39 ● 39   8. 88 ● 78

9. How do you know your answer to problem 4 is true?

Mental Math (Chapter 2)
Find 500 + 300 and 500 − 300.

Here's A Way!

Use a basic fact.

$5 + 3 = 8$ $5 - 3 = 2$

$$\begin{array}{r} 500 \\ + 300 \\ \hline 800 \end{array}$$ $$\begin{array}{r} 500 \\ - 300 \\ \hline 200 \end{array}$$

Find the sum or difference.

10. 80 − 50   11. 800 − 500

12. 8000 − 5000   13. 30 + 60

14. 300 + 600   15. 3000 + 6000

16. Describe the pattern in exercises 13, 14, and 15.

3-Digit Addition (Chapter 3)
Add 466 and 385.

Here's A Way!

• Add and regroup the ones.
• Add and regroup the tens.
• Add the hundreds.

$$\begin{array}{r} \overset{1\ 1}{466} \\ + 385 \\ \hline 851 \end{array}$$

Find the sum.

17. $$\begin{array}{r} 495 \\ + \ 36 \\ \hline \end{array}$$ 18. $$\begin{array}{r} 784 \\ + 196 \\ \hline \end{array}$$

19. $$\begin{array}{r} 373 \\ + \ 89 \\ \hline \end{array}$$ 20. $$\begin{array}{r} 577 \\ + 398 \\ \hline \end{array}$$

21. $$\begin{array}{r} 634 \\ + 287 \\ \hline \end{array}$$ 22. $$\begin{array}{r} 279 \\ + 137 \\ \hline \end{array}$$

23. Suppose you are adding two 3-digit numbers. The sum of the ones is 14. What digit should you write for the ones? What else should you do?

2-Digit Subtraction (Chapter 3)
Find 73 − 28.

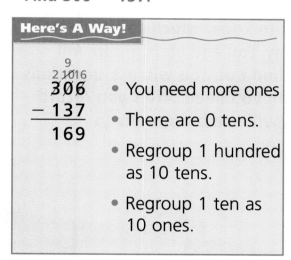

Here's A Way!

  ⁶¹³
  73   Since 8 > 3, you
− 28   need to regroup
  45   1 ten as 10 ones.

Find the difference.

24.	53	25.	42
	− 18		− 29

26.	74	27.	81
	− 36		− 17

28.	65	29.	32
	− 49		− 15

Subtracting with Zeros (Chapter 3)
Find 306 − 137.

Here's A Way!

    9
  2 10 16
  3 0 6   • You need more ones
− 1 3 7   • There are 0 tens.
  1 6 9   • Regroup 1 hundred
             as 10 tens.
           • Regroup 1 ten as
             10 ones.

Find the difference.

30.	400	31.	603
	− 270		− 317

32.	708	33.	201
	− 431		− 145

34.	509	35.	100
	− 284		− 75

36. Explain why you sometimes need to regroup the tens twice in subtraction.

Problem Solving

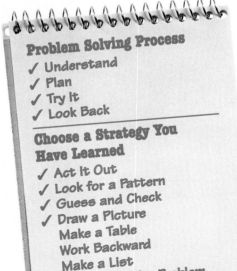

Problem Solving Process
✓ Understand
✓ Plan
✓ Try It
✓ Look Back

Choose a Strategy You Have Learned
✓ Act It Out
✓ Look for a Pattern
✓ Guess and Check
✓ Draw a Picture
  Make a Table
  Work Backward
  Make a List
  Work a Simpler Problem

Solve the problem. Show your work.

37. To advertise a school food drive, you stack a triangle of cans in the lobby. There are 5 cans on the bottom, then 4 cans, and so on, up to 1. How many cans in all are in the triangle?

38. At the end of the food drive, your class collected 197 cans. Another class collected 209 cans. Your goal is 500 cans. Estimate to decide if you have more or less than your goal. Then check to see if you are right.

4

I N V E S T I G A T I O N

Tennis Anyone?

Health Connection   **With Your Group**

A local television station is planning its sports programs. They want to know which sports your classmates like to play. You and your group will conduct a survey to find out. You will ask questions to get the information you need. After you record the information, you will use bar graphs to display the results.

1

Plan It

- Think of sports you and your classmates like to play or watch.
- Pick what you think are eight favorite sports.
- Create a tally sheet like the one shown at the right. Leave space for other sports. Also, make a space for "None" in case someone does not like sports.

Sport	Play	Watch
soccer	卌 卌 IIII	卌
football	III	卌 II
basketball	卌 III	卌 卌
tennis	卌	I
hockey		卌
swimming		卌 卌
gymnastics		卌
ping pong	卌 I	

2

Put It Together

- Ask your classmates which three sports they like to play and which three sports they like to watch.
- Use tally marks to record their answers.

3

Wrap It Up

- Make two bar graphs. One is for the sports your class plays. The other is for the sports your class watches.
- Total the tally marks to make the bar graphs.
- Put a title and labels on your graphs.

4

Discuss Your Results

- Did you meet all of the goals in Keep In Mind?
- Which sports are the favorites?
- Does your class like to play and watch the same sports?

Internet

> Visit the **Math Center** at
Houghton Mifflin Education Place.
http://www.eduplace.com

155

Use What You Know

$4 \times 3 = 12$

- how to multiply

$2, 4, 6, 8, 10, 12$

$5, 10, 15, 20, 25, 30$

- how to skip-count by 2's and 5's

multiply

equal groups

product

- the vocabulary

CHAPTER 5

Multiplication and Division to 5

Try This!

You can skip-count and multiply to find totals. Look for ways to skip-count and multiply in this number code activity.

What You'll Need

paper, pencil

1

Look at the number code. Notice what the different letters are worth.

A	B	C	D	E	F	G	H	I	J	K	L	M
5¢	1¢	1¢	1¢	5¢	1¢	1¢	1¢	5¢	1¢	1¢	1¢	1¢

N	O	P	Q	R	S	T	U	V	W	X	Y	Z
2¢	5¢	2¢	2¢	2¢	4¢	4¢	5¢	2¢	2¢	2¢	4¢	2¢

1 One red rooster went cock-a-doodle-doo.

3

2

Find a sentence in a story. Estimate the total value of the letters. Write your estimate as a money amount. Find the exact value. You can skip-count, multiply, or use a calculator. Write the total money amount.

estimate 95¢

One red rooster
5 2 5   2 5 1   2 5 5 4 4 5 2

went cock-a-doodle-doo.
2 5 2 4   1 5 1 1   5   1 5 5 1 1 5   1 5 5

$1.02

3

Can you write a sentence that is worth $1.00? More than a dollar?

How did you use multiplication or skip-counting as you worked?

Gina likes to ride
1 5 2 5   1 5 1 5 4   4 5   2 5 1 5

her bike to the park.
1 5 2   1 5 1 5   4 5   4 1 5   2 5 2 1

$1.00

What math did you use in the activity?

Ready to Go!

157

LESSON 1

Understanding Multiplication

Cooperative Learning
Checklist

☐ Work alone.
☑ Work with a partner.
☑ Work with a group.

You can show repeated addition and multiplication by making arrays of counters.

Getting Started

What You'll Need:
▶ counters

Activity

> In an array, all the rows are equal.

1

- Copy the chart on the next page.
- Make 3 rows of 4 counters.
- In your chart, write an addition sentence to describe the array.

$$4 + 4 + 4 = 12$$

2

Use words to describe the array. Record.

3 rows of 4 counters is 12 counters.

3

You can also write a multiplication sentence to describe the array. Record the multiplication sentence.

$$3 \times 4 = 12$$

4

Complete the chart. Repeat
steps 1–3 for these arrays.

a. 3 rows of 3 counters

b. 2 rows of 4 counters

c. 3 rows of 5 counters

Addition Sentence	Words	Multiplication Sentence
4 + 4 + 4 = 12	3 rows of 4 counters is 12 counters	3 × 4 = 12

Show What You Know!

1. How many 7's are added in 7 + 7 + 7 = 21?

2. Write a multiplication sentence that means the same as 7 + 7 + 7 = 21.

3. **Critical Thinking** Explain why your multiplication sentence means the same as the addition sentence.

Write an addition sentence and a multiplication sentence for the array.

4.

5.

6.

7. **Critical Thinking** Which was shorter to write for the arrays, an addition sentence or a multiplication sentence? Explain.

8. **Number Sense** Can you write a multiplication sentence for this picture? Explain your answer.

Write a related multiplication sentence. Then, draw an array if you can. If you can't, explain why not.

9. 2 + 2 + 2 = 6   10. 1 + 1 + 1 = 3   11. 0 + 0 + 0 = 0

12. 4 + 4 + 4 + 4 = 16   13. 5 + 5 + 5 + 5 = 20

14. 2 + 2 + 2 + 2 + 2 = 10   15. 3 + 3 + 3 = 9

2

Multiplying with 2

You and a friend are searching the beach for sea treasures. Each of you finds 3 sand dollars. How many sand dollars do you and your friend have in all?

You can find the answer in many ways.

Here's A Way! Find 2 × 3.

You can...

① Use counters.

② Draw.

③ Add.

$$3 + 3 = 6$$

④ Skip-count.

3 6

⑤ You can also write a multiplication sentence.

2	×	3	=	6
factor		factor		product

numbers you multiply   answer

You read 2 × 3 = 6 as "two times three equals six."

You and your friend have 6 sand dollars altogether.

Talk About It!

How is multiplying by 2 like adding doubles?

1. Copy and complete the chart.

2. **Patterns** What patterns do you notice on the chart?

3. **Critical Thinking** What is another way to find the answer when you multiply by 2?

Addition	Multiplication
2 + 2 = 4	2 × 2 = 4
2 + 2 + 2 = 6	3 × 2 = 6
?	4 × 2 = 8
?	?
?	?

Work It Out!

Draw a picture to the show the number sentence. Write the product.

4. 4 × 2 = ■   5. 3 × 2 = ■   6. 5 × 2 = ■   7. 2 × 5 = ■

Write the product.

8. 2 × 1   9. 2 × 2   10. 2 × 3   11. 2 × 4   12. 2 × 5

13. 2 × 0   14. 1 × 2   15. 4 × 2   16. 3 × 2   17. 5 × 2

18. **Write About It** If you multiply a whole number by 2, will the product ever be an odd number? Explain.

19. **Number Sense** How is 2 + 2 + 2 + 2 like 4 × 2?

Problem Solving

20. You walked 6 blocks to the beach. Then you walked home the same way. How many blocks did you walk in all?

21. Yesterday you started collecting some shells. Today you added 13 more. Now you have 43 shells in all. How many of them did you find yesterday?

Mixed Review

Write the answer.

22.
$$\begin{array}{r} 777 \\ +\ 222 \end{array}$$

23.
$$\begin{array}{r} \$441 \\ -\ \$118 \end{array}$$

24.
$$\begin{array}{r} 54 \\ +\ 16 \end{array}$$

25.
$$\begin{array}{r} 121 \\ -\ 65 \end{array}$$

26.
$$\begin{array}{r} 369 \\ +\ 84 \end{array}$$

More Practice Set 5.2, p. 454

Problem Solving
Make a Table

In science class, you learn that a 4 oz bat will eat 8 oz of insects each day. How many ounces of insects will it eat in one week?

Some problems can be solved by making a table.

Here's A Way! Make a Table to solve the problem.

1 Understand

- What does a bat eat in 1 day?
- How many days are in 1 week?

2 Plan

- How can a table help you find out what the bat eats in 1 week?
- What will you label each column?

3 Try It

- Make a table.
- Fill in a few rows.
- Do you see a pattern?
  Use the pattern to complete the table.

4 Look Back

- The bat will eat 56 ounces of insects in 1 week.
  How did making the table help you to solve the problem?
  What pattern did you use?

What the Bat Eats

Number of Days	Ounces of Insects
1	8
2	16
3	24
4	

Make a Table to solve the problem.

1. You want to buy some nature cards. Each card costs 10¢. You have 98¢, but you need to save 25¢ for bus fare. How many nature cards can you buy?

Cards Bought	Money Left
0	98¢
1	88¢
2	78¢

2. **Critical Thinking** How is this table different from the one you used on page 162?

Work It Out!

Use Make a Table or another strategy to solve these problems.

3. Suppose you earn $6 a week by collecting cans to recycle. You have earned $12 so far. In how many more weeks will you be able to buy a game that costs $38?

4. Three dimes and 1 nickel equal 35¢. What other combinations of dimes and nickels equal 35¢?

5. Suppose you have 38¢ in two pockets. In one pocket you have 2 nickels and 3 pennies. There are no pennies in your other pocket. What coins could you have in your other pocket?

6. In a cave there were 7 bats, 4 crickets, and 3 lizards. Some of these animals left the cave. Now there are 2 of each kind. What animals left the cave?

7. You have a mystery number. You add 5 to it. Your friend has the same mystery number. He multiplies it by 2. You both get the same answer. What is the mystery number?

8. In gym you are learning to do exercises on the floor mat. You learn 2 new exercises each week. So far you have learned 4 exercises. How many exercises will you know in 5 more weeks?

Share Your Thinking

9. What table could you make to solve problem 8? What pattern do you see in the table?

Understanding Division

Cooperative Learning Checklist

☐ Work alone.
☑ Work with a partner.
☐ Work with a group.

Getting Started

What You'll Need:
► 30 counters
► recording sheet

When you separate one set of objects into two or more equal sets, you use division.

- Division can tell you how many objects are in each set.
- Division can also tell you how many sets you can make.

Activity

How Many in Each Set?

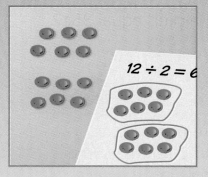

$12 \div 2 = 6$

The division sentence tells how many are in each set.

1 Divide 12 counters into 2 equal sets. Draw a picture to show what you did.

2 Write the division sentence that goes with your picture. Talk about what it means.

3 Repeat Steps 1 and 2 to show
- 3 equal sets.
- 12 equal sets.

4 Make a chart like the one below or use the recording sheet. Take 30 counters. Complete the top chart. Write the division sentence that tells how you got each number.

Name _____ Date _____

RECORDING SHEET

Total number of counters	Number of equal sets	How many in each set?	
30	2	15	$30 \div 2 = 15$
30	3		
30	6		
16	2		
16	4		
16	8		
21	3		

5 Take 12 counters. Separate them into sets of 2 until all the counters are gone. Draw a picture to show what you did.

$12 \div 2 = 6$

The division sentence tells how many sets you can make.

6 Write the division sentence that goes with your picture. Talk about what the division sentence means.

7 Repeat Steps 1 and 2 to show
- 3 in each set.
- 12 in each set.
- 1 in each set.

8 Make a chart or use your recording sheet. Take 30 counters. Complete the bottom chart. Write the division sentence that tells how you got each number.

Show What You Know!

1. **Algebraic Reasoning** What happens to the number in each set as the number of sets gets larger? Why?

2. **Algebraic Reasoning** What happens to the number of sets as the number in each set gets larger? Why?

Write the number of nickels you get if you trade the pennies. Use counters if you wish.

3. 20 pennies   4. 15 pennies   5. 30 pennies

6. 5 pennies   7. 10 pennies   8. 27 pennies

9. **Write About It** Tell how you found the answer to exercise 7.

10. **Critical Thinking** Explain what happened when you traded 27 pennies for nickels.

11. How many different ways can you separate 24 counters into equal groups?

Use What You Know

A nickel has the same value as 5 pennies.

Dividing by 2

Your neighborhood bike shop sells racing bikes. The owner of the shop has 10 bike tires. How many bikes can she put together?

You can find the answer in many ways.

How is this bike different from other bikes you have seen?

Getting Started

Vocabulary:
dividend
divisor
quotient
Glossary, p. 480

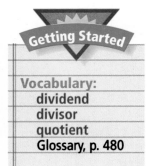

Here's A Way!   Find $10 \div 2$.

You can...

1 Use counters.

2 Draw.

3 Subtract.

10	8	6	4	2
− 2	− 2	− 2	− 2	− 2

You subtracted 5 times.

4 You can also write a division sentence

You read $10 \div 2 = 5$ as "ten divided by two equals five."

$$10 \div 2 = 5$$

dividend · divisor · quotient

| number you divide | number you divide by | answer |

The bike shop owner can put together 5 bikes.

Talk About It!   How is dividing a number by 2 like taking half of it?

Write a division sentence that answers the question.

1. How many bike helmets are in each group?

2. How many groups of bike reflectors are there?

Draw two pictures for the division sentences. Group your objects in a different way in each picture.

3. 8 ÷ 2 **4.** 6 ÷ 2 **5.** 10 ÷ 2 **6.** 4 ÷ 2 **7.** 2 ÷ 2

8. Critical Thinking When you divide by 2, can the answer ever be an odd number? Explain.

Work It Out!

Write a division sentence. Solve.

9. 8 baseball cards shared by 2 friends.

10. 6 socks put into pairs

Find the quotient.

11. 6 ÷ 2 **12.** 2 ÷ 2 **13.** 4 ÷ 2 **14.** 10 ÷ 2 **15.** 8 ÷ 2

Problem Solving Using Data

16. Nick starts at the beach, rides his bike halfway to town, then rides to the pond. You start from the beach, ride to town, and then ride to the pond. How many more miles did you ride than Nick?

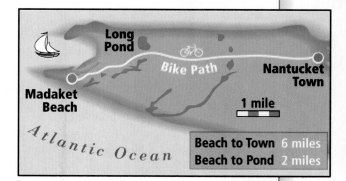

17. Create Your Own Write another problem that goes with the map. Give it to a friend to solve.

More Practice Set 5.5, p. 455

Math Journal

Would you rather subtract or divide to find out how many groups of 2 are in 10? Why?

Problem Solving

Is the Answer Reasonable?

Both Washington and Oregon have coasts, or land that is next to an ocean. Oregon's coast is 296 miles long. Washington's coast is 157 miles. How much longer is Oregon's coast? Is 453 miles a reasonable answer?

Is the Answer Reasonable?

Ask Yourself:

Did I answer the question?

Did I calculate correctly?

Is the answer labeled with the right units?

Does my answer need to be rounded to a whole number to make sense?

You Decide

- Can the answer be greater than the longer coast? Why?
- Is the answer reasonable? Explain.

Work It Out!

Decide if the answer is reasonable. If it is not, explain why not.

1. A seagull's wings measure 47 inches from wingtip to wingtip. A pelican's wings measure 98 inches. How much longer are the pelican's wings?
Answer: 51 feet

2. You give your friend 20 feathers. Now you have 45 left. How many feathers did you have before?
Answer: 65 feathers

3. A pail holds 3 quarts of water. You use it to fill a fish tank with 20 quarts of water. How many times will you fill the pail?
Answer: 10 times

4. Rehearsals for your play are 3 times a week. Each rehearsal lasts 2 hours. How many hours do you rehearse in 2 weeks?
Answer: 6 rehearsals

Share Your Thinking

5. By just reading problem 4, could you tell that the answer is not reasonable? Explain.

Midchapter Review

for Pages 156–168

Problem Solving

Use any strategy to solve the problem. Show your work. (page 162)

1. Suppose your class goes on a field trip to a farm. There are 5 hens living on the farm. If each hen lays 1 egg every day, how many days will it take the hens to lay 24 eggs?

2. The European kingfisher raises 2 broods of chicks each year. If there are 6 chicks in each brood, how many chicks will the kingfisher raise in 3 years?

Concepts

Answer the question. (pages 160, 166)

3. How is multiplying by 2 like doubling a number? Write a number sentence that shows a way to double 7.

4. How is dividing a number by 2 like taking half of it? Write a number sentence that shows a way to take half of 10.

Skills

Find the product. (page 160)

5. 2×3 6. 2×5 7. 3×2 8. 2×7

9. 2×6 10. 2×4 11. 4×2 12. 6×2

13. 5×2 14. 2×8 15. 9×2 16. 7×2

Find the quotient. (page 166)

17. $8 \div 2$ 18. $4 \div 2$ 19. $12 \div 2$ 20. $6 \div 2$

21. $14 \div 2$ 22. $18 \div 2$ 23. $16 \div 2$ 24. $2 \div 2$

25. Divide 10 by 2.   26. Divide 20 by 2.

Math World

**Find out how people have used
multiplication and division at home,
work, and play throughout history.**

Three Times As Much

Would you rather have 1 slice, 2 slices,
or 3 slices of this Mexican tostada (toh
STAH dah)? Three slices, of course!
It's 3 times as much. When people say
"3 times," they are thinking about
multiplication. The word *multiplication*
originally came from a Latin word that
means to fold many times.

No Batteries Required

About 500 years ago, a calculator was a
person, not a machine. In Germany, only
a few people were masters of addition,
subtraction, multiplication, and division.
Regular schools did not teach these skills.
"Human calculators" were needed by
everyone—both governments
and businesses.

Try This! ANCIENT BRAHMI NUMERALS

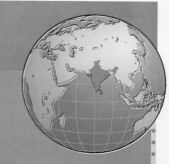

Brahmi (BRAH mee) is an ancient Indian writing system that is thousands of years old. Try using the Brahmi numerals to multiply and divide.

1 Look at the Brahmi numbers for 1–10. Practice writing them a few times.

一	二	三	Ƴ	↑
1	2	3	4	5
6	7	9	9	ɑ
6	7	8	9	10

2 In Brahmi, the problem $4 \times 2 = 8$ might look like this: Ƴ × 二 = 9

3 The problem $3 \div 3 = 1$ might look like this in Brahmi: 三 ÷ 三 = 一

4 Make up some multiplication and division problems of your own using the Brahmi numbers.

5 Give your Brahmi problems to a friend to solve.

Stars and Slashes

Some computers have a built-in calculator. The keys for addition and subtraction have the + and − symbols on them. The keys for multiplication and division are harder to find. On this keyboard, you press * to multiply and / to divide.

Respond

Work with a partner . . .
to solve more Brahmi math problems.

Internet:
Houghton Mifflin Education Place
Explore the Math Center at
http://www.eduplace.com

Multiplying and Dividing with 3

Both multiplication and division answer questions about groups of things. They can answer different questions about the same group.

Here's A Way! Multiply and divide with 3.

Multiply

There are 3 rows of corn. There are 5 cornstalks in each row. How many cornstalks are in the garden?

You can write multiplication in two ways.

$3 \times 5 = 15$

$$\begin{array}{r} 5 \\ \times\ 3 \\ \hline 15 \end{array}$$

There are 15 cornstalks in the garden.

Divide

There are 15 cornstalks in all. There are 3 rows. How many cornstalks are in each row?

You can write division in two ways.

$15 \div 3 = 5$

$$3\overline{)15}$$ with quotient 5

There are 5 cornstalks in each row.

Talk About It! What other question about the garden can you answer using a division sentence?

Follow the directions to make each array on squared paper. Then write a multiplication sentence for the array.

1. Color 3 rows of 4 squares green.

2. Color 2 rows of 3 squares blue.

3. Color 5 rows of 3 squares red.

4. Think of each row as a group. Then write a division sentence to find how many groups are in each array.

5. **Critical Thinking** Look at the division sentence and the multiplication sentence you wrote for 3 rows of 4 squares. What do you notice about the numbers in both sentences?

Write the answer. Use counters or draw a picture if you like.

6. 1×3 7. $\begin{array}{r} 4 \\ \times\,3 \\ \hline \end{array}$ 8. $\begin{array}{r} 3 \\ \times\,3 \\ \hline \end{array}$ 9. $3\overline{)6}$ 10. $9 \div 3$ 11. $3\overline{)12}$

Work It Out!

Find the product.

12. 3×1 13. 3×2 14. 3×3 15. 3×4 16. 3×5

17. $\begin{array}{r} 2 \\ \times\,1 \\ \hline \end{array}$ 18. $\begin{array}{r} 2 \\ \times\,2 \\ \hline \end{array}$ 19. $\begin{array}{r} 2 \\ \times\,3 \\ \hline \end{array}$ 20. $\begin{array}{r} 2 \\ \times\,4 \\ \hline \end{array}$ 21. $\begin{array}{r} 2 \\ \times\,5 \\ \hline \end{array}$

22. $\begin{array}{r} 5 \\ \times\,3 \\ \hline \end{array}$ 23. $\begin{array}{r} 3 \\ \times\,2 \\ \hline \end{array}$ 24. $\begin{array}{r} 3 \\ \times\,3 \\ \hline \end{array}$ 25. $\begin{array}{r} 4 \\ \times\,3 \\ \hline \end{array}$ 26. $\begin{array}{r} 1 \\ \times\,3 \\ \hline \end{array}$

27. **Critical Thinking** How are the answers to exercises 12–16 and 17–21 like skip-counting?

Find the quotient.

28. $15 \div 3$ 29. $12 \div 3$ 30. $6 \div 3$ 31. $3 \div 3$

32. $3\overline{)3}$ 33. $3\overline{)15}$ 34. $2\overline{)8}$ 35. $3\overline{)9}$

36. **Algebraic Reasoning** Suppose you divide some pennies into 3 equal groups. Will each group have more than or less than half the pennies? Why?

More Practice Set 5.7, p. 455

Multiplying and Dividing with 4

You are going camping. You have 4 tents. Each tent needs 4 stakes. Multiplying and dividing with 4 can help you plan your trip.

What would you enjoy about camping?

Tent stakes are made of new, high-strength plastics.

Here's A Way! Multiply and divide with 4.

Multiply

You have 4 tents and 3 people can sleep in each tent. How many people can go camping?

One way to multiply by 4 is to use doubles twice.

$4 \times 3 = \blacksquare$

- First find 2×3.

$2 \times 3 = 6$

- Then multiply that answer by 2.

$2 \times 6 = 12$

So, 12 people can sleep in 4 tents.

Divide

Each tent needs 4 stakes. You have 12 stakes. How many tents can you set up?

One way to divide by 4 is to divide by 2 two times.

$12 \div 4 = \blacksquare$

- First find $12 \div 2$.

$12 \div 2 = 6$

- Then divide that answer by 2.

$6 \div 2 = 3$

So, you can set up 3 tents with 12 stakes.

Talk About It! How can you use multiplication facts for 2 to find facts for 4?

Find the answer. Use doubles or halves if they help.

1. 5
   × 4

2. 4
   × 4

3. 3
   × 4

4. 2
   × 4

5. 1
   × 4

6. 0
   × 4

7. 20 ÷ 4

8. 16 ÷ 4

9. 12 ÷ 4

10. 8 ÷ 4

11. 4 ÷ 4

12. **Critical Thinking** Suppose the number 4 key on your calculator is broken. How could you use the calculator to find 4 × 588? 588 ÷ 4? Explain.

Work It Out!

Find the answer.

13. 4 × 4

14. 4 × 1

15. 4 × 3

16. 4 × 5

17. 4 × 2

18. 4)‾4

19. 4)‾8

20. 4)‾20

21. 4)‾12

22. 4)‾16

Estimation Decide if the product is greater than or less than 20. Write > or <. (Hint: 4 × 5 = 20.)

23. 4 × 7 ● 20

24. 4 × 4 ● 20

25. 4 × 9 ● 20

26. 4 × 2 ● 20

Problem Solving

27. You and three friends are going hiking. You each have a backpack with 2 water bottles. How many water bottles do the four of you have?

28. A group of 16 hikers have only 4 compasses. They plan to divide into equal groups so that each group has a compass. How many hikers will be in each group?

Mixed Review

Write the time. Then write the time 2 hours later.

29.

30.

31.

32.

33.

More Practice Set 5.8, p. 455

175

Multiplying and Dividing with 5

Skip-counting can help you multiply or divide with 5.

Good Dog!

Here's A Way! Multiply and divide with 5.

Skip-Count by 5's to Multiply

For 4 days you give your dog treats for obeying. She gets a treat 5 times a day. How many treats does she get in all?

Skip-count by 5's four times to find the answer.

$$5 \longrightarrow 10 \longrightarrow 15 \longrightarrow 20$$

Your dog gets 20 treats.

You can also multiply. $4 \times 5 = 20$

Skip-Count by 5's to Divide

Each dog treat costs 5¢. How many treats can you buy with 20¢?

Skip-count by 5's until you reach 20.

$$5 \longrightarrow 10 \longrightarrow 15 \longrightarrow 20$$

You said 4 numbers, so you can buy 4 treats.

You can also divide. $20 \div 5 = 4$

Talk About It!

How is the pattern you used to multiply like the pattern you used to divide?

Find the answer. Use what you know about skip-counting patterns to help if you want to.

1. 2×5 2. 3×5 3. 4×5 4. 5×5 5. 1×5

6. $5 \div 5$ 7. $25 \div 5$ 8. $20 \div 5$ 9. $15 \div 5$ 10. $10 \div 5$

11. **Critical Thinking** How is multiplying by 5 like counting nickels?

Work It Out!

Multiply or divide.

12. $\begin{array}{r} 5 \\ \times 3 \\ \hline \end{array}$
13. $\begin{array}{r} 5 \\ \times 2 \\ \hline \end{array}$
14. $\begin{array}{r} 5 \\ \times 1 \\ \hline \end{array}$
15. $\begin{array}{r} 5 \\ \times 5 \\ \hline \end{array}$
16. $\begin{array}{r} 3 \\ \times 5 \\ \hline \end{array}$
17. $\begin{array}{r} 4 \\ \times 5 \\ \hline \end{array}$

18. $5\overline{)25}$ 19. $5\overline{)10}$ 20. $5\overline{)20}$ 21. $5\overline{)5}$ 22. $5\overline{)15}$

23. 5×2 24. 5×1 25. 5×3 26. 5×4

Use each group of numbers to write a multiplication sentence and a division sentence.

27. 3, 5, 15   28. 5, 25   29. 5, 2, 10   30. 1, 5   31. 4, 5, 20

32. There are 5 school days in a week. Copy and complete the table to find the number of school days in 9 weeks.

Number of Weeks	1	2	3	4	5	6	7	8	9
Number of School Days	5	10	15	?	?	?	?	?	?

Problem Solving

33. The bus fare to the dog show is 75¢. The driver cannot give change. What coins can you use to ride the bus?

34. You have only nickels. Can you have exactly 73¢? Explain.

35. **Critical Thinking** Could you use skip-counting to solve exercises 33 and 34? Explain.

More Practice Set 5.9, p. 456

L · E · S · S · O · N

10

Problem Solving
Using Make a Table and Other Strategies

Your class is going to see *The Ancient Reptiles*. It is the new dinosaur movie at the science museum.

THE ANCIENT REPTILES

**SHOWS BEGIN
EVERY 30 MINUTES**

FIRST SHOW: 9:00 A.M.
LAST SHOW: 2:30 P.M.

Problem Solving Process
✓ Understand
✓ Plan
✓ Try It
✓ Look Back

Choose a Strategy You Have Learned
✓ Act It Out
✓ Look for a Pattern
✓ Guess and Check
✓ Draw a Picture
✓ Make a Table
   Work Backward
   Make a List
   Work a Simpler Problem

On Monday, 23 classes are going to see *The Ancient Reptiles*. The movie is 30 minutes long. The theater can hold 2 classes at each showing. Can all the classes see the movie in one day?

• What problem needs to be solved?

• Look at the sign. When does the first show start? The second show? The last show?

• How many classes can watch each show?

• Describe a strategy you can use to solve the problem. Then solve it.

Work It Out!

**Use any strategy to solve the problem.
Show your work.**

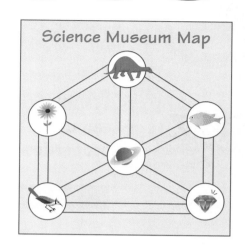

Science Museum Map

1. Copy the map of the museum. Plan a route for yourself. Make sure that you will see every exhibit without going over the same path twice.

2. The children's hands-on exhibit area is open from 9:00 A.M. to 2:00 P.M. Only 6 children can visit the exhibit each hour. How many can visit in a day?

3. Your class has 25 students. Each row in the theater has 10 seats. How many rows will your class need?

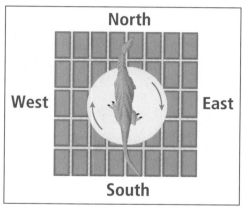

North

West   East

South

4. This dinosaur was built on a revolving stand. The stand takes 1 hour to make a complete turn. At 9:00 A.M. the dinosaur faces north. At 9:15 A.M. it faces east. What direction will it face at 3:45 P.M.?

5. You are planning a dinosaur exhibit. You will place dinosaurs along a wall 100 feet long. There must be 5 feet of space between dinosaurs and at each end. Which 3 dinosaurs will fit just right?

Dinosaur	Length
Tyrannosaurus	40 feet
Euoplocephalus	20 feet
Montanoceratops	15 feet
Triceratops	35 feet
Hypsilophodon	5 feet

6. You decide to place all 5 of the dinosaurs along one wall. Remember: You need 5 feet of space between dinosaurs and at each end. How long must the wall be?

Share Your Thinking

7. What strategy helped you to solve problem 6? Could you have used another strategy? Explain.

Exploring Properties of Multiplication

Multiplication, like addition, has properties. You can use arrays to learn about some multiplication properties.

Activity

The Order Property

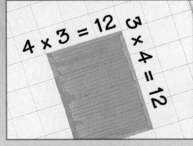

$4 \times 3 = 12$ $3 \times 4 = 12$

The Order Property
When you change the order of the factors in a multiplication sentence, the product stays the same.

1. Make an array diagram to show 3 rows of 4. Write a multiplication sentence for your diagram.

2. Turn your diagram on its side to make a different array. Write a multiplication sentence for the new array.

3. Look at your two multiplication sentences. How are they alike? How are they different?

4. Color diagrams for these arrays. Repeat steps 1–3 for each array.

   a. 5 rows of 7   b. 3 rows of 6   c. 8 rows of 2

The Property of One

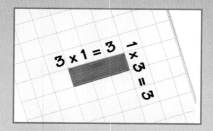

The Property of One
If 1 is a factor, the product always equals the other factor.

1. Make an array diagram with 1 row of 3 squares. Write a multiplication sentence for 1 row of 3 squares and for 3 rows of 1 square.

2. Now repeat step 1 for 1 row of 4 squares and for 1 row of 7 squares.

3. What do you notice about the product when one of the factors is 1?

The Zero Property

The Zero Property
If zero is a factor, the product always equals zero.

1. Use a calculator to find the products.
   a. $7 \times 0 = $ ▦
   b. $0 \times 56 = $ ▦
   c. $229 \times 0 = $ ▦
   d. $0 \times 9783 = $ ▦

2. What do you notice about the product when one of the factors is zero?

3. Now try these:
   a. 0×8
   b. 49×0
   c. 143×0
   d. 0×5746

Show What You Know!

1. Explain each property of multiplication in your own words. Write a number sentence that shows an example.

Use the multiplication properties to find the products. Use a calculator if you need to. Name the property you used.

2. 4×3 and 3×4

3. 25×14 and 14×25

4. 9×0

5. 1×5

6. 798×1

7. 8×0

8. 0×850

9. 9654×1

10. 5×2 and 2×5

11. 234×1

12. 999×0

13. 1×333

14. **Critical Thinking** How is the order property of multiplication like the order property of addition?

Problem Solving
Using Strategies

Read more about city gardeners in the pages of *Newsweek* magazine.

In 1992 a group of high-school students in Los Angeles created a special garden in an empty city lot. The students gave some of the food from the garden to homeless families. They sold the rest at local markets.

Problem Solving Process
✓ Understand
✓ Plan
✓ Try It
✓ Look Back

Choose a Strategy You Have Learned
✓ Act It Out
✓ Look for a Pattern
✓ Guess and Check
✓ Draw a Picture
✓ Make a Table
  Work Backward
  Make a List
  Work a Simpler Problem

Today's Vegetables

corn	45¢
lettuce	75¢
cucumber	25¢
broccoli	50¢
tomato	55¢

Suppose you want to buy some vegetables. You have 3 quarters and 2 dimes. What can you buy for exactly that amount of money?

- What problem needs to be solved?

- What is the price of each vegetable?

- How much money do you have?

- Explain a strategy you can use to solve the problem. Then solve it.

Use Make a Table or another strategy to solve the problem.

1. You want to put "Garden Sale" signs at five street corners in your neighborhood. The corners are marked with dots on the map. Copy the map onto squared paper. Starting from home, draw the shortest route to all 5 places and back. Move only on streets, not from corner to corner.

2. You are selling carrots for $.60 a bag. How many bags must you sell to make $9.00?

3. Corn seeds need to be planted 12 inches from each other. What is the greatest number of seeds you can plant in a row 72 inches long?

4. A customer buys 4 radishes and 1 onion from you. Radishes cost 10¢ each. Onions cost 30¢ each. The customer gives you 3 quarters. How much change should you give the customer?

5. You have 1 watermelon to sell. You cut it in half. Then you cut each half into 4 slices. You charge $.25 for 1 slice. How much money will you make if you sell all the slices?

6. Ears of corn can be stacked in a triangle shape. How many ears of corn would be in a stack that had 6 ears on the bottom layer?

7. You want to stack 15 large cucumbers in a triangle shape. How many cucumbers will be on the bottom row? Why?

Share Your Thinking

8. What strategy did you use to solve problems 6 and 7? Is there more than one way to solve these problems? Explain.

Chapter 5 Test

for Pages 156–183

Test-Taking Tips
Use mental math when you can for multiplication and division exercises.

Problem Solving

Big Peak
Ski Rental
$8.00 a day

Solve using any strategy. Show your work. (page 162, 168, 178, 182)

1. Suppose your class is having a field trip to a ski slope. What will it cost to rent skis for 20 students for the day?

2. The chair lift moves 400 feet each minute. How long will it take to go 6000 feet to the top of the ski slope?

3. Half-day lift tickets cost $20 each. How much will half-day tickets cost for you and 4 friends?

4. Full-day lift tickets cost twice as much as half-day tickets. What will it cost for you and 2 friends to use the lift all day?

Concepts

Use the order property to rewrite the multiplication. Then find the product. (page 180)

5. 6×2

6. 5×3

7. 7×0

8. 30×1

9. 5×4

10. 8×2

11. $\begin{array}{r} 3 \\ \times\ 6 \\ \hline \end{array}$

12. $\begin{array}{r} 4 \\ \times\ 9 \\ \hline \end{array}$

13. $\begin{array}{r} 8 \\ \times\ 2 \\ \hline \end{array}$

14. $\begin{array}{r} 6 \\ \times\ 4 \\ \hline \end{array}$

15. $\begin{array}{r} 8 \\ \times\ 5 \\ \hline \end{array}$

16. $\begin{array}{r} 7 \\ \times\ 3 \\ \hline \end{array}$

Find the product. (pages 172, 174, 176)

17. $3 \times 6 = $ ■   18. $4 \times 0 = $ ■   19. $5 \times 7 = $ ■

20. $3 \times 3 = $ ■   21. $4 \times 2 = $ ■   22. $3 \times 4 = $ ■

23. $6 \times 5 = $ ■   24. $1 \times 5 = $ ■   25. $9 \times 5 = $ ■

26. $3 \times 9 = $ ■

Find the quotient. (pages 166, 172, 176)

27. $5 \div 5 = $ ■   28. $12 \div 3 = $ ■   29. $14 \div 2 = $ ■

30. $18 \div 3 = $ ■   31. $27 \div 3 = $ ■   32. $25 \div 5 = $ ■

33. $21 \div 3 = $ ■   34. $30 \div 5 = $ ■

Performance Task

(pages 162, 172, 182)

Your class wants to sell grab bags at the school fair. You will put 3 items in each bag and sell the bags for $1.00 a piece. How many items will you need to fill all of the bags?

- Do you have all the information you need to solve the problem? If not, what do you need to know?

- Rewrite the problem to include what is missing. Then solve the problem.

- Write a new problem. Change the number of bags. Then solve the new problem.

Keep In Mind . . .

Your work will be evaluated on the following:

☑ Plan to find information

☑ Complete written problems

☑ Strategy for solving

☑ Correct solutions and method for checking

Cumulative Review

Addition (Chapter 1)
Find 4 + 3 + 6 + 7.

Here's A Way!

4 + 3 + 6 + 7
10 + 10 = 20 (order)
Choose an addition property.
Check with a calculator.

Choose a property of addition and solve.

1. 129 + 0 + 11   2. 60 + 25 + 60

3. 4 + 30 + 700   4. 64 + 400 + 6

5. 370 + 0 + 30   6. 80 + 20 + 17

7. Which property of addition was most helpful in problem 5? Why?

Place Value (Chapter 2)
Which is greater, 779 or 776?

Here's A Way!

Compare the hundreds. If the digits are the same, compare the tens. If those digits are the same, compare the ones.

Hundreds	Tens	Ones
7	7	9
7	7	6

779 > 776.

Compare. Write >, <, or =.

8. 332 ● 223   9. 251 ● 255

10. 888 ● 800   11. 525 ● 552

Order from greatest to least.

12. 689, 986, 972, 699

13. 1111, 1011, 1001, 1100

14. How did understanding place value help you in exercise 13?

Addition (Chapter 3)
Find 475 + 398.

Here's A Way!

$\overset{1\ 1}{475}$
+ 398
873

- Add the ones. Regroup.
- Add the tens. Regroup.
- Add the hundreds.

Find the sum. Regroup if necessary.

15. 45   16. 79   17. 318
   + 88   + 154   + 622

18. 432   19. 312   20. 384
     150   895   112
   + 267   + 413   + 570

21. In what order do you add the columns in an addition problem? Why is this important?

Pictographs (Chapter 4)
How many dog stickers are there?

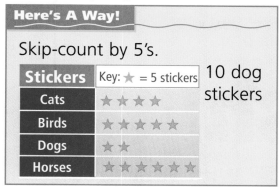

Here's A Way!

Skip-count by 5's.

Stickers	Key: ★ = 5 stickers
Cats	★ ★ ★ ★
Birds	★ ★ ★ ★ ★
Dogs	★ ★
Horses	★ ★ ★ ★ ★ ★

10 dog stickers

Answer the question.

22. How many bird stickers are there?

23. Of which kind are there the fewest?

24. How many more bird stickers are there than dog stickers?

25. Of which kind are there the most stickers?

26. If a star was 10 stickers, how many stars would there be in the last row?

Line Graphs (Chapter 4)
How much snow fell in March?

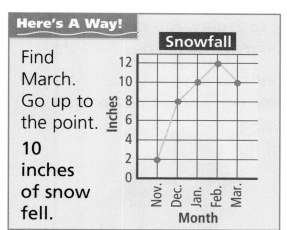

Here's A Way!

Find March. Go up to the point.

10 inches of snow fell.

Snowfall

(line graph: Inches vs. Month — Nov. 2, Dec. 8, Jan. 10, Feb. 12, Mar. 10)

Read the line graph. Answer the question.

27. What month had the most snowfall?

28. How many inches did it snow in that month?

29. What is the difference between November's snowfall and the greatest monthly snowfall?

30. How many inches of snow fell in November?

31. Why is a graph useful for this data?

Problem Solving

Problem Solving Process
✓ Understand
✓ Plan
✓ Try It
✓ Look Back

Choose a Strategy You Have Learned
✓ Act It Out
✓ Look for a Pattern
✓ Guess and Check
✓ Draw a Picture
✓ Make a Table
  Work Backward
  Make a List
  Work a Simpler Problem

Solve using any strategy. Show your work.

32. What 5 coins equal 75¢?

33. The bookshelf in your room is 33 inches long. You have a 10-volume set of nature books. The thickest book is 3 inches wide. The thinnest is 2 inches wide. Will the whole set fit on your bookshelf? Explain.

Go Fish!

Science Connection   **With Your Group**

Your class is working at an aquarium to learn about how different animals behave. You will feed the animals from Monday to Friday. You need to make a plan for feeding the animals four times each day.

Your challenge is to find out how many animals you can feed in a shift. Once you know this, you can make a schedule showing when everyone should do his or her chores.

5 Day Schedule

Animals	Number of Feedings	Minutes for Each Feeding
Penguins	15	45 min.
Turtles	10	15 min.
Octopus	5	5 min.
Herring	20	5 min.
Eels	5	10 min.
Piranha	15	5 min.
Sea Lions	20	20 min.
Seals	15	15 min.
Tropical Fish	20	5 min.
Crabs	5	20 min.

1 Plan It

- Think about the animals and fish shown on the schedule. Which would you like to work with most?
- As a group, list the animals from the most to least interesting.

2 Put It Together

- The schedule shows how many times each animal is fed in 5 days. Divide to find the daily feedings.
- Copy the chart below. In the top row, write 5 animals that your group wants to feed.
- Fill in the shifts you will be feeding each animal. Write the number of minutes it takes to feed the animal.
- Add the minutes in each row. Is there enough time on your shift to get your animals fed? If not, change your chart.

3 Wrap It Up

- Make a final chart. Include the names of who will work at each time.
- Are the jobs different? How?

4 Discuss Your Results

- Did you meet all of the goals in Keep In Mind?
- Does another group want to work with the same animals as your group?

Internet

> Visit the **Math Center** at
Houghton Mifflin Education Place.
http://www.eduplace.com

Daily Feedings

shift	turtle	eels	seals	octopus	fish	total min.
8 am	15		15		5	35min
11 am		10	15		5	30min
2 pm	15			5	5	25min
5pm			15		5	20min

189

Use What You Know

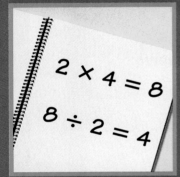

2 rows of
4 counters

• about arrays

2 × 4 = 8

8 ÷ 2 = 4

• related facts

• factor
• product
• divisor
• dividend
• quotient

• the vocabulary

Multiplication and Division to 9

Try This!

Plan a store display for 24 school mugs. Each mug is packaged in a box.

What You'll Need

connecting cubes, paper, pencil

1

How could you arrange the boxes in 8 rows? Use your connecting cubes to show a display.

Plan two other ways to show the 24 boxes in rows of the same size.

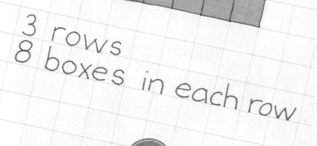

3 rows
8 boxes in each row

Draw your ideas. Describe the number of rows and the number of boxes in each row.

What number sentences can you write for each of your displays?

$3 \times 8 = 24$

How have you shown multiplication or division in your displays? Have you shown addition or subtraction too? Explain.

Ready to Go!

LESSON 1

Multiplication and Division

Cooperative Learning Checklist

☐ Work alone.
☑ Work with a partner.
☐ Work with a group.

Use counters to explore how a multiplication sentence with a missing factor is related to a division sentence.

Getting Started

What You'll Need:
▶ 30 counters
▶ 8 blank number cards

Activity

- **Make number cards for the numbers 6, 8, 12, 15, 18, 24, 25, and 30.**

- **Make charts like the ones on the next page. Each partner will use one chart.**

1 Choose a number card. Take that many counters. Record the total number of counters on both charts.

2 Divide the counters into equal groups and record. Write a multiplication and a division sentence with a missing factor.
- The missing factor is the number of counters in each group.

3 Record the number of counters in each group. Complete the related multiplication and division sentences.

4 If you can, find another way to make equal groups. Record the results.

5 Repeat steps 1–4 with the other number cards.

Show What You Know!

1. **Critical Thinking** Do you think 10 ÷ 2 = ■ asks the same question as 10 × ■ = 2? Why or why not?

Find the missing factor. Complete the multiplication sentence.

2. 4 × ■ = 28   3. ■ × 6 = 18   4. ■ × 2 = 10

5. 3 × ■ = 6   6. 4 × ■ = 12   7. ■ × 6 = 12

Divide. Use a related multiplication sentence to help you.

8. 15 ÷ 3 = ■   9. 10 ÷ 2 = ■   10. 8 ÷ 4 = ■

11. 9 ÷ 3 = ■   12. 16 ÷ 8 = ■   13. 12 ÷ 4 = ■

14. **Critical Thinking** How could you use a related multiplication and division sentence to write a fact family?

Complete each number sentence. Then write a related number sentence.

15. ■ × 4 = 8   16. 3 × ■ = 12   17. 5 × ■ = 15   18. ■ × 2 = 20

19. 12 ÷ 3 = ■   20. 20 ÷ 2 = ■   21. 8 ÷ 4 = ■   22. 15 ÷ 5 = ■

23. **Mental Math** How can knowing 2 × 3 = 6 help you find 6 ÷ 3?

Multiplication

Number of Groups	Counters in Each Group	Total Number of Counters	Multiplication Sentence
		6	2 × □ = 6
2			

Division

Total Number of Counters	Number of Groups	Counters in Each Group	Division Sentence
6			
	2		
			6 ÷ 2 = □

Exploring Rules for Division

What do you think would happen if you divided a number by itself? What about by 1 or 0? Use counters and a calculator to find out.

Getting Started

What You'll Need:
► counters
► calculator

Use What You Know

You know that the answer to a division problem is called the **quotient**.

Activity

Dividing a Number by Itself

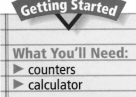

When a number, except zero, is divided by itself, the quotient is 1.

① Take 5 counters. Make 5 groups with them.

② Find the number of counters in each group.

③ Write the division sentence.

④ Divide. What do you notice about the quotient?
   a. $4 \div 4 =$ ■   b. $8 \div 8 =$ ■   c. $7 \div 7 =$ ■

Dividing by 1

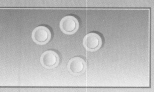

When a number is divided by 1, the quotient is the number.

5 Take 5 counters. Make 1 group with the counters.

6 Complete the division sentence. $5 \div 1 = $ ▨

7 Divide. What do you notice about the quotient?

a. $9 \div 1 = $ ▨   b. $6 \div 1 = $ ▨   c. $3 \div 1 = $ ▨

Zero Divided by a Number

When zero is divided by any number except zero, the quotient is zero.

 8 Use a calculator to divide.

a. $0 \div 4 = $ ▨   c. $0 \div 5 = $ ▨

b. $0 \div 3 = $ ▨   d. $0 \div 2 = $ ▨

9 What do you notice about the quotient?

Show What You Know!

1. **Critical Thinking** Use your calculator. Try $5 \div 0$ and $6 \div 0$. Write what you see on the calculator display. Try to divide other numbers by 0. What happens? What do you think the error message means?

 Predict the quotient. Write your prediction. Then use counters or a calculator to divide. Compare the quotient to your prediction.

2. $8 \div 8 = $ ▨   3. $0 \div 17 = $ ▨   4. $7 \div 1 = $ ▨

5. $0 \div 8 = $ ▨   6. $234 \div 1 = $ ▨   7. $709 \div 709 = $ ▨

8. $629 \div 1 = $ ▨   9. $0 \div 18 = $ ▨   10. $25 \div 25 = $ ▨

11. $17 \div 17 = $ ▨   12. $543 \div 1 = $ ▨   13. $0 \div 2 = $ ▨

Math Journal

How can division rules help you do mental math?

Patterns in the Multiplication Table

You have learned to multiply some factors. Use what you know to create a multiplication table.

Activity

- **Make a multiplication table or use the one on the recording sheet.**

1
- Find the 2 in the row of factors above the table.
- As you move down the 2's column, skip-count by 2's.
- Write the numbers you say to complete the column.

2
- Find the 2 in the column of factors to the left of the table.
- As you move across the row, skip-count by 2's.
- Write the numbers you say to complete the row.

3

- Find the 3 in the top row of factors at the top.
- Fill in as much of the 3's column as you can.
- Then do the same for the 3's row.

4

- Continue with the columns and rows for 4 and 5.
- Use skip-counting or other strategies to help you fill in the table.

Show What You Know!

1. What strategies have you used to make the table?

2. What is the product of 1 and any number? How can knowing this property help you fill in more of the table?

3. How does knowing the product of 2×6 help you find 6×2? Look for other places in the table to use this property.

4. What pattern do you notice about the products in the 1's row and the 2's row? The 2's row and the 4's row? Can this pattern help you fill in more of the table? Explain.

5. Which products in the table do you still need to find? Shade them.

6. How could you use the table to find quotients?

7. **Critical Thinking** How could you use the products you have filled in to find other products in the table?

8. **Create Your Own** Choose three products from the table. Each person in your group should write a pair of factors for each product.

9. **Critical Thinking** Do the factors your group wrote match? Explain why they might be different.

10. **Write About It** Start at the upper left-hand corner of your chart. Make a 2×4 array with counters. Is the product under the counter in the bottom right corner? Try 3×3 and 4×5. Write about your results.

Problem Solving
Guess and Check

A display box is to be divided into 15 equal sections. To fit on a shelf, the box should have 2 more columns than rows. How many columns and rows will the box have?

Some problems can be solved by using Guess and Check.

Here's A Way! Use Guess and Check.

1 Understand

- What shape will the box be? How do you know?
- What problem do you need to solve?

2 Plan

- What would be a good first guess? Why?

3 Try It

- Suppose you guess 6 columns and 4 rows.

- What would be a good second guess? Why?

4 Look Back

- The box needs 5 columns and 3 rows. Would 3 columns and 5 rows also work? Explain.

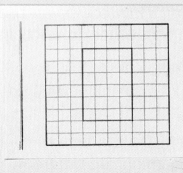

First guess: 6 columns
and 4 rows
Check: 6 x 4 = 24
24 > 15
6 columns and 4 rows
is too high

Show What You Know!

Use Guess and Check to solve the problem.

1. What two numbers come one after the other and have a product of 20?

2. **Critical Thinking** Since $2 \times 10 = 20$, could 2 and 10 also be a correct answer? Explain.

First guess: 3 and 4
Check: 3 × 4 = 12
12 is less than 20
3 and 4 are too low

Work It Out!

Use Guess and Check or any other strategy to solve the problem.

3. There are twice as many boxes of crayons as boxes of markers. There are 15 boxes in all. How many boxes of markers are there?

4. You have 7 coins that total $1.25. What coins do you have?

5. Suppose you want to put up posters in three places about free kittens. The map shows the places. Copy the map onto squared paper. Draw the shortest route from your house to all three places and back. How many blocks long is the route?

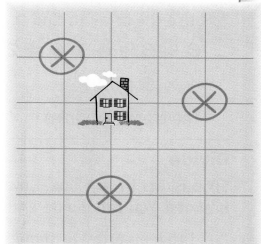

6. You have a mystery number. If you add 4 to it or multiply it by 2, you get the same answer. What is the mystery number?

7. One of your classmates has 3 more sisters than brothers. If your classmate has 5 sisters and brothers all together, how many brothers does she have?

Share Your Thinking

8. What strategy did you use to solve problem 7? Explain your solution step-by-step.

9. Describe a different strategy that you could have used for problem 7.

Multiplying and Dividing with 6

A small apple-picking basket can hold 6 apples.

You can multiply and divide with 6 to answer questions about the baskets.

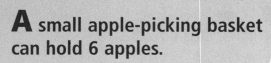

Here's A Way!　**Multiply and divide with 6.**

Multiply

How many apples are in 4 full baskets? Find 4×6.

1 Draw an array to show 4×6.

2 Use the array to find the product.

$$6 + 6 + 6 + 6 = 24$$

$$4 \times 6 = 24$$

There are 24 apples in 4 full baskets.

Divide

Six baskets fit in 1 box. How many boxes do you need for 24 baskets? You can divide 24 by 6 to find out.

1 Draw an array to show $24 \div 6$.

2 Think of a related multiplication fact to find the quotient.

$$4 \times 6 = 24$$

$$24 \div 6 = 4$$

You need 4 boxes for 24 baskets.

Talk About It!　How would you draw an array for 6×4 and $24 \div 4$?

Write the answer.

1. 18 ÷ 6
2. 30 ÷ 6
3. 48 ÷ 6
4. 36 ÷ 6
5. 6 ÷ 6

6. 7
   × 6

7. 6
   × 7

8. 5
   × 6

9. 3
   × 6

10. 2
    × 6

11. **Critical Thinking** How can you use the answer to exercise 9 to check your answer to exercise 10?

Work It Out!

Write the answer.

12. 6
    × 3

13. 4
    × 6

14. 1
    × 6

15. 6
    × 2

16. 6
    × 5

17. 42 ÷ 6
18. 0 ÷ 6
19. 24 ÷ 6
20. 12 ÷ 6
21. 54 ÷ 6

22. Add any new facts you have learned to your multiplication table. If your table is filled, check the products.

Problem Solving   Using Data

23. Charoset (hah ROH seht) is served at the Jewish holiday Passover. Which would use more apples: 4 batches of charoset or 3 batches of applesauce?

24. Picadillo (pee kah DEE yoh) is a Latin American dish made with beef and apples. How many apples would you need to serve 54 people?

Apple Recipes

Food	Number of Apples
Applesauce (1 batch)	6
Charoset (1 batch)	4
Picadillo (serves 6)	2

Mixed Review

Write the answer. Use mental math when you can.

25. 72 + 19 + 33
26. $304 + $629 + $481
27. 500 + 200 + 100
28. $900 − $50
29. 408 − 129
30. 653 − 53

More Practice Set 6.5, p. 457

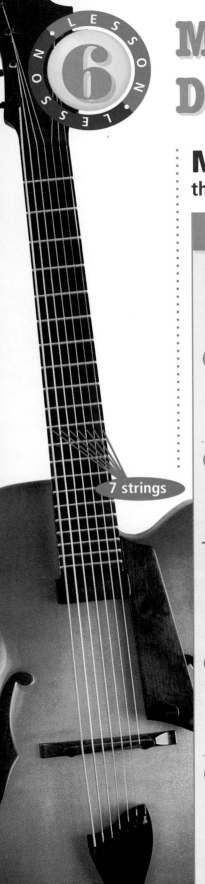

Multiplying and Dividing with 7

LESSON 6

Most guitars have 6 strings. This is a rare guitar from the 1960's. It has 7 strings instead.

7 strings

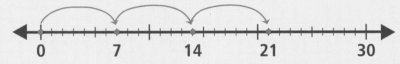

Here's A Way! Multiply and divide with 7.

Multiply

How many strings do you need to put new strings on 3 of these guitars? Find 3 × 7.

1 Use a number line to help you.

```
0    7    14    21    30
```

2 Write a multiplication sentence.

$$3 \times 7 = 21$$

You need 21 strings.

Divide

How many 7-string guitars could get all new strings if you have 21 strings? Find 7)21.

1 To divide by 7, think of a related multiplication fact.

To find 21 ÷ 7 = ■,
think ■ × 7 = 21.

There are 2 ways to show division.

$$21 \div 7 = 3$$
dividend divisor quotient

divisor → 7)21 ← dividend, 3 ← quotient

2 Complete the division sentence.

Since 3 × 7 = 21, 21 ÷ 7 = 3.
Three guitars could get new strings.

Talk About It! How did multiplication help you find the quotient of 21 ÷ 7?

Copy and write the answer.

1. 7×7 2. 3×7 3. $28 \div 7$ 4. $56 \div 7$

5. $\begin{array}{r} 4 \\ \times 7 \\ \hline \end{array}$ 6. $\begin{array}{r} 7 \\ \times 8 \\ \hline \end{array}$ 7. $\begin{array}{r} 5 \\ \times 7 \\ \hline \end{array}$ 8. $\begin{array}{r} 6 \\ \times 7 \\ \hline \end{array}$ 9. $\begin{array}{r} 1 \\ \times 7 \\ \hline \end{array}$

10. $7\overline{)63}$ 11. $7\overline{)42}$ 12. $7\overline{)14}$ 13. $7\overline{)49}$ 14. $7\overline{)35}$

15. **Critical Thinking** Rewrite exercise 14 using the $\div$ symbol. How did you decide where to write the 7?

Work It Out!

Write the answer.

16. $\begin{array}{r} 7 \\ \times 2 \\ \hline \end{array}$ 17. $\begin{array}{r} 3 \\ \times 7 \\ \hline \end{array}$ 18. $\begin{array}{r} 7 \\ \times 3 \\ \hline \end{array}$ 19. $\begin{array}{r} 7 \\ \times 6 \\ \hline \end{array}$

20. $6\overline{)42}$ 21. $7\overline{)42}$ 22. $7\overline{)28}$ 23. $7\overline{)56}$

24. 7×0 25. 7×5 26. $49 \div 7$ 27. $7 \div 7$

28. Write two division sentences for 6, 7, and 42.

29. **Mental Math** If you know that $6 \times 7 = 42$, how can you use that fact to find the product of 7×7?

30. Fill in your multiplication table with any new facts you have learned. If your table is filled, check the products.

31. **Patterns** Copy and complete the table.

32. **Estimation** About how many weeks is 25 days? 36 days?

33. **Logical Reasoning** A song is 7 minutes long. If 7 guitar players play the song together, how long will it take?

Weeks	Days
1	7
2	?
3	21
?	28
?	35

More Practice Set 6.6, p. 457

Problem Solving
Choose a Computation Method

Choose a Computation Method

Ask Yourself:

Do I need an exact answer or an estimate?

Should I use a model, paper and pencil, mental math, or a calculator?

What operation should I use?

Suppose you want to buy a ball, socks, and laces. Is $25 enough to buy everything?

You Decide

- Do you need to find the exact total for the items?

- How could you use mental math to solve the problem?

- Would a calculator be quicker? Why or why not?

Work It Out!

Decide whether to use a calculator or mental math. Explain your decision. Solve the problem.

$1.00

$4.00

1. Last week your soccer team practiced 5 times. Each practice lasted 2 hours. How many hours did your team practice last week?

2. Your coach bought snacks for your team twice. The first time, she spent $11.58. The second time, she spent $8.56. How much did she spend in all?

3. **Create Your Own** Write a problem that could be solved with mental math.

4. Your team played 12 games. It lost 3 games and tied 2. How many games did you win?

Share Your Thinking

5. How did you decide whether to use a calculator or mental math?

$13.00

More Practice Set 6.7, p. 458

Midchapter Review

for Pages 190–204

for Pages 190–204

Problem Solving

Use any strategy to solve the problem. Show your work. (page 198)

1. Your class goes on a trip to the local animal shelter. The shelter has 21 cats and dogs in all. There are twice as many cats as dogs. How many dogs are there?

2. You have 2 quarters, 2 dimes, and 3 nickels. How many ways can you use these coins to buy exactly 50¢ worth of dog treats? Write your answer in a chart like the one below.

Quarters	Dimes	Nickels
?	?	?
?	?	?
?	?	?

Concepts

Find the answers. (pages 192, 194)

3. $9 \div 1$

4. $7 \div 1$

5. What do exercises 3 and 4 tell you about dividing by 1?

6. Write a multiplication sentence for the division sentence $0 \div 5 = 0$.

7. Can you find $5 \div 0$? Explain.

Skills

Multiply. (pages 200, 202)

8. 7×2

9. 7×7

10. 3×6

11. $\begin{array}{r} 3 \\ \times 5 \\ \hline \end{array}$

12. 4×6

13. 7×6

14. 6×5

Divide. (pages 200, 202)

15. $42 \div 7$

16. $6 \overline{)36}$

17. $7 \overline{)21}$

18. $18 \div 6$

Math World

See how people in different times

remembered numbers and used their

fingers to help with multiplication facts.

Show Your Work

Did you know that the Chinese knew how to make paper and kept it a secret for about 600 years? Long ago people also used other materials to write math problems.

Clay Tablets, Mesopotamia
(MEHS uh puh TAY mee uh)
Writers wrote on wet clay and smoothed it out to erase their work.

Slates, Europe
Later people used slates, which are like some chalkboards. Slates were easier to erase.

Dust Table, Europe
Colored sand was sprinkled on a table to work out problems.

Is This Table Set?

People in the past used multiplication tables to multiply and divide faster. Why do you think only half the table is filled in? (Hint: Is the answer for 3 × 6 different from the answer for 6 × 3?)

Try This!

EUROPEAN FINGER MULTIPLICATION

This way to find multiplication facts with 9 was used in Europe for hundreds of years. Follow these steps to find 9 × 7.

1 Spread out the fingers of both hands. Hold up your hands side by side in front of you.

2 You are multiplying 7 by 9. So count to 7 on your fingers starting from the left. Bend down the seventh finger.

3 The number of fingers to the left of the bent finger is the number of tens in the product. There are 6 fingers, so there are 6 tens. The number of fingers to the right of the bent finger is the number of ones in the product. There are 3 fingers, so there are 3 ones. So, 9 × 7 = 63.

Try 9 × 9.

×	1	2	3	4	5	6	7	8	9	10
1	1	2	3	4	5	6	7	8	9	10
2		4	6	8	10	12	14	16	18	20
3			9	12	15	18	21	24	27	30
4				16	20	24	28	32	36	40
5					25	30	35	40	45	50
6						36	42	48	54	60
7							49	56	63	70
8								64	72	80
9									81	90
10										100

Respond

Work with a partner . . .
to make your own multiplication table.

Internet:
Houghton Mifflin Education Place
Explore the Math Center at
http://www.eduplace.com

Multiplying and Dividing with 8

The octopus gets its name from the Greek word *okto*. It means "eight." An octopus has 8 arms that help it move and catch food.

Here's A Way! Multiply and divide with 8.

Multiply

How many arms do 4 octopuses have?

Find 8 × 4.

1 Use a pattern to multiply. Think

8 is the double of 4, so 8 × 4 is double 4 × 4.

$4 \times 4 = 16$

2 Double the result.

$16 + 16 = 32$

So, 8 × 4 = 32.

The octopuses have 32 arms.

Divide

An aquarium has 32 octopuses. Each tank can hold 8 octopuses. How many tanks does the aquarium need? Find 32 ÷ 8.

1 You know that 8 × 4 = 32. Write a fact family.

$8 \times 4 = 32 \quad 4 \times 8 = 32$

$32 \div 8 = 4 \quad 32 \div 4 = 8.$

2 Complete the division sentence.

$32 \div 8 = 4$

The aquarium needs 4 tanks.

Talk About It! Why is this a fact family?

Write the answer.

1. 8 × 5
2. 8 × 3
3. 8 × 2
4. 8 × 8
5. 8)56
6. 8)40
7. 8 ÷ 1
8. 24 ÷ 8

9. **Number Sense** How can 4 × 5 help you find 8 × 5?

Work It Out!

Write the answer.

10. 7
    × 8
11. 2
    × 8
12. 4
    × 8
13. 6
    × 8
14. 3
    × 8

15. 56 ÷ 8
16. 8 × 1
17. 0 ÷ 8
18. 32 ÷ 8
19. 8 × 0
20. 8)40
21. 8)16
22. 8)56
23. 8)24
24. 8)48

25. **Algebraic Reasoning** Copy and complete the table.

Octopuses	1	8	?	?	5	6	?	?	9
Arms	8	16	24	?	40	?	56	64	?

26. Fill in your multiplication table with any new facts that you have learned. If your table is filled, check the products.

Problem Solving

27. An octopus has 2 rows of suction cups on each arm. How many rows of suction cups does an octopus have?

28. Squid are related to octopuses, but squid have 10 arms. Which has more arms, a group of 3 squid or a group of 4 octopuses?

Mixed Review

Write the value of the digit 8 in the number.

29. 18
30. 802
31. 387
32. 6283
33. 8096

More Practice Set 6.8, p. 458

Multiplying and Dividing with 9

The dogs that pull a dogsled are called a team. This team has 9 dogs.

Here's A Way! Multiply and divide with 9.

Multiply

Three teams of dogs race. Each team has 9 dogs. How many dogs race? Find 3×9.

Thinking of tens can help you multiply nines.

3 tens = 30

3 nines = 3 tens − 3 ones

30 − 3 = 27

$3 \times 9 = 27$

27 dogs are in the race.

Divide

A racing club has 27 dogs. How many teams of 9 could the dogs form? Find $27 \div 9$.

To find $27 \div 9 = $ ■, think of ■ $\times 9 = 27$.

Since $3 \times 9 = 27$, $27 \div 9 = 3$. The dogs could form 3 teams.

Talk About It!

- Why can you subtract 3 from 30 to find 3×9?
- How could you use $7 \times 10 = 70$ to find the product of 7×9?

Show What You Know!

Copy. Write the answer.

1. 5 × 9
2. 6 × 9
3. 3 × 9
4. 45 ÷ 9
5. 54 ÷ 9
6. 18 ÷ 9
7. 63 ÷ 9
8. 1 × 9
9. 2 × 9
10. 0 × 9
11. 4 × 9
12. 8 × 9
13. 9)54
14. 9)27
15. 9)72

16. **Critical Thinking** How could you use the fact 10 ÷ 2 = 5 to help you find 10 ÷ 5?

Work It Out!

Write the answer.

17.
$$\begin{array}{r} 9 \\ \times\ 4 \\ \hline \end{array}$$
18.
$$\begin{array}{r} 8 \\ \times\ 9 \\ \hline \end{array}$$
19.
$$\begin{array}{r} 7 \\ \times\ 9 \\ \hline \end{array}$$
20.
$$\begin{array}{r} 2 \\ \times\ 9 \\ \hline \end{array}$$
21.
$$\begin{array}{r} 9 \\ \times\ 6 \\ \hline \end{array}$$

22. 9)63
23. 9)45
24. 9)81
25. 3)27
26. 9)36

27. 9 × 6
28. 9 × 3
29. 27 ÷ 9
30. 9 ÷ 9

31. Fill in your multiplication table with any new facts you have learned. Is your table complete? Fill in any missing products.

32. **Create Your Own** Write multiplication facts using the factor 9. Add the digits in each product. What pattern do you see? What other patterns do you see in the products?

Problem Solving

33. Each team of 9 dogs has 1 lead dog. In 9 teams, how many of the dogs are not lead dogs?

34. Sled dogs sometimes wear booties to keep their paws warm. A dog owner wants to buy booties for 9 dogs. How many booties does he need?

More Practice Set 6.9, p. 459

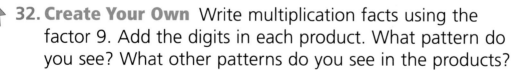

Problem Solving
Using Guess and Check and Other Strategies

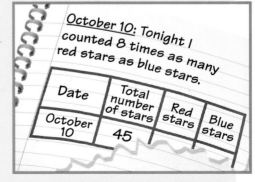

Astronomers are scientists who study stars, planets, and other objects in space. They know that the color of a star can tell them important things about it. Red stars are usually cooler than blue stars, for example.

Problem Solving Process
- ✓ Understand
- ✓ Plan
- ✓ Try It
- ✓ Look Back

Choose a Strategy You Have Learned
- ✓ Act It Out
- ✓ Look for a Pattern
- ✓ Guess and Check
- ✓ Draw a Picture
- ✓ Make a Table
- Work Backward
- Make a List
- Work a Simpler Problem

Oh no! The dog chewed part of your notes for your astronomy project! How can you figure out how many red and blue stars you saw?

- What problem do you need to solve?

- How does the number of red stars compare to the number of blue stars?

- How many stars are there in all?

October 10: Tonight I counted 8 times as many red stars as blue stars.

Date	Total number of stars	Red stars	Blue stars
October 10	45		

- Explain a strategy that can help you to solve the problem. Then solve it.

Work It Out!

Use any strategy to solve the problem. Show your work.

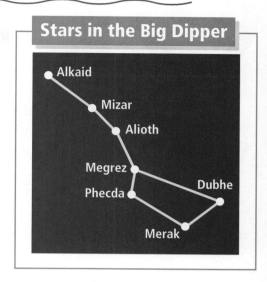

1. Look at the picture on the right. Your class is using star stickers to show the Big Dipper. How many pictures can your class make with 56 stickers?

2. Star stickers come in a packet of 5. You want to make 2 Big Dipper pictures. How many packets would you need to buy to make your pictures?

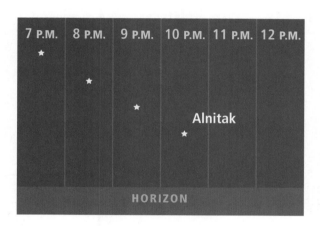

3. Alnitak (AL nih tak) is a star in the constellation Orion. At what time will it be below the horizon line? How can you tell?

4. Orion has more than 4 times as many stars as the Big Dipper, but fewer than 5 times as many. Could you make 2 pictures of Orion with 70 stickers?

5. Stars can be put into four basic color groups. The sun is yellow. Orange stars are hotter than red stars but cooler than the sun. Blue stars are hotter than yellow stars. Which color are the hottest stars?

6. You count 15 meteors, or shooting stars, each hour. How many meteors will you count in 3 hours?

Share Your Thinking

7. Describe the strategy you used to solve problem 6.

8. Did you use Guess and Check for any of the problems? Explain.

Exploring Patterns in Multiplication

You know how to multiply 3 by 2. How can that help you multiply 30 by 2 and 300 by 2? You can use place-value blocks to find out.

Here's A Way! Multiply 3, 30, and 300 by 2.

1 Make 2 groups of 3 ones blocks. Write the multiplication sentence.

$2 \times 3 = 6$

2 Make 2 groups of 3 tens blocks. Write the multiplication sentence.

$2 \times 30 = 60$

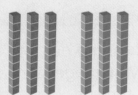

3 Now make 2 groups of 3 hundreds blocks. Write the multiplication sentence.

$2 \times 300 = 600$

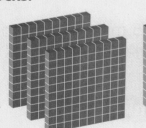

Talk About It!

• What patterns do you notice in the factors and products?

• How can the patterns help you use mental math to multiply greater numbers?

Show What You Know!

Use blocks if you want. Complete the multiplication sentences.

1. 3 groups of 4 ones $3 \times 4 = \blacksquare$ 2. $2 \times 5 = \blacksquare$
   3 groups of 4 tens $3 \times 40 = \blacksquare$ $2 \times 50 = \blacksquare$
   3 groups of 4 hundreds $3 \times 400 = \blacksquare$ $2 \times 500 = \blacksquare$

3. $2 \times 200 = \blacksquare$ 4. $6 \times 40 = \blacksquare$ 5. $7 \times 300 = \blacksquare$ 6. $5 \times 80 = \blacksquare$

7. **Critical Thinking** How could the patterns you have learned help you find 3×8000?

Work It Out!

Complete the multiplication sentence.

8. $2 \times 2 = \blacksquare$ 9. $1 \times 5 = \blacksquare$ 10. $5 \times 4 = \blacksquare$
   $2 \times 20 = \blacksquare$ $1 \times 50 = \blacksquare$ $5 \times 40 = \blacksquare$
   $2 \times 200 = \blacksquare$ $1 \times 500 = \blacksquare$ $5 \times 400 = \blacksquare$

Find the product.

11. 3×20	12. 2×400	13. 5×20	14. 9×30
15. 3×30	16. 4×300	17. 6×100	18. 7×400
19. 4×10	20. 2×300	21. 3×50	22. 5×30

Problem Solving

23. Suppose you build a tower with 20 alphabet blocks. Each block is 2 inches high. How high is the tower?

24. Suppose you have one dollar. A wooden block costs 20¢. Do you have enough money to buy 4 blocks? 5 blocks? 6 blocks?

Math Journal

Write rules for multiplying 1, 10, and 100 by the same number. What is the same? What is different?

Exploring Patterns in Division

$8 \div 2 = 4$

Getting Started

What You'll Need:
▶ place-value blocks

How would you find 80 ÷ 2? What about 800 ÷ 2? You can use basic facts to help.

Here's A Way! **Divide 8, 80, and 800 by 2.**

1 Take 8 ones blocks. Make 2 equal groups with them. Write the division sentence.

$8 \div 2 = 4$

---

2 Take 8 tens blocks. Make 2 equal groups with them. Write the division sentence.

$80 \div 2 = 40$

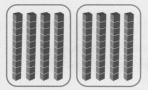

---

3 Now, take 8 hundreds blocks. Make 2 equal groups. Write the division sentence.

$800 \div 2 = 400$

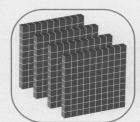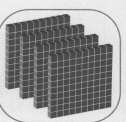

Talk About It!

• What patterns do you notice? How do basic facts help you?

• How can these patterns help you do mental math?

Use blocks if you wish. Complete the division sentence.

1. 12 ones in 2 sets $12 \div 2 = $ ▣   2. $2 \div 1 = $ ▣

    12 tens in 2 sets $120 \div 2 = $ ▣ $20 \div 1 = $ ▣

    12 hundreds in 2 sets $1200 \div 2 = $ ▣ $200 \div 1 = $ ▣

3. **Critical Thinking** How is dividing 10 and 100 by 2 like multiplying 10 and 100 by 2? How is it different?

4. **Mental Math** How can you use the division fact $27 \div 3 = 9$ to help you solve $270 \div 3$ mentally?

Work It Out!

Complete the division sentence. Write the division fact you used.

5. $400 \div 4 = $ ▣   6. $560 \div 7 = $ ▣   7. $4000 \div 8 = $ ▣   8. $600 \div 6 = $ ▣

Use the patterns to find the quotient.

9. $60 \div 1$ 10. $3000 \div 6$ 11. $210 \div 7$ 12. $4200 \div 6$

13. $30 \div 3$ 14. $400 \div 2$ 15. $150 \div 3$ 16. $1600 \div 8$

17. $800 \div 8$ 18. $100 \div 5$ 19. $60 \div 6$ 20. $250 \div 5$

21. **Estimation** Estimate $24,000 \div 6$. Record how you estimated. Then use a calculator to find the exact answer.

Problem Solving

22. Beads cost 3¢ each. How many beads could you buy with 2 quarters and a dime?

23. Bears can hibernate for more than 140 days. How many weeks is 140 days?

Mixed Review

Write the amount in dollars and cents.

24. 156 cents   25. 375 cents   26. 415 cents   27. 263 cents

LESSON 13

Problem Solving
Using Strategies

You can read more about the trip in the pages of *National Geographic.*

In 1994 three men traveled across Baffin Island in Canada. They skied, paddled kayaks, and hiked. They crossed almost 1900 miles of wilderness. The map shows Baffin Island.

Baffin Island

Hudson Bay

U.S.A. CANADA

Problem Solving Process

✓ Understand
✓ Plan
✓ Try It
✓ Look Back

Choose a Strategy You Have Learned

✓ Act It Out
✓ Look for a Pattern
✓ Guess and Check
✓ Draw a Picture
✓ Make a Table
✓ Work Backward
  Make a List
  Work a Simpler Problem

Sometimes the men carried their food on sleds. A sled can hold up to 200 pounds. Suppose the men had 6 packages of food. How could they divide the packages between 2 sleds?

- What is the question you need to answer?

- How many pounds can each sled hold?

- How much does each package weigh?

- Explain a strategy that can help you solve the problem.

28
120
145
47
27
33

Use any strategy to solve the problem. Show your work.

1. The trip began on March 27. The men skied about 10 miles a day. How far had they skied by the end of March (Hint: March has 31 days.)?

2. The men stopped at Inuit villages along the way. Here is an Inuit bead design that has been broken. How many beads of each color are needed to fix the design?

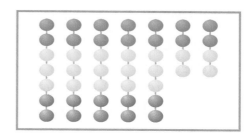

3. Each man needed to eat 5500 calories a day to keep up his energy. One ounce of cheese has 115 calories. How much cheese would have 805 calories?

4. The trip took 192 days. March 27 was the first day. On May 1, how many days had they traveled?

5. The men used about 2 pounds of food each day. Would 400 pounds of food be enough for the trip? How do you know?

6. One day the men put sails on their kayaks. That day they traveled 22 miles. How many days would it take them to travel 100 miles at this speed?

7. The men have 2-ounce and 7-ounce cups. They need 16 ounces of water to cook their dinner. How can they measure the water?

Share Your Thinking

8. What strategy did you use to solve problem 6? How did you use it?

9. Compare your solution of problem 6 to a classmate's. How are the solutions alike? How are they different?

Chapter 6 Test
for Pages 192–219

Test-Taking Tips
Remember to look for patterns when doing multiplication exercises.

Problem Solving

Solve. Show your work. (pages 198, 212, 218)

1. Suppose your class goes on a field trip to the Natural History Museum to see a special show. The show is open from 9:00 A.M. to 5:00 P.M. every day. Suppose 50 people see the show each hour. How many people will see the show in 1 day?

2. The theater at the museum is showing a special film. The cost is $5 for adults and $4 for children. If you order the tickets by phone, they add $1 to the total bill. Suppose you call up and order tickets for 2 adults and 2 children. How much will it cost you?

Concepts

Use a basic fact to find the product. (page 214)

3. 6 × 5   4. 60 × 5   5. 600 × 5

6. 50 × 3   7. 500 × 3   8. 400 × 2

9. What pattern do you see in exercises 3–5?

10. Write a multiplication sentence for 50 + 50 + 50 + 50.

Which group of numbers gives the correct products?
Write *a*, *b*, *c*, or *d*. (pages 202, 208, 214)

11. 3 × 7	a. 27	b. 21	c. 21	d. 21
30 × 7	270	280	201	210
300 × 7	2700	3500	2001	2100

12. 8 × 2	a. 16	b. 16	c. 18	d. 18
8 × 20	160	180	160	180
8 × 200	1600	1600	1800	1800

Find the product. (pages 200, 202, 208, 210)

13. 4×6 14. 7×6 15. 7×5 16. 8×3

17. $\begin{array}{r} 9 \\ \times\, 2 \\ \hline \end{array}$ 18. $\begin{array}{r} 4 \\ \times\, 9 \\ \hline \end{array}$ 19. $\begin{array}{r} 7 \\ \times\, 8 \\ \hline \end{array}$ 20. $\begin{array}{r} 8 \\ \times\, 9 \\ \hline \end{array}$

21. 5×8 22. 9×6 23. 4×7 24. 8×6

Find the quotient. (pages 200, 202, 208, 210)

25. $6\overline{)36}$ 26. $7\overline{)56}$ 27. $9\overline{)63}$

28. $8\overline{)40}$ 29. $9\overline{)45}$ 30. $8\overline{)64}$

31. $7\overline{)21}$ 32. $9\overline{)81}$ 33. $63 \div 7$

34. $16 \div 8$ 35. $42 \div 6$ 36. $36 \div 9$

Performance Task

(pages 194, 200, 218)

You and 5 friends want to make friendship bracelets. Together you have materials to make 30 bracelets with rainbow colors and 12 bracelets with pastel colors. Each of you will make an equal number of bracelets. How many bracelets will you each be able to make?

- Choose a strategy and solve the problem.

- Explain how you found the answer.

Keep In Mind . . .

Your work will be evaluated on the following:

☑ Clear plan for solving

☑ Correct math

☑ Written explanation

☑ Method for checking

Cumulative Review

Subtraction (Chapter 1)
Find 15 − 8.

Here's A Way!

Use an addition fact to help.
Think: 8 + ■ = 15.
8 + 7 = 15
So, 15 − 8 = 7.

Find the difference.

1. 18 − 9   2. 13 − 8   3. 11 − 7
4. 17 − 7   5. 11 − 6   6. 7 − 4

7. Write the fact family for these
   numbers: 4, 3, 7. Then, find 7 − 3.
   How did writing a fact family help
   you find the difference?

Rounding (Chapter 2)
**Round 22 to the nearest ten, and
179 to the nearest hundred.**

Here's A Way!

22 is closer to **20** than 30.

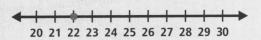
20 21 22 23 24 25 26 27 28 29 30

180 is closer to **200** than 100.

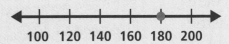
100 120 140 160 180 200

Round all halfway numbers up.

Round to the nearest ten.

8. 51   9. 35   10. 96

Round to the nearest hundred.

11. 120   12. 250   13. 380

14. How would you round 150 to the
    nearest hundred? Explain.

Estimating (Chapter 3)
**Estimate 492 + 286 and
492 − 296.**

Here's A Way!

Round both numbers to the
nearest hundred. Then, add or
subtract.
500 + 300 = 800
500 − 300 = 200

**Write an estimate for the sum or the
difference. Check your estimate. Find the
answer on a calculator.**

15. 184 + 206   16. 875 − 110
17. 585 − 111   18. 198 − 101
19. 999 − 222   20. 685 + 289

21. Estimate which is greater,
    289 + 312 or 795 − 501.
    How do you know?

Bar Graphs (Chapter 4)
How many liked the zoo best?

Here's A Way!

Read the bar for *zoo*.
8 students chose the zoo.

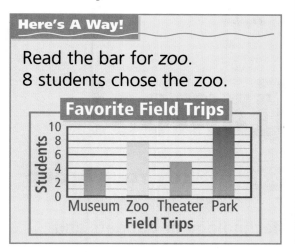

Use the bar graph to answer the question.

22. Did more students vote for the museum or the theater?

23. How many students liked visiting the museum best of all?

24. Which field trip was chosen by more students than any other?

25. How many in all voted for the 2 most popular field trips?

26. There are 27 students in the class. Why do the labels only go to 10?

Multiplying, Dividing (Chapter 5)
Find 3 × 4. Find 12 ÷ 3.

Here's A Way!

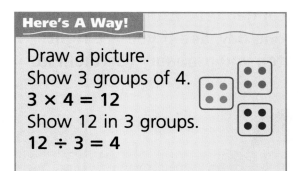

Draw a picture.
Show 3 groups of 4.
3 × 4 = 12
Show 12 in 3 groups.
12 ÷ 3 = 4

Draw a picture. Write a multiplication sentence.

27. 5 groups of 3   28. 3 groups of 2

Draw a picture. Write a division sentence.

29. 18 in 3 groups   30. 9 in 3 groups

31. Do you think of the whole first in multiplication or division?

Problem Solving

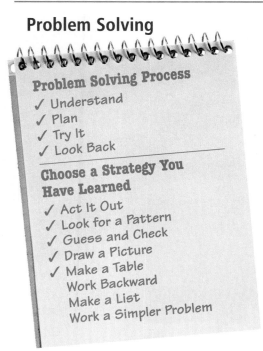

Problem Solving Process
✓ Understand
✓ Plan
✓ Try It
✓ Look Back

Choose a Strategy You Have Learned
✓ Act It Out
✓ Look for a Pattern
✓ Guess and Check
✓ Draw a Picture
✓ Make a Table
   Work Backward
   Make a List
   Work a Simpler Problem

Solve. Show your work.

32. Suppose your class is selling calendars as a way to raise money to buy computer programs. For every 5 calendars they sell, the class earns enough money for 2 programs. How many programs will the class be able to buy when it sells 25 calendars?

33. If 4 calendar sales earn enough for 1 computer program, how many programs will you get selling 20 calendars?

6

I N V E S T I G A T I O N

Gadgets & Gizmos!

Technology Connection   **With Your Group**

Keep In Mind . . .

Your work will be evaluated on the following:

☑ Whether you multiply correctly

☑ How well you compare your estimated use and actual use

☑ How clear and easy to understand your chart is

☑ How well your group works together to make the chart

Whether you call it technology or gadgets and gizmos, you use many electrical things every day. Look for gadgets that plug in, have a switch, or use batteries. Find out how often you use them.

Make a list of electrical gadgets. Estimate how often you will use them in one day. See if you are right! Then find out how often you probably use them in one week.

Electrical Items
- TV
- computer
- flashlight
- lamp
- refrigerator
- radio

1

Plan It

- As a group, write a list of electrical gadgets that you use every day. The picture may help you.
- Choose 10 items that everyone can keep track of for one day.
- Talk about how you can use tally marks to keep track of how much you use each gadget.

It uses electricity if it . . .

has a plug,

uses batteries,

or has a switch.

2

Put It Together

- Make a chart like the one below.
- Estimate how often you think you will use each gadget. Record.
- Now, actually tally how often you use each item in one day. Count your tallies and record the results.
- Multiply your results by the number of days in a week. Record how often you might use each gadget in a week. You can use a calculator.

3

Wrap It Up

- Compare your estimate to your actual results. How close was your estimate?

4

Discuss Your Results

- Did you meet all of the goals in Keep In Mind?
- Did any of your results surprise you?

Use of Electrical Items

Item	Guess	1 day	1 week
TV	4	3	21
light	3	5	35
radio	2	1	7

Internet

> Visit the **Math Center** at **Houghton Mifflin Education Place.** http://www.eduplace.com

Use What You Know

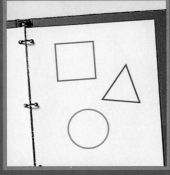

- what a square looks like

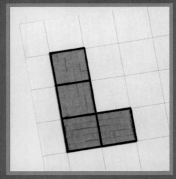

- how to draw figures

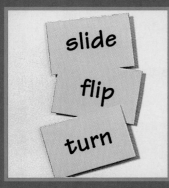

- words to describe figures

Geometry

Try This!

Find different ways to connect 3, 4, and 5 squares. Each square needs to share a side with another square.

What You'll Need

graph paper, pencil

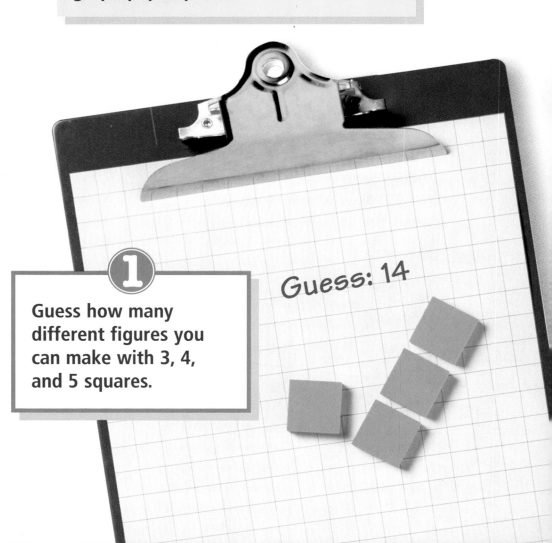

1

Guess how many different figures you can make with 3, 4, and 5 squares.

Guess: 14

Now, draw as many different figures as you can. Check to be sure that all the squares share at least one side. Move figures around to be sure they do not match.

How many different figures did you make? Was your guess close? Compare your results with the results of others.

How did you check to see whether your figures were alike or not?

What other shapes do you know besides squares?

Ready to Go!

Slides

Cooperative Learning
Checklist

☑ Work alone.
☑ Work with a partner.
☑ Work with a group.

Getting Started

What You'll Need:
▶ tracing paper
▶ ruler
▶ scissors
▶ recording sheet

Vocabulary:
slide
Glossary, p. 480

This blanket was made in the Central American country of Guatemala. What shapes do you see in its design?

Activity

1 Trace the part of the design that is outlined in white onto a piece of paper. What shape is it?

2 Move your tracing along the blanket in a straight line and match it to other parts of the design. Do not turn the tracing.

Moving a figure along a line is a **slide**.

3

Draw a line on a piece of paper. Cut a corner off another piece to make a triangle. Put a side of the triangle on the line. Trace the triangle. Move it along the line. Trace it again. Compare the tracings. What do you notice?

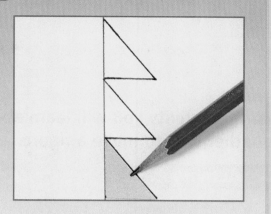

Show What You Know!

Answer the question.

1. **Critical Thinking** What happens to a figure in a slide? Tell what changes and what stays the same.

Does the picture show a slide? Write *yes* or *no*.

2. 　　　3.　　　4.　　　5.

Draw another figure to show a slide. Use your recording sheet or dot paper.

 6.　　　7. 　　　8. 　　　9.

 10. **Create Your Own** Use your recording sheet or dot paper. Make your own slides. Draw the figures.

Math Journal

Use your own words to tell what a slide is.

LESSON 2

Flips

Cooperative Learning Checklist

☐ Work alone.
☑ Work with a partner.
☑ Work with a group.

Getting Started

What You'll Need:
▶ tracing paper
▶ recording sheet

Vocabulary:
flip
Glossary, p. 480

In this activity you will learn about another way to move a figure.

Activity

1 Fold a sheet of tracing paper in half. Then unfold it. Draw around your hand on one side of the paper. Your thumb should be toward the fold.

2 Fold the paper in half again. Make sure that the blank side is on top. Trace your drawing through the paper.

3 Unfold the paper. The two thumbs should face each other. The picture you have made shows a **flip**.

4

Look at these pictures. Which show flips? Explain. Use tracing paper if it helps.

Show What You Know!

Does the figure show a flip? Write *yes* or *no*.

1.

2.

3.

4.

5. **Critical Thinking** What stays the same when you flip a figure?

 Continue the pattern. Use your recording sheet or dot paper.

6.

7.

8.

9. **Critical Thinking** If you look at your name in a mirror, will you see a flip or a slide? Try it to check your prediction.

Draw another figure to show a flip. Use your recording sheet or dot paper.

10.

11.

12.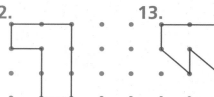

13.

231

LESSON 3

Turns

stem

A turn can be made by rotating a figure around a point. These musical notes show a **half turn**.

Getting Started

What You'll Need:
- ► paper
- ► tracing paper
- ► scissors
- ► crayons
- ► glue
- ► recording sheet

Vocabulary:
half turn
Glossary, p. 480

Cooperative Learning Checklist

- ☑ Work alone.
- ☑ Work with a partner.
- ☑ Work with a group.

Activity

1 Fold a piece of tracing paper in half. Trace the large note. Cut out the tracing to make two notes.

2 Paste one note at the top of a piece of paper with the stem down. Put the other note over the pasted one so it matches.

3 Put a pencil point on a corner of the bottom of the stem. With your other hand, turn the note.

4 Turn the note until the stem points up. Paste the note down. Your figure shows a half turn.

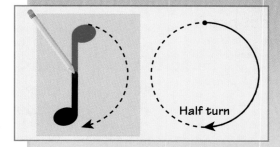

Half turn

Show What You Know!

1. Does the turned note have the same shape and size as the first note? How do you know?

2. How is the turned note different from the first note?

3. Cut six *L*-shaped figures from your recording sheet or trace these. Paste them on a piece of paper to show half turns.

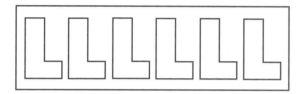

Use your recording sheet or dot paper. Draw one more figure to continue the pattern.

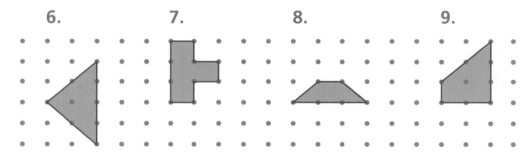

4.

5.

Look at the figure below. On your recording sheet or dot paper, draw another figure that shows a half turn.

6.   7.   8.   9.

10. **Critical Thinking** How would the note at the top of page 232 look if you made a full turn? Draw a picture.

11. **Create Your Own** Create a pattern that shows slides, flips, and turns. Give your pattern to a classmate to continue.

Mixed Review

Write the answer.

12. 56 ÷ 8	13. 4 × 9	14. 30 ÷ 6	15. 2 × 8	16. 5 × 0
17. 6 × 4	18. 7 ÷ 7	19. 72 ÷ 8	20. 4 × 4	21. 64 ÷ 8

Problem Solving
Look for a Pattern

What You'll Need:
▶ pattern blocks

You have 5 pieces of wrapping paper. Which 3 could be part of one large sheet of paper?

You can look for a pattern to help you solve some kinds of problems.

Here's A Way! Use Look for a Pattern to solve.

1 Understand

- What problem are you solving?
- Would the larger sheet have many different patterns?

2 Plan

- Why would looking for a pattern help you to solve this problem?

3 Try It

- Do you see any patterns of slides, flips, or turns?
- Do any of the pieces show the same pattern?

4 Look Back

- Pieces A, B, and D are part of the same larger picture. How did looking for a pattern help you to solve this problem?

Show What You Know!

Use Look for a Pattern to help you finish the problem.

1. Draw the next 3 figures.

2. Critical Thinking Describe the pattern in problem 1.

Work It Out!

Use Look for a Pattern or any other strategy to solve the problem.

3. A restaurant uses triangular tables. One person can sit at each side of a table. How many people can sit at a row of 7 tables pushed together?

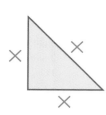 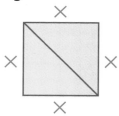 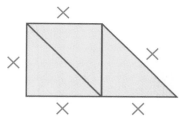

4. What 7 coins equal 25 cents?

5. Draw a shape that can be covered by 4 green pattern blocks but not by 2 blue pattern blocks.

6. If you face north and then make a half turn, you will be facing south. What direction will you be facing if you face north and make 4 half turns? 10 half turns? 11 half turns?

7. On March 1, you save one penny. On March 2, you save 2 pennies. On March 3, you save 3 pennies. At that rate, how many pennies will you save on the last day of March?

Share Your Thinking

8. What strategy did you use for problem 6? Explain why you chose that strategy.

9. When can finding a pattern help you to solve problems?

Cooperative Learning Checklist

☑ Work alone.
☑ Work with a partner.
☐ Work with a group.

Angles

Getting Started

What You'll Need:
► oaktag
► paper fastener

Vocabulary:
angle
square corner
right angle
Glossary, p. 480

This maze has corners and **angles** of different sizes. How can you copy the angles to draw the maze?

Activity

• **Cut two strips of oaktag. Use a paper fastener to join the strips at one end. You now have an angle maker!**

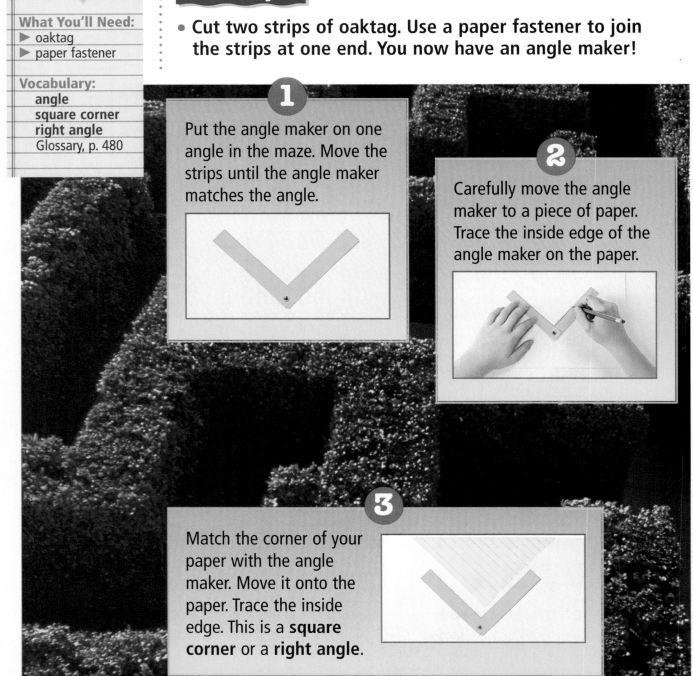

1 Put the angle maker on one angle in the maze. Move the strips until the angle maker matches the angle.

2 Carefully move the angle maker to a piece of paper. Trace the inside edge of the angle maker on the paper.

3 Match the corner of your paper with the angle maker. Move it onto the paper. Trace the inside edge. This is a **square corner** or a **right angle**.

1. Critical Thinking Compare the first angle you made to the right angle. Was the first angle greater than a right angle, less than a right angle, or equal to a right angle?

Use the pictures to answer exercises 2–4.

a.   b.    c.    d.

2. Which angles are right angles?

3. Which angle is greater than a right angle?

4. Which angle is less than a right angle?

Use your angle maker to answer exercises 5–7.

a.   b.   c.   d.   e.

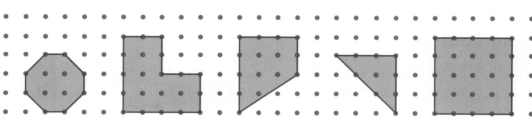

5. How many right angles can you find in each figure?

6. Which figure has the most right angles? The fewest?

7. Which figure has the most angles in all?

8. Critical Thinking Does the angle maker show a right angle? How can you tell?

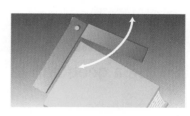

⌐∠⌐∠⌐∠⌐   **9. Patterns** Describe this pattern. Then draw the next angle.

More Practice Set 7.5, p. 460

237

Congruence

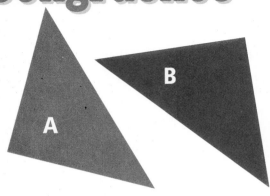

These pieces are congruent.

This is a set of tangram pieces. Figures that are the same size and shape are **congruent**.

Are pieces A and B congruent?

Here's A Way! **Check for congruence.**

Find congruent figures.

1 Trace figure A.

2 Match your tracing to figure B.

Figures A and B are congruent.

Make congruent figures.

You can use a geoboard to make congruent figures.

1 Make a figure on a geoboard.

2 Make a congruent figure. Each side and angle must match the original.

Talk About It! Why did you make the sides and angles match?

Show What You Know!

Predict whether the figures are congruent.

1.

2.

3.

4. Choose one pair of figures from exercises 1–3. Copy one figure and cut it out. Place it on the other figure to check your prediction.

5. **Critical Thinking** If two figures show a flip, are the figures congruent? Explain.

Work It Out!

Copy each figure. Use square dot paper, a geoboard, or a tracing. Then make a figure that is the same shape and size.

6.   7.   8.   9.

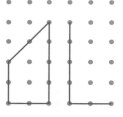 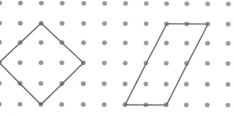

10. **Critical Thinking** Look at your figures from exercise 8. How are they the same? How are they different?

11. Suppose a figure has exactly 4 right angles. Another figure is congruent to the first figure. How many right angles does the second figure have?

12. **Problem Solving** Which figures in this tangram are congruent? How do you know? (Hint: You can use tracing paper.)

More Practice Set 7.6, p. 461

LESSON 7

Symmetry

Does the left side of the small snowflake below match the right side? If a figure is folded in half and the two parts match, the fold line is called a **line of symmetry**.

Getting Started

What You'll Need:
▶ square dot paper
▶ scissors
▶ tracing paper
▶ recording sheet

Vocabulary:
line of symmetry
Glossary, p. 480

Activity

● **Make a chart like the one below.**

1
● Use dot paper. Draw and cut out a square.
● Fold the square in half so the two sides match.
● Draw a line along the fold to show a line of symmetry.

2
● Find and draw another line of symmetry on the square.
● Find as many lines of symmetry as you can.

3
Make figures with
● 0 lines of symmetry
● 1 line of symmetry
● 2 lines of symmetry
● more than 2 lines of symmetry
Sketch the figures on your chart.

line of symmetry

Number of Lines of Symmetry			
0	1	2	More than 2
■	♥	⧖	✳

Show What You Know!

1. **Critical Thinking** Explain how to find lines of symmetry.

Use your recording sheet or dot paper. Draw the other half of the design. The first one is started for you.

2.
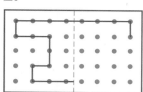

3.

4.

Use your recording sheet or trace the figures. Draw a line of symmetry on the figures that have them.

5.   6.   7.   8.   9.

10. Which of the figures in exercises 5–9 could be folded from top to bottom so the two parts match?

11. Use your recording sheet or print the numbers 0–9. Circle the numbers that have a line of symmetry.

12. **Critical Thinking** How many lines of symmetry does a square have? Would a smaller square have the same number of lines of symmetry?

13. Trace and cut out each of these figures. Find as many lines of symmetry as you can for each figure. Record the lines of symmetry.

      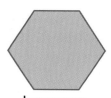

square   triangle   hexagon   circle

14. **Create Your Own** Draw a figure with exactly two lines of symmetry.

Circles

What You'll Need:
▶ strip of oaktag
▶ 2 pencils
▶ scissors

Vocabulary:
center
diameter
Glossary, p. 480

Circles are everywhere! All these objects you might see every day look like circles. What makes a circle different from other figures? Make circles of your own to find out.

Here's A Way! **Make a circle.**

1 Use the strip of oaktag. Make a small hole at each end of the strip. Place the strip on a piece of paper. Put one pencil point in one hole. Hold it steady. This will be the **center** of the circle.

2 Put another pencil point in the other hole. With this pencil, turn the strip around. You will draw a circle.

3 Cut out the circle you drew. Fold it in half. Does the fold line pass through the center? A line that passes through the center of a circle is called a **diameter**.

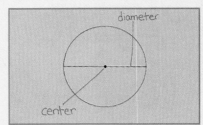

Talk About It!

• How could you change your circle maker to make a smaller circle?

• Think of a way to draw a very large circle.

Show What You Know!

Is the figure a circle? Write *yes* or *no*.

1.

2.

3.

4.

5.

6.

7. **Critical Thinking** How is a circle different from a square, a triangle, and a rectangle?

8. **Write About It** Is every figure that has curves a circle? Draw some figures to support your answer.

Work It Out!

Is the line inside the circle a diameter? Write *yes* or *no*, and explain your answer.

9.

10.

11.

12.

13. **Logical Reasoning** If you make a circle, how can you find the center by folding? (Hint: Start by folding the circle in half.)

14. **Problem Solving** You are setting up chairs for a storytelling performance. How can you make sure that all the chairs are in an exact circle around the storyteller?

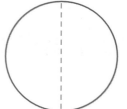

Math Journal

Is a diameter of a circle always a line of symmetry? Explain.

Problem Solving
Choose a Computation Method

Suppose your aunt and uncle work in a bookstore. They ask you to help them find the total number of books to be ordered.

You Decide

- Is it important for you to know the exact number of books you are ordering? Why or why not?

- Is there a way to group the numbers to make them easier to work with mentally?

- Decide whether to use mental math or paper and pencil to find the sum. Explain your decision.

Choose a Computation Method

Ask Yourself:

Do I need an exact answer or an estimate?

Should I use a model, paper and pencil, mental math, or a calculator?

What operation should I use?

Work It Out!

Decide whether to use mental math or paper and pencil. Explain.

1. You order 216 books and receive 149 books. How many more books should you receive?

2. The store receives 3 boxes with 25 books in each. How many books are received?

3. You order *Jumanji* for $4.99 and 2 copies of *Lyle, Lyle Crocodile* for $4.95 each. What does your order cost?

4. You buy a copy of *Loo-Loo, Boo, and Art You Can Do* for $8.79 You pay with a $10 bill. What should be your change?

ORDER FORM

James and the Giant Peach	76 books
The Kids' Guide to Money	68 books
Raptors, Fossils, Fins, and Fangs	54 books
Charlotte's Web	82 books

Share Your Thinking

5. How do you know when to use mental math?

Midchapter Review

for Pages 226–244

for Pages 226–244

Problem Solving

Use any strategy to solve. Show your work. (pages 234, 242)

1. You order a cake with a border of frosting roses. The baker makes a blue rose, then a pink rose, then blue, then pink, and so on. Between each rose are 3 leaves. How many roses of each color will there be if there are 24 leaves in all?

2. There are 4 boys and 4 girls sitting at a rectangular table. One student sits at each short end and 3 students sit at each long side. They sit boy-girl-boy-girl. If a boy sits at one end, is there a boy or a girl at the other end?

Concepts

Write whether each picture shows a slide, a flip, or a half turn.
(pages 228, 230, 232)

3. 　4. 　5.

Look at the figure. Draw a congruent figure. Draw the lines of symmetry. (pages 238, 240)

6. 　　　7.

Skills

Compare the figures. (page 236)

8. Which has the most angles?

9. Which has no angles?

10. Which has 1 square corner?

a.　　b.　　c.

245

Math World

Explore the different ways that lines of symmetry, straight lines, and slides have all been used.

Tasty Symmetry

In Mexico, people make this pastry for special occasions. The designs are made by dipping a piece of fancy iron into batter and frying it. How many lines of symmetry do you see in the pastry?

Straight Ahead

Straight lines have always been very important to builders. Here are two of the tools that have been used to make straight lines.

Sighting Tube

At first the Chinese only used sighting tubes, which are like telescopes, to look at the stars. Later the sighting tubes helped Chinese builders to make terraces and dams.

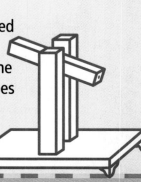

Try This!

PUEBLO BORDER PATTERN

The Pueblo (PWEHB loh) people are Native Americans who live mainly in New Mexico and Arizona. They have been been making clay pots for more than 3000 years. Follow these steps to make a pattern like one made by the San Ildefonso Pueblo people.

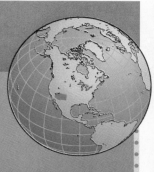

1 Draw the shape below on cardboard or thick paper. Then, cut the shape out.

2 Cut a strip of black construction paper. Make the strip a little taller than the shape you drew. Make the strip long enough to put several designs on.

3 Place the shape from step 1 at the left edge of your strip of paper. Trace around it with a bright-colored crayon or chalk.

4 Use slides to fill the rest of the strip. Wrap your border pattern around a can and tape it. Use the decorated can for pencils.

Laser Tools

In the 1960s, builders started to make straight lines with a beam of light from a laser. This laser is used in Africa.

Respond

Work with a partner . . .
to learn more about Pueblo patterns.

Internet:
Houghton Mifflin Education Place
Explore the Math Center at
http://www.eduplace.com

Solids

Cooperative Learning Checklist

☐ Work alone.
☑ Work with a partner.
☑ Work with a group.

Getting Started

What You'll Need:
▶ straws
▶ clay
▶ recording sheet

Vocabulary:
face
square pyramid
triangular prism
Glossary, p. 480

Solid figures like cubes have flat surfaces. Each flat surface of a solid figure is called a **face**. Try making some solid figures of your own!

Activity

Cube

Triangular Prism

Square Pyramid

1 Make a cube and a **square pyramid** like those in the picture. Use clay balls for corners. Use straws for edges. Count the corners, edges, and faces. Record your results.

2 Make the **triangular prism** next. Two faces of the prism are triangles. The rest are rectangles. Count the corners, edges, and faces and record your results.

3

Make a rectangular prism with your clay and straws. How many faces does it have? What shape are they? Count he corners and edges. Record your results.

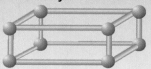

4

Think of a way to sort your figures into 2 different groups.

- Draw a picture of the groups. Write your rule.
- Sort your figures again using a different sorting rule.

Show What You Know!

Name the shape of the red face on each solid.

1.

Triangular Pyramid

2.

Rectangular Prism

3.

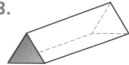

Triangular Prism

4. The bottom face of a cube and a square pyramid are squares. What shapes are the other faces in each solid?

5. Look at the triangular pyramid. How is it like a square pyramid? How is it different?

6. You have seen two prisms. What is the same about them? What is different?

7. **Critical Thinking** Study these solids. Could you build each solid with your straws and clay? Explain.

Sphere

Cone

Cylinder

8. **Write About It** Build a solid with straws and clay. Write a description that tells about the faces, corners, and edges. Give only the description to a friend. Can your friend make the same shape from it?

Visualization

Getting Started

What You'll Need:
► connecting cubes

Are these two figures the same or different? You can find out by making the figures with cubes.

Activity

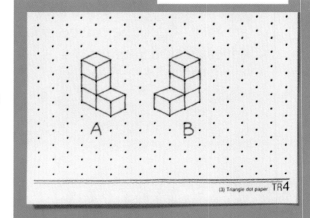

1

One partner uses the picture to make a stack of cubes that looks like Figure A. The other makes a stack of cubes that looks like Figure B.

2

Count how many cubes are in each model. Do Figure A and Figure B have the same number of cubes?

3

Can you make Figure A look like Figure B? Move Figure A to match Figure B.

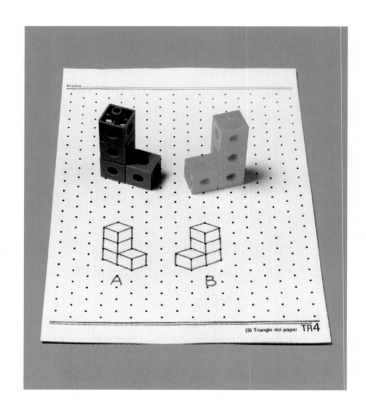

4

Compare Figure A and Figure B. Are they the same shape and the same size?

• Make two more figures that are the same shape and size, but in different positions.

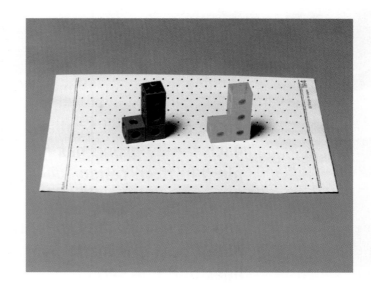

Show What You Know!

Use the picture to build each figure. Write the number of cubes. Tell if any figures are the same size and shape.

1.

2.

3.

4.

Use the pictures to build the figures. Then fit figures a and b together to make figure c. (Hint: Some cubes may be hidden.)

5.   a.   b.   c.
 +   →

6.   a.   b.   c.
  + 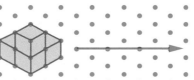 →

7. Logical Reasoning Is there a cube you cannot see in any of the pictures in exercise 6? How do you know?

Lines and Line Segments

What You'll Need:
- ▶ square dot paper
- ▶ markers
- ▶ ruler

Vocabulary:
- line
- line segment
- parallel
- Glossary, p. 480

In some parts of Scotland, each family group has a plaid pattern called a tartan.

You can use tartans to learn about patterns made by lines and line segments.

Activity

Lines

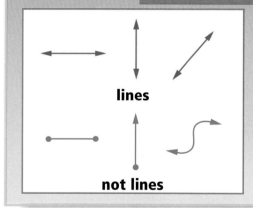

lines

not lines

A **line** is a straight path that goes in both directions. Arrows at both ends show that the line does not end.

1 Draw your own lines. Use a ruler or straight edge to help.

Line Segments

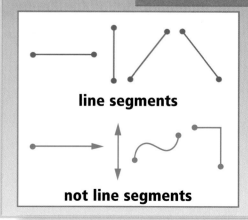

line segments

not line segments

A **line segment** is part of a line. The ends of a line segment do not have arrows. A line segment has two endpoints.

2 Draw a picture on your dot paper using only line segments.

a. Can you use curves? Why or why not?

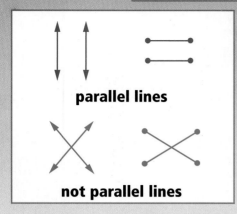

parallel lines

not parallel lines

Parallel lines are always the same distance apart. Line segments are parallel when they are part of parallel lines.

3 Draw a square, a rectangle, and a triangle on your paper.

4 Which shapes have sides that are parallel line segments? Mark each pair of parallel line segments with a different color.

Show What You Know!

1. **Critical Thinking** Is the design on the blanket on page 252 made of lines or line segments? Explain.

Use the pictures to answer questions 2 and 3.

a.
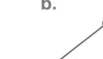

b.

c.

d.

e.

2. Which pictures show lines? Explain.

3. Which pictures show line segments? Explain.

Do the colored parts of the drawing show parallel line segments? Explain your answer.

4.

5.

6.
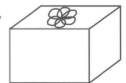

7. **Create Your Own** Use a ruler and markers to create your own tartan on dot paper. Use parallel line segments and line segments that cross.

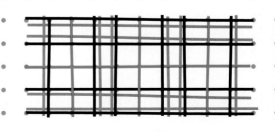

Ordered Pairs

What You'll Need:
▶ tracing paper

Vocabulary:
ordered pair
Glossary, p. 480

This map shows places you might see if you visited Philadelphia, Pennsylvania. The numbers at the bottom and side of the grid help you find places on the map.

Independence Hall is located at point (3,0). The pair of numbers used to describe the point on the grid is called an **ordered pair**. What is at point (3,2)?

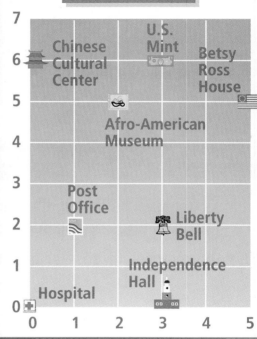

Philadelphia

Chinese Cultural Center
U.S. Mint
Betsy Ross House
Afro-American Museum
Post Office
Liberty Bell
Independence Hall
Hospital

Here's A Way! | **Locate point (3,2).**

1 Put your finger at point (0,0). Move your finger 3 spaces across the bottom of the map.

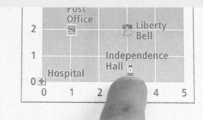

2 Now move your finger up 2 spaces. The Liberty Bell is at point (3,2).

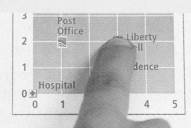

Talk About It! How do you know which direction to move your finger to find the point (3,2)?

Use the map of Philadelphia on page 254. Find each place. Write the ordered pair of the point it is nearest to.

1. U.S. Mint

2. Betsy Ross House

3. Independence Hall

4. the post office

5. **Critical Thinking** Does it matter whether you give the ordered pair of a place as (3,2) or (2,3)? Explain.

Work It Out!

Use this map of Philadelphia for exercises 6–12. Find the ordered pair for each place.

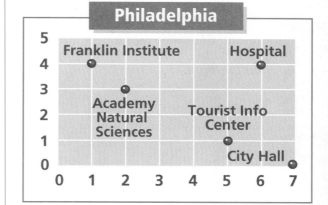

6. City Hall

7. the Franklin Institute

8. the Tourist Information Center

9. What is located at (2,3)?

10. What is located at (6,4)?

11. Is (5,7) on the map? Explain.

12. Trace the grid map above. Draw a straight line between the Academy of Natural Sciences and the Franklin Institute. Draw another between the Tourist Information Center and City Hall. Are the lines parallel? Explain.

13. **Create Your Own** Trace this grid. Draw your own map. Give a friend the ordered pair for a place. Can your friend find it?

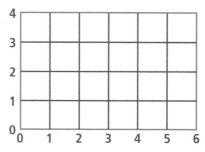

Mixed Review

Write < or >.

14. 741 ● 714   15. 2113 ● 987   16. $601 ● $599   17. 1033 ● 1303

More Practice Set 7.13, p. 462

LESSON 14

Problem Solving
Using Look for a Pattern and Other Strategies

Problem Solving Process
✓ Understand
✓ Plan
✓ Try It
✓ Look Back

Choose a Strategy You Have Learned
✓ Act It Out
✓ Look for a Pattern
✓ Guess and Check
✓ Draw a Picture
✓ Make a Table
  Work Backward
  Make a List
  Work a Simpler Problem

Suppose your class is making decorations for your classroom. You want to make a flower with a red center and yellow and orange petals.

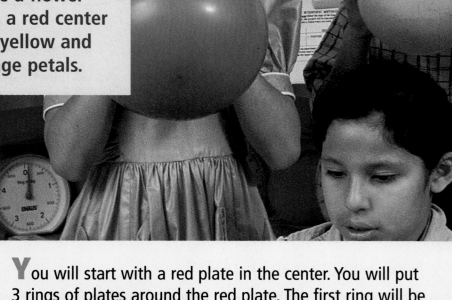

You will start with a red plate in the center. You will put 3 rings of plates around the red plate. The first ring will be yellow, the second ring orange, and the third ring yellow. How many plates will you need to make the flower?

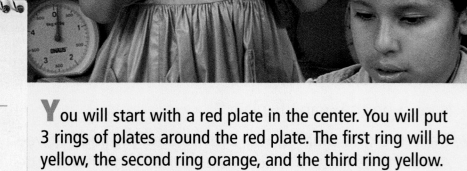

- What problem needs to be solved?

- How can you find out how many yellow plates will fit around the red plate? How many orange plates will fit around the ring of yellow plates?

- Do you see a pattern? Describe it.

- Explain a strategy you can use to solve this problem. Then solve it.

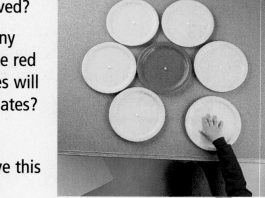

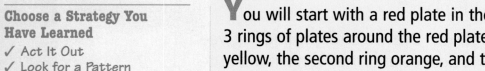

Use any strategy to solve the problem. Show your work.

1. Extend the pattern by drawing the next three circles.

2. If you fold a circle in half, you can see a line of symmetry. How many times would you fold a circle to get exactly 4 lines of symmetry?

3. You want to make a flower for each person in the class. Eight people want red flowers. The rest want yellow flowers. There are 26 people in the class. How many yellow flowers do you need?

4. **Create Your Own**
   Create a pattern with circles or figures. See if a classmate can continue your pattern.

5. You buy decorations. Your change is $11. How many different combinations of both $1 and $5 bills can you get?

6. Show the next three figures in this pattern.

F ⅂ t Ⅎ F

7. You need 35 plates for a party. You have 6 packages of 5 plates each. Do you have enough plates? If not, how many more do you need?

8. You want to make a border out of 15 plates. Put a red plate first. Then put an orange one, and then a yellow one. Then start over with red. What color will the last plate be?

Share Your Thinking

9. What strategy did you use to solve problem 8? Explain your choice.

10. Did you look for patterns to solve any of the problems? Which ones? Choose one problem and explain how you used patterns to help you to solve it.

LESSON 15
Exploring Area

Getting Started

What You'll Need:
- ► square dot paper
- ► ruler

Vocabulary:
area
Glossary, p. 480

To find out how much paper you would need to make a kite, you can find its area. **Area** is the number of square units needed to cover a figure.

Activity

Area in Whole Squares

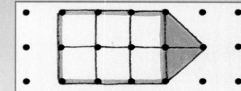

1. Draw the shape of a rectangular kite on dot paper.
2. Connect all the dots inside the picture.
3. Count the squares. Each square equals one square unit. The area of this picture is 6 square units.

Whole and Half Squares

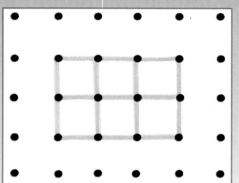

1. Copy the shape of the kite above onto dot paper. Connect the dots to divide it into squares and half squares.
2. Count the whole squares.
3. Then count the half squares. Two half squares equal 1 whole square.
4. Add the whole and half squares. The area of this figure is 7 square units.

Show What You Know!

Copy the figure onto dot paper. Find the area. Show your work.

1. 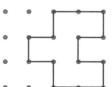 **2.** 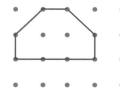 **3.** **4.**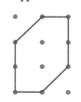

5. Critical Thinking Which of the figures above has the greatest area? How do you know?

Draw a figure that has the area given.

6. 6 square units **7.** 15 square units **8.** 45 square units

Guess which figure below has the largest area. Then count the squares to find the area. Compare the result with your guess.

9.  **10.**   **11.**   **12.**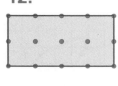

13. Critical Thinking How can you use multiplication to find the area of exercise 12?

14. Patterns Copy this pattern onto dot paper. Then draw the next two figures in the pattern.

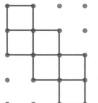

15. Copy and complete the chart. Count the number of squares to find the area of each figure in exercise 14.

Figure Number	1	2	3	4	5
Area	2	?	?	?	?

16. Algebraic Reasoning How many squares would there be in the sixth figure? What would the area be?

LESSON 16

Area of Irregular Figures

People who study dinosaurs can learn a lot from fossil footprints. How could you estimate the area of a footprint?

A dinosaur made this footprint millions of years ago.

Here's A Way! Estimate area by counting squares.

1 Count the whole squares.

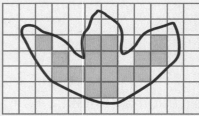

17 whole squares

2 Count the squares that are "almost whole."

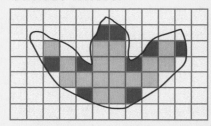

9 "almost whole" squares

3 Count the squares that are "about half." Two of these will equal about one square.

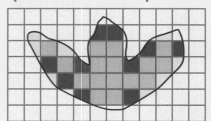

8 "about half" squares, or 4 squares

4 Add to find the total.

$$\begin{array}{r} \overset{2}{1}7 \\ 8 \\ +\ 5 \\ \hline 30 \end{array}$$

The area of this figure is about 30 square units.

Talk About It! What if a figure has "almost empty" squares? How would you estimate them?

Show What You Know!

Estimate the area. Count the squares in each footprint drawing.

1. deer

2. elephant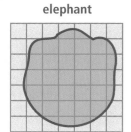

3. duck

4. bear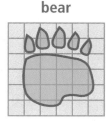

5. **Critical Thinking** What did you do with any "almost empty" squares when you estimated? Explain.

Work It Out!

Estimate the area of each figure.

6.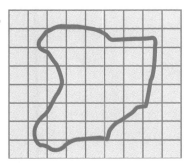

7.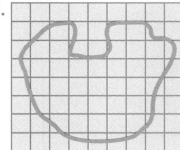

8. Trace your shoe on grid paper. Estimate the area of your shoeprint.

9. Find something in your classroom that you predict covers a smaller area than your shoeprint. Trace it on grid paper and estimate the area. Compare the area to your shoeprint.

10. **Create Your Own** Use grid paper. Draw a footprint. Estimate the area. Tell how you estimated.

11. **Problem Solving** About how many duck footprints from exercise 3 could fit inside this footprint?

Problem Solving
Using Strategies

LESSON 17

You can read more about Washington, D.C., in the pages of *Cobblestone*.

COBBLESTONE
A Historical Look at
Washington, D.C.

There are many exciting places to visit in Washington, D.C. This drawing shows the original plan for Lincoln Park, near the Capitol. To make it easier to get across the park quickly, the designers added straight paths.

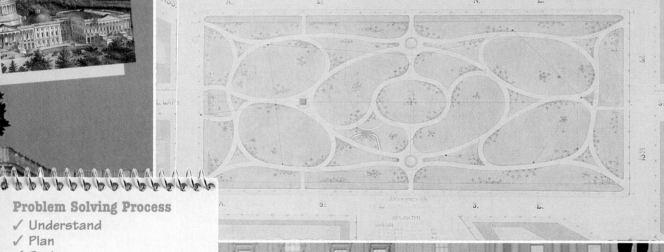

Problem Solving Process
✓ Understand
✓ Plan
✓ Try It
✓ Look Back

Choose a Strategy You Have Learned
✓ Act It Out
✓ Look for a Pattern
✓ Guess and Check
✓ Draw a Picture
✓ Make a Table
  Work Backward
  Make a List
  Work a Simpler Problem

You want to connect all the entrances to the center oval with straight paths. What is the smallest number of paths you can make?

• How many entrances are there?

• What is the smallest number of paths that can connect two entrances?

• How many paths do you need to connect 3 entrances?

• Explain a strategy that can help you to solve the problem. Then solve it.

Work It Out!

Use any strategy to solve the problem. Show your work.

1. Suppose the grid lines are paths and the distance from (0,0) to (0,1) is 1 block. What is the least number of blocks you could walk to go from the Science Museum to the Space Museum?

2. Start at (0,0). Walk 1 block up and 2 blocks to the right. Where will you be if you do this twice more?

The Mall

3. This park has a tunnel under it. Suppose the tunnel goes from A to B. Would you go a shorter distance if you drove from A to B around the park or through the tunnel? Explain.

4. How could you plant a row of shrubs in this park to show a line of symmetry?

Thomas Circle, Washington, D. C

5. Your class has volunteered to help repair this wall in a park in Washington. How many square and rectangular bricks do you need to replace all the missing and broken ones?

6. You are planting tulips and irises in Lincoln Park. Each row of tulips has 4 plants. You want 2 iris plants for every tulip plant. You plant 3 rows of tulips. How many iris plants do you need?

Share Your Thinking

7. What strategy did you use to solve problem 6? Explain why you chose it.

8. In which problems did you look for a pattern? Explain how you used this strategy.

263

Chapter 7 Test

for Pages 226–263

Problem Solving

Solve using any strategy. (pages 234, 256)

1. You are packing lunches for a class picnic. You put a tuna sandwich and an apple in the first bag, a tuna sandwich and an orange in the next, and a cheese sandwich and an orange in the third bag. If you pack 2 more of each kind of lunch, how many more oranges will you use?

2. Extend the pattern. Draw the next 3 figures.

Concepts

Copy the figure on dot paper. Then, show a slide, a flip, or a half turn. (pages 228, 230, 232)

3. Show a slide.

4. Show a flip.

5. Show a half turn.

Tell which pairs show congruent figures. (page 238)

6. a.

b.

c.

Copy the figure on dot paper. Then draw a congruent figure. (page 238)

7.

Find the area. Count square units and parts of square units. (page 258)

8.

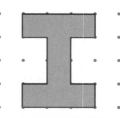

9.

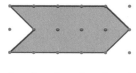

Choose what the picture shows. Write *a, b,* or *c.* (pages 236, 252)

10.
a. a line
b. a corner
c. a line segment

11.
a. a square corner
b. an angle
c. a line

12.
a. a square corner
b. a triangle
c. a line

How many lines of symmetry does the figure have? (page 240)

13.

14.

15.

Write the name of each solid figure. (page 248)

16.

17.

18.

19.

20.

21.

Use the map to find an ordered pair. (page 254)

22. Write the ordered pair for Colorado's capital city, Denver.

23. Write the ordered pair for the mountain Pike's Peak.

24. Which river can be found at (7,6)?

Performance Task

(page 254)

- Copy the grid. Make a map by drawing a house, tree, and pond.

- Write directions that use ordered pairs.

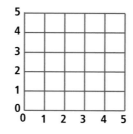

Keep In Mind . . .
Your work will be evaluated on the following:
☑ Correct map
☑ Clear directions
☑ Correct use of ordered pairs
☑ Labels for all parts

Cumulative Review

Ordering Numbers (Chapter 1)
What number comes just before 47?

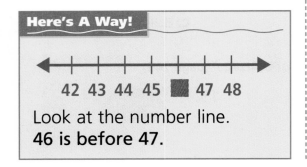

Here's A Way!

42 43 44 45 ■ 47 48

Look at the number line.
46 is before 47.

Write the missing number.

1. 56, 57, ■, 59   2. 33, ■, 35, 36
3. 70, 71, ■, 73   4. 18, 19, ■, 21
5. 39, 40, ■, 42   6. ■, 85, 86, 87

7. How does counting backward change the order of numbers? Explain.

Writing Numbers (Chapter 2)
Write three thousand eight hundred fifty-nine in standard form.

Here's A Way!

Thousands	Hundreds	Tens	Ones
3	8	5	9

Write 3859.

Write the number in standard form.

8. two thousand thirty-five
9. nine hundred seventy-one
10. six thousand four hundred
11. five hundred sixty-eight
12. seven hundred five
13. one hundred ninety-four
14. Look at exercise 13. Does the digit 4 have a greater value than the digit 1? Explain.

Adding Four Numbers (Chapter 3)
Find 48 + 51 + 13 + 77.

Here's A Way!

```
  1
  48      Add the ones.
  51      Regroup. Then,
  13      add the tens and
+ 77      regroup.
 189
```

Find the sum.

```
15.    37     16.    38     17.    42
       22            25            76
       90            75            20
     + 46          + 46          + 74
```

18. How can you use doubles or sums of ten to help you add four numbers?

Interpreting Data (Chapter 4)

How many students like in-line skating best?

Here's A Way!

Favorite Type of Skating

Activity	Tally	Number
Roller Skating	~~IIII~~ II	
Ice Hockey	IIII	
Figure Skating	III	
In-Line Skating	~~IIII~~ ~~IIII~~ ~~IIII~~	15

Skip-count the tally marks by 5's. **15 students like in-line skating best.**

Use the chart to answer the question.

19. What number would you write for roller skating?

20. How many students voted for ice hockey?

21. What number would you write for figure skating?

22. How many more students voted for in-line than for roller skating?

23. Which kind of skating did the fewest students vote for?

24. How many students in all voted?

Properties of Multiplication

(Chapter 5)

Find 1496×0, 1×58, and 7×5.

Here's A Way!

Zero Property: $1496 \times 0 = 0$
Property of One: $1 \times 58 = 58$
Order Property: $7 \times 5 = 5 \times 7$

Find the product. Use the properties of multiplication.

25. 138×1

26. 1×49

27. 27×0

28. 0×356

29. 4×10

30. 4×5

31. Explain in your own words what the Zero Property means.

Problem Solving

Problem Solving Process
✓ Understand
✓ Plan
✓ Try It
✓ Look Back

Choose a Strategy You Have Learned
✓ Act It Out
✓ Look for a Pattern
✓ Guess and Check
✓ Draw a Picture
✓ Make a Table
   Work Backward
   Make a List
   Work a Simpler Problem

Solve. Show your work.

32. Two numbers have a product of 42. One follows right after the other. What are the two numbers?

33. Suppose there are 180 glue sticks. One teacher takes 25 for her class. Another teacher takes 23. A third teacher takes 24. Are there more than 100 glue sticks left in the art closet? Explain how you can estimate to find out.

Mask Task!

Drama Connection   **With Your Group**

Wearing a mask is a great way to "put on" the character of a play or a story that you are acting out. Now you are going to use what you know about shapes to make a fun mask! It can be a mask of an animal, a person, or a creature that you make up. It does not have to be flat. Then, your group will use your masks to act out a story.

Keep In Mind . . .

Your work will be evaluated on the following:

☑ How you decide what shapes to use in your mask

☑ How you show symmetry

☑ How you use flips, turns, and slides

☑ How well your group works together to act out your story

Plan It

①

- Decide on the story your group would like to act out.
- Decide what kind of mask to make and choose some shapes to use.
- Plan your mask on graph paper. Begin by folding the paper in half. Draw a dark line on the fold to use as a line of symmetry.
- Design half of the mask. Use slides and turns.
- Use flips to draw the other half of the design.

Put It Together

②

- Cut out your mask. Tape it on construction paper. Cut around the pattern.
- Decorate your mask.
- Glue your mask to a craft stick to hold it up to your face.

Wrap It Up

③

- Find the lines of symmetry in your group's masks.
- Act out your story for another group.

Discuss Your Results

④

- Did you meet all of the goals in Keep In Mind?
- Talk about how the masks were made. How well did the masks fit the characters?

Internet

> Visit the **Math Center** at **Houghton Mifflin Education Place.** http://www.eduplace.com

- what a fraction is

- how to write a fraction

- equal parts
- fractions
- one half
- one third
- one fourth

- words to describe parts of a whole

Fractions

Try This!

Show some things you know about fractions in a cartoon.

What You'll Need

paper, pencil, markers, or crayons

1

Think about when and where fractions are used. Draw one or more cartoon frames to show something you know about fractions.

Write fractions as you need them.

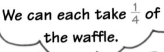
We can each take $\frac{1}{4}$ of the waffle.

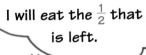
I will eat the $\frac{1}{2}$ that is left.

3

Show your cartoon to others to see if they understand the fractions.

Use your cartoon idea with different fractions. How do the pictures and words change?

How does your cartoon help you remember things about fractions?

Ready to Go!

Cooperative Learning
Checklist

☐ Work alone.
☑ Work with a partner.
☑ Work with a group.

LESSON 1

Exploring Fractions

What You'll Need:
▶ recording sheet
▶ pattern blocks

A fraction is a number that names a part of a whole or part of a set. Use pattern blocks and a recording sheet to find out more about fractions.

Activity

• Use pattern blocks to explore figures with equal parts.

1

Figure 1 is divided into 2 parts, or 2 halves. Place a green triangle on Figure 1.

• How many of the equal parts are covered by the triangle?

• One of the halves, or one half, of the whole figure is covered.

2

Figure 2 is divided into 3 parts or 3 thirds. How many equal parts are in Figure 2?

- Place a green triangle on Figure 2.
- How much of the whole figure is covered? One of the thirds, or one third, is covered.
- Figure 3 is divided into 4 fourths. How much can you cover with a green triangle?

3

- Use a green triangle. Cover a part in Figures 4 and 5. How much is covered?
- Use a blue block. Cover a part in Figures 6 and 7. How much is covered?
- Use a red block. Cover a part in Figure 8. How much is covered?

Show What You Know!

Discuss each question. Explain your answer.

1. **Critical Thinking** How are Figures 1–5 alike? How are they different?

2. Would you need more than one green block to cover half of Figure 3? Explain why.

3. The red block covers half of some figures. Which ones?

4. The blue block covers half of some figures. Which ones?

5. The green block covers five of the eight parts of figure 5. Write this as a fraction.

6. Place one blue block on Figure 2. How much of the whole figure is covered?

7. **Critical Thinking** Could you use green blocks to cover exactly half of figure 2? Explain.

Math Journal

Use your own words. Explain the difference between equal and unequal parts of a whole figure.

Writing Fractions

You can use fractions to describe this flag that is divided into equal parts.

This is Italy's flag.
The capital of Italy is Rome.

Here's A Way! | Write a fraction.

1 Count how many equal parts are in the flag.

3 equal parts

2 Tell what fraction of the flag is white.

One of the three parts is white.
So, one third is white.

3 Write the fraction for the white part.

One third is written $\frac{1}{3}$.

number of white parts ➡ **1** ⬅ numerator

number of equal parts ➡ **3** ⬅ denominator

Talk About It!

How do you know that $\frac{1}{3}$ tells about the white part of the whole flag?

Other Examples What fraction of each flag is red?

a. Mali   b. Indonesia   c. Benin

Show What You Know!

Write the fraction for the shaded part of the figure.

1.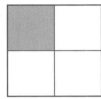

2.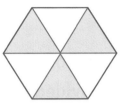

3.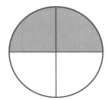

4.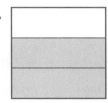

5. **Critical Thinking** Write a fraction for the unshaded part of exercise 4.

Work It Out!

Draw a flag. Use the fraction to show the shaded part of the flag.

6. $\frac{2}{4}$ 7. $\frac{2}{6}$ 8. $\frac{4}{4}$ 9. $\frac{3}{8}$ 10. $\frac{1}{3}$ 11. $\frac{3}{5}$

Look at the chart. Write the missing fractions.

Fraction Name	Fraction	Picture
one half	$\frac{1}{2}$	
one third	12. ?	
one fourth	13. ?	
one fifth	14. ?	
15. ?	$\frac{1}{6}$	
one seventh	16. ?	
17. ?	$\frac{1}{8}$	

Look at the set of blocks.

18. How many blocks are in the whole set?

19. What fraction of the whole set is one block? Two blocks? Three blocks? Four blocks? Five blocks?

20. **Create Your Own** Design a school flag. Divide a rectangle into fourths and color it in. Write fractions for the parts.

More Practice Set 8.2, p. 463

LESSON 3

Cooperative Learning
Checklist
☐ Work alone.
☑ Work with a partner.
☑ Work with a group.

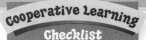

Comparing Fractions

Which is greater, $\frac{1}{4}$ or $\frac{2}{4}$? Find out by comparing fraction models divided into the same number of equal parts.

Activity

Compare $\frac{1}{4}$ and $\frac{2}{4}$.

The fractions $\frac{1}{4}$ and $\frac{2}{4}$ have the same denominator but they have different numerators.

1. Use fraction models for $\frac{1}{4}$ and $\frac{2}{4}$. Both fractions have a denominator of 4. Both models show 4 equal parts.

2. Compare the models. Which model shows more shading?

3. Write > or < between the fractions to tell which is greater.

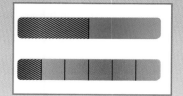

Compare $\frac{1}{2}$ and $\frac{1}{6}$.

The fractions $\frac{1}{2}$ and $\frac{1}{6}$ have the same numerator but they have different denominators.

1 Use fraction models for $\frac{1}{2}$ and $\frac{1}{6}$. The denominators are different. Each model is divided into a different number of equal parts.

2 Compare the models. Which model shows more shading?

3 Write > or < between the fractions to tell which is greater.

Show What You Know!

Use fraction models to compare the pair of fractions. Write > or <.

1. $\frac{3}{6}$ ▩ $\frac{5}{6}$ 2. $\frac{2}{4}$ ▩ $\frac{3}{4}$ 3. $\frac{1}{3}$ ▩ $\frac{2}{3}$ 4. $\frac{1}{2}$ ▩ $\frac{2}{2}$ 5. $\frac{1}{6}$ ▩ $\frac{2}{6}$

6. $\frac{1}{2}$ ▩ $\frac{1}{3}$ 7. $\frac{1}{6}$ ▩ $\frac{1}{4}$ 8. $\frac{1}{3}$ ▩ $\frac{1}{4}$ 9. $\frac{1}{2}$ ▩ $\frac{1}{6}$ 10. $\frac{1}{4}$ ▩ $\frac{1}{2}$

11. In exercises 1–5, each pair of fractions has the same denominator. What do you notice about the size of the numerator and the size of the fraction?

12. In exercises 6–10, each pair of fractions has the same numerator. What do you notice about the size of the denominator and the size of the fraction?

13. The fractions $\frac{2}{3}$ and $\frac{3}{4}$ have different numerators and denominators. Which is greater, $\frac{2}{3}$ or $\frac{3}{4}$? Why?

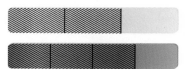

Use fraction models to compare the fractions. Write > or <.

14. $\frac{2}{3}$ ▩ $\frac{2}{2}$ 15. $\frac{2}{4}$ ▩ $\frac{2}{6}$ 16. $\frac{2}{4}$ ▩ $\frac{3}{3}$ 17. $\frac{1}{4}$ ▩ $\frac{3}{4}$ 18. $\frac{2}{5}$ ▩ $\frac{4}{5}$

19. $\frac{2}{3}$ ▩ $\frac{4}{6}$ 20. $\frac{3}{6}$ ▩ $\frac{3}{5}$ 21. $\frac{3}{6}$ ▩ $\frac{1}{2}$ 22. $\frac{1}{4}$ ▩ $\frac{2}{3}$ 23. $\frac{4}{6}$ ▩ $\frac{2}{4}$

24. **Critical Thinking** When you compare fractions with the same denominator, how can you tell which fraction is greater without using fraction models?

Equivalent Fractions

Getting Started

What You'll Need:
▶ drawing paper
▶ scissors
▶ crayons or markers
▶ Fraction Bars

Vocabulary:
equivalent
fractions
Glossary, p. 480

Different fractions can name the same amount. How can that be? Make fraction models to find out.

Activity

• **Cut three strips of paper the same size.**

1

Fold a strip of paper in half so the short ends meet. Draw a dark line along the fold. Shade one part.

• Write the fraction for the shaded part on the model.

2

Fold another strip of paper in half twice to make fourths. Draw a dark line along each fold. Shade two parts.

• Write a fraction for the shaded parts.

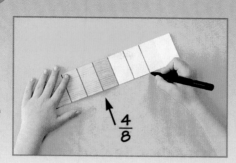

3 Fold another strip into eighths. Darken the fold lines. Shade four parts.

- Write a fraction for the shaded parts. Compare the strips. Are the same amounts shaded? What 3 fractions name this amount?

$\frac{4}{8}$

Show What You Know!

Use Fraction Bars to answer the question.

1. Use the $\frac{1}{2}$ bar. Find a sixths bar that has the same amount shaded as the $\frac{1}{2}$ bar. Write the fraction for the sixths bar.

2. Use the $\frac{1}{2}$ bar. Find a tenths bar that has the same amount shaded as the $\frac{1}{2}$ bar. Write the equivalent fraction.

Find a Fraction Bar with the same amount of shading. Write an equivalent fraction.

3. $\frac{1}{3}$ 4. $\frac{1}{4}$ 5. $\frac{4}{6}$ 6. $\frac{2}{5}$ 7. $\frac{2}{3}$ 8. $\frac{3}{4}$

9. $\frac{3}{6}$ 10. $\frac{2}{4}$ 11. $\frac{1}{5}$ 12. $\frac{1}{6}$ 13. $\frac{1}{2}$ 14. $\frac{6}{8}$

Copy and complete the equivalent fractions.

15. 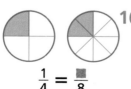   16.   17. 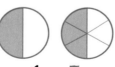   18.

$\frac{1}{4} = \frac{\blacksquare}{8}$ $\frac{1}{2} = \frac{\blacksquare}{6}$ $\frac{1}{2} = \frac{\blacksquare}{10}$ $\frac{2}{3} = \frac{\blacksquare}{6}$

19. **Algebraic Reasoning** Explain when two fractions are equivalent.

Problem Solving
Choose a Computation Method

You ask people to give $2 for each mile you walk for the Walk for Hunger. Five people will pay that. You hope to raise $20. How far do you need to walk?

Walk for Hunger,
Boston, Massachusetts

You Decide

• Can you solve the problem in your head?

• Would using a calculator be quicker? Why?

Work It Out!

Decide whether to use mental math or a calculator. Explain your decision. Then answer the question.

1. Would you raise more money washing 12 cars or selling 12 cakes?

2. You earned $16 from the bake sale. How many cakes did you sell?

3. Twelve students danced in the dance-a-thon. Each student danced an hour. How much did they raise?

 4. **Create Your Own** Look at the chart. Write a problem that you could solve with a calculator rather than with mental math. Explain.

Share Your Thinking

5. How do you decide when to use mental math or a calculator?

Raising Money for a Food Bank	
Activity	**Amount**
Ten-pin Bowling	$5.00 each strike
Car Wash	$3.50 each car
Dance-a-thon	$2.50 each hour
Bake Sale	$2.00 each cake
Recycling Drive	$1.00 each bag

Choose a Computation Method

Ask Yourself:

Do I need an exact answer or an estimate?

Should I use a model, paper and pencil, mental math, or a calculator?

What operation should I use?

Midchapter Review

for Pages 270–280

Problem Solving

Solve using any strategy. Show your work. (page 280)

1. A recipe for clown cookies says to put 2 nuts for eyes and 5 raisins for a mouth on each cookie. You have 15 nuts and 45 raisins. How many clown cookies can you make?

2. You make a spinner that has 16 equal spaces. You color $\frac{1}{2}$ of the spaces blue. Then you color $\frac{1}{2}$ of the leftover spaces green. How many spaces are green?

Concepts

Use models to compare the fractions. Write > or <. (page 276)

3. $\frac{1}{4}$ ● $\frac{2}{4}$

4. $\frac{3}{3}$ ● $\frac{2}{3}$

5. $\frac{4}{5}$ ● $\frac{4}{6}$

6. $\frac{2}{5}$ ● $\frac{1}{2}$

7. Write the fractions $\frac{1}{2}$ $\frac{1}{6}$ $\frac{5}{6}$ $\frac{1}{3}$ in order from least to greatest. Use fraction models to help you.

Skills

Write the fractions for the shaded and unshaded parts. (page 274)

8.

9.

10.

11.

Use fraction models. Write an equivalent fraction. (page 278)

12. $\frac{2}{4}$

13. $\frac{1}{5}$

14. $\frac{6}{10}$

15. $\frac{2}{6}$

Use the models to write the equivalent fractions. (page 278)

16. $\frac{1}{2} = \frac{\blacksquare}{8}$

17. $\frac{2}{3} = \frac{\blacksquare}{6}$

18. $\frac{3}{5} = \frac{\blacksquare}{10}$

Math World

Use fractions to describe the weather and
to play a game; then write them the way
the Egyptians and Greeks did.

Fractions in the Sky

Scientists watch the sky at weather stations all around the world. They use fractions to describe what they see. They use the same fractions in the United States, in Argentina (AHR juhn TEE nuh), and in Kenya (KEHN yuh). When there aren't any clouds, scientists write $\frac{0}{8}$. If clouds cover half the sky, they write $\frac{4}{8}$. If clouds cover all the sky, they write $\frac{8}{8}$. What fraction would you use to describe the sky where you are?

Egyptian Fraction Symbols

People in ancient Egypt used these special symbols for the $\frac{1}{2}$ and $\frac{1}{4}$ fractions. Use the symbol for $\frac{1}{2}$ to draw a symbol for 1. Then, use the symbol for $\frac{1}{4}$ to make a different symbol for 1.

 $\frac{1}{2}$ $\times$ $\frac{1}{4}$

Try This!

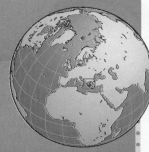

Learn a method for writing fractions that was sometimes used by writers in ancient Greece. Follow these steps to write the fraction for $\frac{3}{4}$.

1 Write the numerator. Put an accent mark after it.

2 Write the first part of the denominator. Put two accent marks after it.

3 Write the rest of the denominator. What pattern do you notice? Write a rule for reading and writing ancient Greek fractions.

Try: Write the following as standard fractions.

1'6"6"   5'8"8"

A "Sticky" Situation

The Pima people of the southwestern United States play a game called Gins. In Gins, players toss 4 sticks that are plain on one side and patterned on the other side. To score points, the player counts what shows on the sticks. Try a simple way to count this toss. How many sticks show a pattern? What fraction of this toss shows a pattern?

Respond

Work with a partner . . .
to make your own fraction symbols.

 Internet:
Houghton Mifflin Education Place
Explore the Math Center at
http://www.eduplace.com

Estimating Fractions

Your pen pal in the Netherlands sends you this postcard. How can you estimate what fraction of the card is yellow tulips?

Here's A Way! Use $\frac{1}{4}$, $\frac{1}{2}$, and $\frac{3}{4}$ to estimate.

1 Suppose the card is divided into 4 equal parts. The marks along the side of the card can help you think about the parts.

2 Compare. Decide if the fraction of the card that is yellow is about $\frac{1}{4}$, $\frac{1}{2}$, or $\frac{3}{4}$.

About 2 of the 4 parts is yellow, so about $\frac{1}{2}$ of the card is yellow.

Talk About It!

Is more than or less than $\frac{1}{2}$ of the postcard yellow? Explain.

Other Examples

Use $\frac{1}{4}$, $\frac{1}{2}$, and $\frac{3}{4}$ to estimate.

a. About what fraction of the row is purple?

b. About what fraction is red?

Estimate the fraction of the garden that is planted. Write $\frac{1}{4}$, $\frac{1}{2}$, or $\frac{3}{4}$.

1.  2.  3.

4. Critical Thinking About what fraction of the garden in exercise 3 is not planted?

Work It Out!

Look at the water. About how full is the vase?

5.   6.   7.

8. Number Sense Look at the vases above. Can you pour all the water from any vase into any other vase? Explain.

Draw a vase with water to show each estimate.

9. About $\frac{3}{4}$ full   10. About $\frac{1}{2}$ full   11. About $\frac{3}{4}$ empty

12. About $\frac{1}{4}$ empty   13. About $\frac{1}{4}$ full   14. About $\frac{1}{2}$ empty

15. About how much of the circle is orange? Write a or b.

    a. $\frac{1}{4}$ b. $\frac{1}{2}$

16. About how much of the strip is shaded? Write a or b.

    a. $\frac{1}{4}$ b. $\frac{1}{2}$

Mixed Review Solve.

17. $6 + 6 + 6 + 6$ 18. $5 + 5 + 5$ 19. 4×6

20. 5×9 21. 4×8

More Practice Set 8.6, p. 464

LESSON 7

Adding and Subtracting Fractions

Getting Started

What You'll Need:
► fraction models
► colored markers

Cooperative Learning Checklist

☑ Work alone.
☑ Work with a partner.
☑ Work with a group.

You can use fraction models to add and subtract fractions with the same denominator. Look at the way the artist used colors and fractions in this painting.

Blue, Green, Yellow, Orange, Red. 1966

Ellsworth Kelly

Solomon R. Guggenheim Museum, New York

Activity

Find $\frac{1}{4} + \frac{2}{4}$.

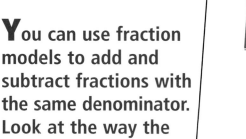

1 Use the fourths fraction model. Shade $\frac{1}{4}$ of the model. Use a different color to shade $\frac{2}{4}$ more.

2 How much is shaded altogether? Write an addition sentence for what you did.

3 Try these.

a. $\frac{1}{4} + \frac{3}{4}$ b. $\frac{1}{4} + \frac{1}{4}$ c. $\frac{1}{3} + \frac{1}{3}$

Find $\frac{5}{6} - \frac{2}{6}$.

1 Use a sixths fraction model. Shade $\frac{5}{6}$ of the model. Use another sixths fraction model. Shade $\frac{2}{6}$.

2 What is the difference in the number of shaded parts? Write a subtraction sentence using $\frac{5}{6}$ and $\frac{2}{6}$.

3 Try these.

a. $\frac{5}{6} - \frac{3}{6}$ b. $\frac{4}{6} - \frac{2}{6}$ c. $\frac{3}{4} - \frac{1}{4}$

Use fraction models to add. Write the sum.

1. $\frac{1}{6} + \frac{1}{6}$ 2. $\frac{2}{3} + \frac{1}{3}$ 3. $\frac{1}{4} + \frac{3}{4}$ 4. $\frac{1}{6} + \frac{2}{6}$ 5. $\frac{1}{4} + \frac{1}{4}$

6. Write whether each sum above is more than, less than, or equal to one half.

Use fraction models to subtract. Write the difference.

7. $\frac{2}{3} - \frac{1}{3}$ 8. $\frac{5}{6} - \frac{1}{6}$ 9. $\frac{2}{2} - \frac{1}{2}$ 10. $\frac{3}{4} - \frac{2}{4}$ 11. $\frac{4}{6} - \frac{2}{6}$

12. Write whether each difference above is more than, less than, or equal to one half.

13. **Algebraic Reasoning** How is adding and subtracting fractions like adding and subtracting whole numbers? How is it different?

14. **Critical Thinking** How could counting on the number line help you add $\frac{3}{6}$ and $\frac{2}{6}$?

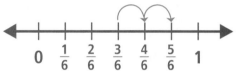

$$0 \quad \frac{1}{6} \quad \frac{2}{6} \quad \frac{3}{6} \quad \frac{4}{6} \quad \frac{5}{6} \quad 1$$

Problem Solving

When red, yellow and blue are mixed, they make all the other colors. Mix these letters to make color words. (Hint: Look at the color wheel.)

15. Write the first $\frac{2}{5}$ of the letters in *blank* with the last $\frac{1}{2}$ of the letters in *glue*.

16. Write the first $\frac{2}{3}$ of the letters in *yes* with the last $\frac{4}{6}$ of the letters in *follow*.

17. Write the first $\frac{1}{4}$ of the letters in *rain* with the last $\frac{1}{2}$ of the letters in *weed*.

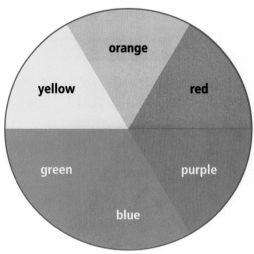

18. **Create Your Own** Use the colors to make up a problem like the one above.

Math Journal

You know the basic facts for adding and subtracting whole numbers. How can they help you add and subtract fractions?

Problem Solving
Draw a Picture

Getting Started

What You'll Need:
▶ unlined paper

There are 12 paintings on display in your classroom. You write labels for $\frac{1}{3}$ of them. How many paintings do you label? Drawing a picture can help you to solve the problem.

Here's A Way! Use Draw a Picture to solve.

1 Understand

- How many paintings are there?
- What fraction of the paintings must you label?

2 Plan

- What picture can you draw to help you?

3 Try It

- Draw a picture of the paintings.
- Into how many equal parts should you divide the paintings to show thirds?
- How many paintings equal one third?

4 Look Back

- How did drawing a picture help you to find that you need to label 4 paintings?

Show What You Know!

Draw a picture to finish the problem.

0   1

1. The art show is 1 mile from your house. You are $\frac{3}{4}$ of the way there. What part of a mile do you have to go before you get there?

2. **Critical Thinking** Why is the number line divided into four equal parts?

Work It Out!

Use Draw a Picture or any other strategy to solve the problem.

3. In another art show, there were 2 rows with 6 paintings in each row. Only $\frac{1}{3}$ of the paintings are left. The rest were sold. How many paintings were sold?

4. One quarter of the 12 paintings were of playgrounds. The remaining paintings were of families. How many paintings were of families?

5. For your artwork you fold a square piece of paper in half 3 times. Then you unfold the paper and paint $\frac{1}{4}$ of the sections green. How many sections are green?

These pieces of art are entered in an art show. Look at the chart to solve the problems.

6. Is the number of paintings more than $\frac{1}{2}$ of the art pieces entered?

Our Art Show

	Class A	Class B	Class C
Paintings	3	1	3
Sculptures	2	2	1
Photos	1	0	1

Share Your Thinking

7. Which problems did you solve by drawing a picture? Why?

8. What strategies did you use to solve other problems?

Mixed Numbers

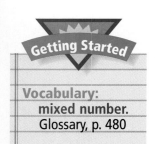
Quesadillas Sold Each Day

Monday	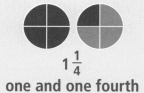
Tuesday	
Wednesday	
Thursday	
Friday	

Key 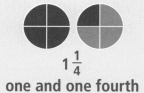 = 1 quesadilla   = $\frac{1}{2}$ quesadilla

A new lunch item at school is quesadillas (kehsaDEEyah). The pictograph shows how many quesadillas your classmates ate last week. What mixed number can you use to tell how many quesadillas were eaten on Tuesday?

> A mixed number has a whole number part and a fraction part.

Here's A Way! Write mixed numbers.

Find the key for the graph. Each stands for a whole quesadilla. Each stands for $\frac{1}{2}$ quesadilla.

1 Find Tuesday on the graph.

How many are there? Write the whole number part of the mixed number.

$3\frac{1}{2}$
three and one half

2 How many are there?

Write the fraction part of the mixed number.

$3\frac{1}{2}$
three and one half

On Tuesday, your class ate $3\frac{1}{2}$ quesadillas.

Talk About It!

How many whole quesadillas were eaten on Tuesday? How do you know?

Other Examples Why does the shading show $1\frac{1}{4}$?

$1\frac{1}{4}$
one and one fourth

Write a mixed number for the shaded parts.

1.   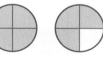 2.   3.

4.   5.   6.

7. **Critical Thinking** Which picture shows a mixed number that is closest to 4?

Work It Out!

Write a mixed number for the quesadillas.

8.   9.   10.

Write a mixed number for the shaded parts.

11. 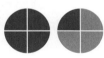 12.   13.

Write the mixed number.

14. two and two thirds

15. one and one fourth

16. three and two eighths

17. one and one sixth

18. eight and one third

19. four and four sixths

Mixed Review

Write the quotient.

20. 6)‾54‾   21. 3)‾18‾   22. 7)‾49‾   23. 6)‾30‾   24. 9)‾72‾   25. 8)‾72‾

Write the missing factor.

26. 5 × ■ = 40   27. ■ × 2 = 18   28. ■ × 4 = 24   29. 7 × ■ = 21

More Practice Set 8.9, p. 464

Problem Solving
Using Draw a Picture and Other Strategies

LESSON 10

In Massachusetts, the ferryboat from Woods Hole carries both passengers and vehicles to the island of Martha's Vineyard. The island is a popular place for summer visitors.

ATLANTIC OCEAN

Massachusetts

Woods Hole

Martha's Vineyard

Problem Solving Process
✓ Understand
✓ Plan
✓ Try It
✓ Look Back

Choose a Strategy You Have Learned
✓ Act It Out
✓ Look for a Pattern
✓ Guess and Check
✓ Draw a Picture
✓ Make a Table
  Work Backward
  Make a List
  Work a Simpler Problem

quarter past

half past

quarter to

$\frac{1}{4}$ of an hour has passed

$\frac{1}{2}$ of an hour has passed

$\frac{3}{4}$ of an hour has passed

A quarter of an hour is $\frac{1}{4}$ of an hour. Three quarters of an hour is $\frac{3}{4}$ of an hour. Fractions can help you to tell time.

Suppose you just miss the 5:15 P.M. boat to Martha's Vineyard. The next ferry leaves at 5:45 P.M. What fraction of an hour must you wait for the next ferry?

- What problem needs to be solved?

- How can you use fractions to help you to tell time?

- Explain how drawing a picture can help you to solve the problem. Then solve it.

Work It Out!

Look at the ferry schedule to answer the problem. Use any strategy to solve the problem. Show your work.

Leave Wood's Hole		
7:15 A.M.	1:15 P.M.	6:15 P.M.
8:00 A.M.	2:45 P.M.	7:45 P.M.
9:45 A.M.	3:45 P.M.	8:45 P.M.
10:45 A.M.	5:15 P.M.	9:45 P.M.
12:15 P.M.	5:45 P.M.	10:45 P.M.

1. The ferryboat ride from Woods Hole to Martha's Vineyard takes $\frac{3}{4}$ of an hour. Is there a boat that will get you there at 1:00 P.M.? Explain.

2. Suppose your family wants to go to Martha's Vineyard at night. How many boats leave after 7:00 P.M.?

3. Which ferryboats leave Woods Hole $\frac{1}{2}$ hour apart?

4. **Critical Thinking** Is the boat that leaves at 12:15 P.M. more than halfway to Martha's Vineyard at 12:30 P.M.? Explain.

5. Suppose you get to Martha's Vineyard at 11:30 A.M. That night you leave on a 7:30 P.M. boat. How long did you stay on Martha's Vineyard?

6. If one-way tickets cost $4.25 for each adult and $2.15 for each child. How much does it cost for a group of two adults and three children to ride one way?

7. **Algebraic Reasoning** In one group, there are twice as many children as adults. Which costs more, the tickets for all the adults or for all the children? Explain.

8. **Create Your Own** Write a problem about the ferryboats for a friend to solve.

Share Your Thinking

9. Choose one of the problems you solved. Talk with a friend about the strategy you used to solve it. Explain how you could solve the problem using another strategy.

293

LESSON 11

Problem Solving
Using Strategies

You can read more about the Vikings from the pages of *Kids Discover Vikings.*

The Vikings lived many years ago in what are now Denmark, Norway, and Sweden. Winters were severe. Animals were kept indoors to protect them from the cold weather.

Problem Solving Process
✓ Understand
✓ Plan
✓ Try It
✓ Look Back

Choose a Strategy You Have Learned
✓ Act It Out
✓ Look for a Pattern
✓ Guess and Check
✓ Draw a Picture
✓ Make a Table
  Work Backward
  Make a List
  Work a Simpler Problem

The Vikings ate food from their farms, such as beef, beans, peas, and cheese. Suppose you were a Viking and had to share a round of cheese equally. You cut the cheese so that each piece is $\frac{1}{8}$ of the round. How can you use only 4 straight cuts to cut the cheese?

- Do the parts have to be equal? Why?

- How many cuts can you make?

- Explain a strategy that can help you to solve the problem. Then solve it.

Work It Out!

Use any strategy to solve the problem. Show your work.

1. Plan to make a pizza with different toppings. Your brother likes cheese and beef. Your sister will not eat beef. Your mother likes cheese and beef, but not beans. You like all three. Design a pie so that your brother, your sister, your mother, and you can each have two slices.

2. A recipe calls for $\frac{3}{4}$ cup of carrots. You have 1 cup of carrots and a $\frac{1}{4}$ cup measure. How can you measure $\frac{3}{4}$ cup? Is there more than one way?

3. If you spent $\frac{1}{4}$ of a 24-hour day working on the farm, how many hours did you work?

4. Mix $\frac{1}{4}$ cup peas with every 1 cup of beans. If you have 16 cups of beans, how many cups of peas do you need?

5. Can you get more peas or more kidney beans into $\frac{1}{2}$ cup? Explain.

6. Look at the Viking alphabet. This alphabet is made up of 16 letters, called runes. The runes were often brightly painted on stones or wood. What fraction of the runes are not painted blue yet?

7. The grid paper shows different ways to cut a square piece of cloth in half. Show two other ways you can cut this cloth in half.

Share Your Thinking

8. What strategy did you use to solve problem 7? What other ways could you have solved it?

9. Make a list of all the different strategies you used to solve these problems. Compare your list with a classmate's.

Chapter 8 Test

for Pages 270–295

Test-Taking Tips
Decide if you can use models or draw a picture.

Problem Solving

Solve. Show your work. (pages 288, 292)

1. You sew together 36 squares of cloth to create a square quilt. Only the squares along the edges will be red. How many of the squares will be red?

2. You have a bookcase with 5 shelves. Tell how you can put books so that:
   - the shelf for spelling is not right above or right below the shelf for math or science.
   - the shelf for math is just above the shelf for science.
   - the shelf for history is not next to reading or science.
   - the shelf for reading is above science but not on the top.

Concepts

Draw fraction models to compare. Write > or <. (page 276)

3. $\frac{5}{10}$ ● $\frac{7}{10}$

4. $\frac{2}{8}$ ● $\frac{1}{2}$

5. $\frac{2}{2}$ ● $\frac{3}{4}$

Which fraction shows about how much of the rectangle is red? (page 284)

6. a. $\frac{1}{4}$ b. $\frac{1}{2}$ c. $\frac{1}{12}$ d. $\frac{3}{4}$

7. a. $\frac{1}{4}$ b. $\frac{3}{4}$ c. $\frac{1}{2}$ d. $\frac{1}{8}$

Which fraction names the _unshaded_ part of the figure? (page 290)

8. a. $\frac{1}{3}$ b. $\frac{2}{6}$ c. $\frac{4}{6}$ d. $\frac{3}{4}$

9. a. $\frac{2}{3}$ b. $\frac{3}{4}$ c. $\frac{1}{2}$ d. $\frac{1}{3}$

Write a mixed number for the shaded part. (page 274)

10.

11.

12.

13.

14.

15.

Use fraction models. Find an equivalent fraction. (page 278)

16. $\frac{3}{6}$ 17. $\frac{6}{8}$ 18. $\frac{2}{10}$ 19. $\frac{1}{3}$

Use fraction models. Find the answer. (page 286)

20. $\frac{3}{4} - \frac{1}{4}$ 21. $\frac{4}{6} - \frac{2}{6}$ 22. $\frac{1}{2} + \frac{1}{2}$

23. $\frac{3}{6} + \frac{2}{6}$ 24. $\frac{2}{5} + \frac{1}{5}$ 25. $\frac{3}{3} - \frac{2}{3}$

 ## Performance Task

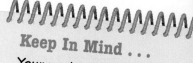

Keep In Mind . . .

Your work will be evaluated on the following:
- ☑ Correctly shaded models
- ☑ Clear description
- ☑ Correct labels for all parts
- ☑ Easy to read models

(pages 272, 274)

$\frac{2}{4}$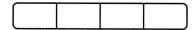

$\frac{5}{6}$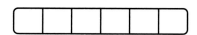

$\frac{1}{10}$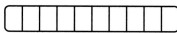

$\frac{3}{8}$

- Copy the fraction models and shade to show the fraction named.

- Explain how you decided how many parts to shade.

- What fraction of each model is unshaded?

Cumulative Review

Rounding (Chapter 2)
Round 57 to the nearest ten, and 219 to the nearest hundred.

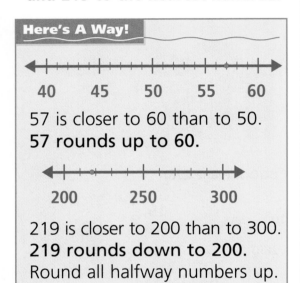

Here's A Way!

57 is closer to 60 than to 50.
57 rounds up to 60.

219 is closer to 200 than to 300.
219 rounds down to 200.
Round all halfway numbers up.

Round to the nearest ten.

1. 94   2. 68   3. 25

Round to the nearest hundred.

4. 327   5. 188   6. 854

7. Explain how you would round 84 to the nearest ten. Then, explain how you would round 84 to the nearest hundred.

Subtracting (Chapter 3)
Subtract 28 from 62.

Here's A Way!

$$\begin{array}{r} \overset{512}{} \\ 62 \\ -\ 28 \\ \hline 34 \end{array}$$

8 > 2, so regroup
1 ten as 10 ones.
Subtract the ones.
Subtract the tens.

Find the difference.

8. $\begin{array}{r} 55 \\ -17 \\ \hline \end{array}$ 9. $\begin{array}{r} 21 \\ -12 \\ \hline \end{array}$ 10. $\begin{array}{r} 43 \\ -29 \\ \hline \end{array}$

11. $\begin{array}{r} 64 \\ -\ 9 \\ \hline \end{array}$ 12. $\begin{array}{r} 85 \\ -36 \\ \hline \end{array}$ 13. $\begin{array}{r} 76 \\ -18 \\ \hline \end{array}$

14. How do you know when you need to regroup the tens?

Multiply by 2 (Chapter 5)
Find 2×4.

Here's A Way!

You can use skip-counting.
Skip-count by 4's two times.
Say: **4, 8.**
Write: $2 \times 4 = 8.$

Write the product.

15. 2×1 16. 2×2

17. 2×3 18. 2×5

19. 2×6 20. 2×7

21. Draw a picture to show 2×8.

Multiplication Patterns (Chapter 6)
Multiply 3 by 6.

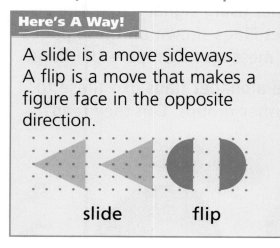

Here's A Way!

×	1	2	3	4	5	6	7	8	9	10
1										
2										
3	3	6	9	12	15					

Copy the table. Then, follow the directions.

22. Complete the last row.

23. Fill in the first row. What property of multiplication could you use?

24. Fill in the middle row. What skip-counting could you use?

Slides and Flips (Chapter 7)
Which pattern shows a slide?
Which pattern shows a flip?

Here's A Way!

A slide is a move sideways.
A flip is a move that makes a figure face in the opposite direction.

slide   flip

Tell if the pattern shows a slide or a flip.

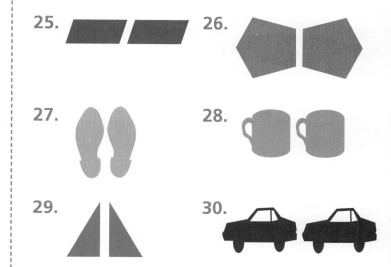

25.   **26.**

27.   **28.**

29.   **30.**

Problem Solving

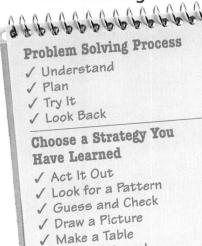

Problem Solving Process
✓ Understand
✓ Plan
✓ Try It
✓ Look Back

Choose a Strategy You Have Learned
✓ Act It Out
✓ Look for a Pattern
✓ Guess and Check
✓ Draw a Picture
✓ Make a Table
  Work Backward
  Make a List
  Work a Simpler Problem

Use any strategy to help answer the question.

31. Describe the pattern: 8, 12, 16, 20 . . .

32. Suppose you are playing a game at a fair. For every 20 points you score, you earn 3 tickets. How many tickets will you win if you score 160 points?

33. You put toppings on a pizza. You put onions around the outer edge, then a ring of green peppers, then onions, then red peppers. If you can continue the pattern for 5 more rings, what is the last topping you will use?

Land Ho!

Art Connection   **With Your Group**

Did you know that ships at sea often send messages to each other using signal flags? The 26 International Alphabet Flags shown on these pages are used to spell out messages. Compare the flags.

Your group will make alphabet flags like these to send a message to other groups. Can they read your message?

1

Plan It

- Decide how big to make each flag. What message will your group send?

2

Put It Together

- Use graph paper to make the alphabet flags for the letters.
- Color in each flag.
- Write the fraction for each color on the back. For example, the flag for "T" is $\frac{1}{3}$ red, $\frac{1}{3}$ white, and $\frac{1}{3}$ black.

3

Wrap It Up

- Send a message to another group with your flags.
- Read the messages sent to you.
- Use fractions to design a new alphabet flag for one of the letters.

4

Discuss Your Results

- Did you meet the Keep In Mind goals?
- Which of the real alphabet flags have the same number of colors?

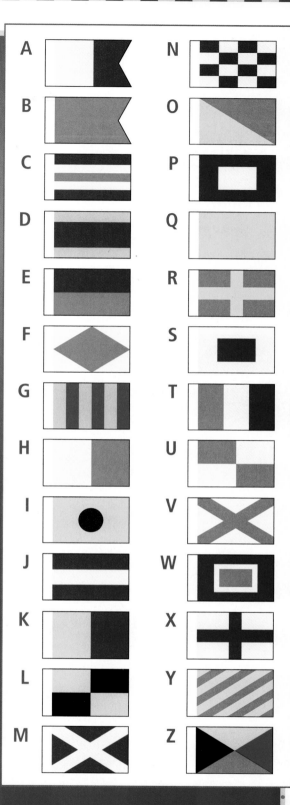

Internet

> Visit the **Math Center** at **Houghton Mifflin Education Place.** http://www.eduplace.com

Use What You Know

• How long?
• How heavy?
• How warm?

• about many kinds of measurement questions

• about measuring tools

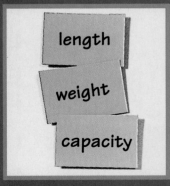

length

weight

capacity

• measurement vocabulary

Measurement and Time

Try This!

Chances are that you use measurement many times each day. Write about it.

What You'll Need

paper, crayons or markers, stapler

Design and staple together a booklet with eight pages.

My Measurement Book

Show different ways of using measurement on six pages.

I use my watch to tell how long it takes to walk to school.

3

Show ways of measuring time on two pages of your booklet.

Show the booklet to others. Do they measure things in the same way?

How many different kinds of measurement have you shown?

Ready to Go!

Cooperative Learning
Checklist

☐ Work alone.
☑ Work with a partner.
☑ Work with a group.

LESSON 1

Inch

Getting Started

What You'll Need:
▶ paper clips
▶ ruler

Vocabulary:
 inch (in.)
 customary
 system
 Glossary, p. 480

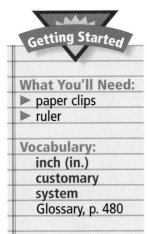

Suppose you want to measure something small, like the length of your pencil. You can measure it in inches. How long is one inch?

One inch is about the length of a paper clip.

An *inch* is a unit of length. Inches are part of the customary system of measurement.

Activity

• Copy the chart.

• Try estimating length. Then measure to find the actual length.

Estimate with Paper Clips

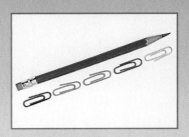

1 Choose a small object. Estimate its length by measuring with paper clips placed end to end. Count and record the number of paper clips you use.

2 Write your estimate in inches. Remember that one paper clip is about 1 inch long.

3 Repeat steps 1–2 with three more objects. Record your results.

	Length		
Object	Number of Paper Clips	Estimated Length	Actual Length
ncil	5 paper clips	about 5 inches	6 inches

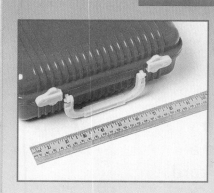

Measure in Inches

1 Now measure one of your objects with a ruler. Remember to line up the end of the object with the 0 mark on the ruler.

2 Record the number of inches. Compare the actual length to your estimate.

3 Repeat steps 1–2 with the rest of your objects. Record your results.

Show What You Know!

1. Number Sense If only half a paper clip fit, how did you write the length?

Estimate the length of each object in inches. Record your estimate. Then measure the length with a ruler.

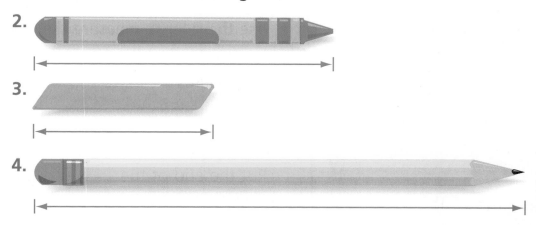

2.

3.

4.

5. Estimation In exercises 2–4, how close were your estimates to the actual length?

Use a ruler to draw the line segment.

6. 4 in.   **7.** 7 in.   **8.** 10 in.   **9.** 12 in.   **10.** 15 in.

Without a ruler, try to draw the line segment. Then measure it. Write the actual length of the line segment.

11. 6 in.   **12.** 11 in.   **13.** 8 in.   **14.** 2 in.   **15.** 5 in.

More Practice Set 9.1, p. 465

Inch and Half Inch

Getting Started

What You'll Need:
▶ half–inch ruler

Suppose you are making a thank-you card for your friend. You want to glue a piece of ribbon across the top of the card. How can you cut the ribbon so it will fit?

You can measure to get the ribbon the right length.

Here's A Way! Measure to the nearest half inch.

Measure from the 0 mark!

1 Look at a ruler with half-inch marks. There are 2 half inches in 1 inch.

2 Use the ruler to measure the width of the card.

It measures $2\frac{1}{2}$ in. to the nearest half inch.

3 Measure and cut $2\frac{1}{2}$ in. of ribbon.

Put the end of the ribbon at the 0 mark. Cut the ribbon at the $2\frac{1}{2}$ in. mark.

Talk About It! Why do you line up the edge of the card at the 0 mark and not at the 1 mark?

Other Examples

Sometimes when you measure to the nearest half inch, you get a whole number.

This piece of yarn measures 2 in. to the nearest half inch and 2 in. to the nearest inch.

Show What You Know!

Measure the length to the nearest inch. Then measure the length to the nearest half inch. Write each length.

1.

2.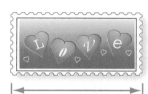

3.

4.

5. **Critical Thinking** How many half inches are in 3 inches? Explain your answer.

Work It Out!

Measure to the nearest inch and to the nearest half inch. Write each length.

6.

7.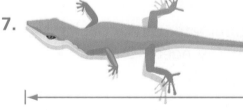

8. length of scissors

9. length of your little finger

10. **Write About It** Did any measurements in exercises 6–9 fall between half-inch marks on your ruler? What did you do?

Use a ruler to draw the line segment.

11. $7\frac{1}{2}$ in.   12. 3 in.   13. $13\frac{1}{2}$ in.

14. 5 in.   15. $4\frac{1}{2}$ in.

16. Copy and complete the chart. Measure the shoe lengths of five people. Measure to the nearest half inch.

Shoe Measurements

Person	Shoe Length
?	?
?	?

More Practice Set 9.2, p. 466

Perimeter

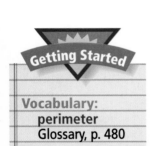
Suppose you are making a poster for your class play. You want to put this cloth around the border. How much cloth do you need?

You can measure around the poster. The distance around a figure is called the **perimeter**.

Here's A Way! Find the perimeter.

1. Measure and record the length of each side of the poster.

2. Add the lengths of all the sides.

   $11 + 9 + 11 + 9 = 40$

3. Explain what the sum means.

   The perimeter of the poster is 40 in. You need 40 in. of cloth.

9 in.

11 in.

11 in.

Anansi
the
Spider
High View School
March 15,
2:00 P.M.

Talk About It!

- How many sides does the poster have? How does this help you know how many numbers to add?

- Could you use mental math to add the lengths? How?

Other Example

$14 + 14 + 9 = 37$
The perimeter is 37 in.

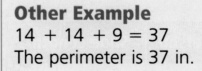

14 in.

9 in.

ANANSI

14 in.

Find the perimeter. The lengths of the sides are labeled.

1.
8 in.
6 in.   6 in.
8 in.

2.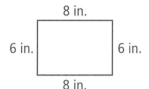
13 in.
5 in.   13 in.

3.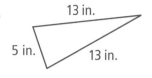
18 in.
7 in.   7 in.
24 in.

4. Draw a figure with a perimeter of 8 in. Label the sides.

5. **Critical Thinking** How could you find the perimeter of a rectangle by measuring only two sides?

Work It Out!

Write the perimeter. The lengths of the sides are labeled.

6.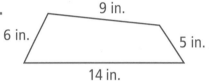
6 in.   6 in.
6 in.   6 in.

7.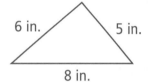
9 in.
6 in.   5 in.
14 in.

8.
6 in.   5 in.
8 in.

9. 10 in., 2 in., 10 in., 2 in.

10. 5 in., 5 in., 5 in.

11. 6 in., 5 in., 2 in., 4 in.

12. 2 in., 9 in., 3 in., 7 in., 2 in.

13. A square has 4 equal sides. Copy and complete the table to show the perimeters of different squares.

One side of a square	1 in.	2 in.	?	4 in.	5 in.	?	?	8 in.	?	?
Perimeter of a square	4 in.	8 in.	12 in.	?	?	24 in.	28 in.	?	36 in.	?

14. **Algebraic Reasoning** Look at your table. Write a rule for finding the perimeter of a square.

Draw a figure with each perimeter. Label the sides.

15. 4 in.   16. 8 in.   17. 10 in.   18. 11 in.   19. 6 in.

More Practice Set 9.3, p. 466

LESSON 4

Foot, Yard, and Mile

You know how to measure in inches. **Feet (ft)**, **yards (yd)**, and **miles (mi)** are other customary units used to measure length.

> 1 ft = 12 in.
> 1 yd = 3 ft or 36 in.
> 1 mi = 5280 ft

Activity

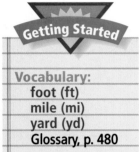

Getting Started

Vocabulary:
  foot (ft)
  mile (mi)
  yard (yd)
  Glossary, p. 480

Cooperative Learning Checklist

☐ Work alone.
☑ Work with a partner.
☑ Work with a group.

Measure in Feet, Yards, and Miles

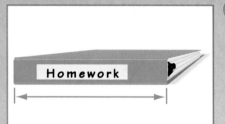

Homework

About 1 ft

1 One foot is 12 in. The length of a notebook is about 1 ft.
  • Find something else that is about 1 ft long. Measure and write its length.

About 1 yd

2 One yard is 3 ft or 36 in. A baseball bat is about 1 yd long.
  • Find something else that is about 1 yd long. Measure and write its length.

3 One mile is 5280 ft. The street distance shown here is about 1 mi long.
  • List some other things that could be measured in miles.

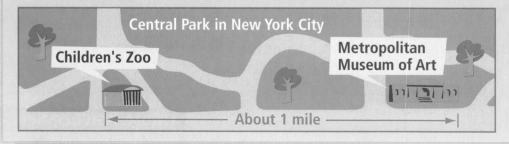

Central Park in New York City

Children's Zoo

Metropolitan Museum of Art

About 1 mile

Rename Feet as Yards

The curtain on a puppet stage is 12 ft long. How many yards is it?

Rename 12 feet as yards.

Feet	3	
Yards	1	

- Make a table. Show 3 ft = 1 yd.

- Continue the table until you fill in a column for 12 ft.

Feet	3	6	9	(12)
Yards	1	2	3	(4)

- Find the number of yards that equals 12 ft.

  12 ft = 4 yd

  So, the curtain is 4 yd long.

Show What You Know!

Which unit would you use to measure each? Write *foot*, *yard*, or *mile.* Explain your choice.

1. distance to the North Pole
2. length of a football field
3. distance to the lunch room
4. length of your desk

Complete. Write >, <, or =.

5. 1 mi ■ 2000 ft
6. 1 ft ■ 29 in.
7. 2 mi ■ 5000 ft
8. 1 yd ■ 3 ft
9. 12 mi ■ 12 yd
10. 4 yd ■ 13 ft
11. 6 ft ■ 2 yd
12. $7\frac{1}{2}$ ft ■ $7\frac{1}{2}$ yd
13. 2 ft ■ 10 in.

Mixed Review

Write a fraction for the shaded part.

14.
15.
16.
17.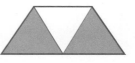

Math Journal

Look at the table at the top of this page. When you rename feet as yards, what pattern do you see?

LESSON 5

Cup, Pint, Quart, and Gallon

Getting Started

What You'll Need:
▶ cup, pint, quart, and gallon containers
▶ water

Vocabulary:
capacity
cup (c)
gallon (gal)
pint (pt)
quart (qt)
Glossary, p. 480

The amount of liquid that a container will hold is its **capacity**. Customary units for measuring capacity are **cup (c)**, **pint (pt)**, **quart (qt)**, and **gallon (gal)**.

Activity

- Make a chart. Label the columns as shown below.
- Use different containers to estimate and measure capacity.

1 Fill the cup container with water. Estimate how many cups of water you will need to fill the pint container. Record your estimate.

2 Empty the cup of water into the pint container. Keep pouring cups of water into the container until it is full. Record your findings.

3 Estimate. Then measure.
- the number of pints in 1 quart
- the number of quarts in 1 gallon

Record your results.

Capacity		
What I'm Finding	Estimate	Exact Number
cups in 1 pint	3 cups	
pints in 1 quart		
quarts in 1 gallon		

1. **Logical Reasoning** You know there are 2 cups in a pint. You also know there are 2 pints in a quart. How can you find the number of cups in a quart without measuring?

Copy and complete.

2.

Cup	2	?	6	8	?	?	14	?	?
Pint	1	2	?	?	5	6	?	8	?
Quart	?	1	$1\frac{1}{2}$	?	?	3	?	?	?

3.

Gallon	1	2	?	?
Quart	4	?	12	?

4. **Algebraic Reasoning** Write a rule for finding the number of quarts when you know the number of gallons.

Write >, <, or =. You can use the tables you completed.

5. 1 qt ■ 1 pt   6. 1 gal ■ 4 qt   7. 8 c ■ 2 pt   8. 4 c ■ 4 pt

Estimation Does the object hold more than or less than 1 quart? Write *more than* or *less than*.

9. kitchen sink   10. baby bottle   11. mug   12. bathtub

Choose the better unit of measure. Write *a* or *b*.

13. glass of milk
    a. cup   b. quart

14. water in a pool
    a. pint   b. gallon

15. water in a fish tank
    a. cup   b. gallon

Write the answer.

16. 493
    + 307

17. 136
    + 249

18. 903
    − 426

19. 39
    + 64

20. 850
    − 50

Ounce and Pound

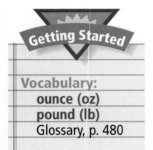
Vocabulary:
ounce (oz)
pound (lb)
Glossary, p. 480

You can measure weight in **ounces (oz)** and **pounds (lb)**. Ounces and pounds are customary units of measure.

1 lb = 16 oz

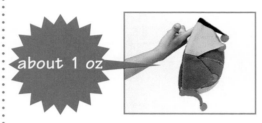

about 1 oz

about 1 lb

Which bag of popcorn weighs more?

You know that there are 16 oz in 1 lb. How many ounces are in 3 lbs?

16 + 16 + 16 = 48

3 lb = 48 oz

48 oz > 30 oz

So, the unpopped corn weighs more.

Show What You Know!

Which unit would you use to weigh? Write *ounce* or *pound*.

1. a box of crayons
2. one apple
3. a large dog
4. ten paper clips
5. a full suitcase
6. a bicycle

· Write the missing weight.

7. $\frac{1}{2}$ lb = ▦ oz
8. 2 lb = ▦ oz
9. 6 lb = ▦ oz

More Practice Set 9.7, p. 468

Midchapter Review

for Pages 302–314

Problem Solving

Solve using any strategy. Show your work. (pages 308, 312)

1. You ran 120 laps in 3 days. Each day you ran 10 more than the day before. How many laps did you run on the third day?

2. Suppose you glue these two figures together to make a house. You will tape the outside edges. About how many inches of tape do you need?

12 in. 12 in. 16 in.

16 in. 13 in. 13 in.

16 in.

Concepts

Estimate the length. Then, measure to the nearest half inch.
(pages 304, 306)

3. ●————————————●

4. ●———————————————————●

5. ●————————————●

6. ●——————●

Choose the better unit of measure. Write *a* or *b*. (pages 312, 314)

7. soup in a bowl
   a. cup
   b. quart

8. a computer
   a. ounce
   b. pound

9. a calculator
   a. ounce
   b. pound

Skills

Write the perimeter. (page 308)

10. 14 in.
    8 in.   8 in.
    7 in.

11. $3\frac{1}{2}$ in.

    $3\frac{1}{2}$ in. $3\frac{1}{2}$ in.

    $3\frac{1}{2}$ in.

Complete. Write >, <, or =. (pages 310, 312)

12. 1 ft ● 12 in.

13. 1 mi ● 100 ft

14. 1 qt ● 1 gal

Complete the number sentence. (page 314)

15. 16 oz = ▇ lb

16. 8 oz = ▇ lb

17. 5 lb = ▇ oz

Math World

Learn how Roman numerals and knotted cords have helped to measure and tell time around the world.

Roman Numerals

Although we use Arabic numbers most of the time, Roman numerals are used on the faces of some clocks. The Roman numeral for number 1 is *I*. The Roman numeral *V* means 5 and *X* means 10. Some people think that *X* came from putting two of the symbols for 5 together.

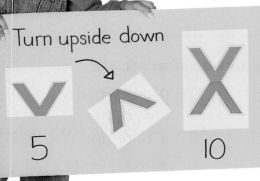

Turn upside down

V → Λ X
5   10

Times Flies

In Nigeria (ny JIHR ee ah), some farmers use sun clocks to tell time. When it is too cloudy to see the sun, the farmers estimate the time with the help of birds. The awe bird cries every four hours, and another bird cries at 6 A.M., 6 P.M., and midnight. What helps you to know the time when you do not have a clock?

Try This! 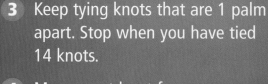 EGYPTIAN MEASURING CORD

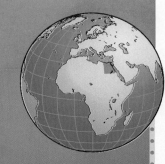

People in ancient Egypt sometimes used knotted cords to measure lengths. Follow these steps to make an Egyptian measuring cord.

1 A *palm* was a unit of length in ancient Egypt. One palm was equal to the width of a person's hand.

2 Tie a knot at the end of a long piece of string. Tie another knot 1 palm away.

3 Keep tying knots that are 1 palm apart. Stop when you have tied 14 knots.

4 Measure at least four objects with your knotted cord. Record the lengths in palms in a chart.

A Step a Day

Thousands of years ago, the Maya built this pyramid in Mexico. All 4 sides of the pyramid have 90 steps, which makes 360 steps in all. The Mayan calendar had 360 regular days. Scientists think that the Maya made a step for every day in their year.

Respond

Work with a partner . . .
to read more Roman numerals.

Internet:
Houghton Mifflin Education Place
Explore the Math Center at
http://www.eduplace.com

Centimeter

See if one of your fingers is 1 cm wide!

Getting Started

What You'll Need:
► centimeter ruler

Vocabulary:
centimeter (cm)
decimeter (dm)
metric system
Glossary, p. 480

Scientists often measure small things in units of length called **centimeters (cm)**. Centimeters are units in the **metric system** of measurement.

Suppose you planted some seeds one month ago. How tall did your plants grow in one month?

You can measure them to the nearest centimeter.

10 centimeters equals 1 decimeter (dm)
10 cm = 1 dm

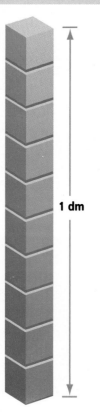

1 dm

| Here's A Way! | Measure in centimeters. |

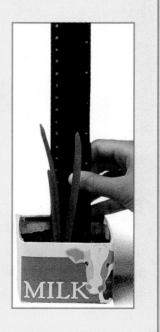

❶ This plant is between 10 cm and 11 cm tall.

❷ The top of the plant is nearer to the 11-cm mark than to the 10-cm mark.

So, the plant is 11 cm tall to the nearest centimeter.

Talk About It!

• How could you use ones blocks to show the height of the plant?

• How tall is the plant to the nearest decimeter?

1. Find two objects that are each about 1 cm long.

2. Find two objects that are each about 1 dm long.

First, estimate. Then measure to the nearest centimeter.

3.

4.

5.

6. length of your little finger   7. perimeter of a box of crayons

8. **Critical Thinking** If you wanted to measure something precisely, would it be better to measure in centimeters or decimeters? Explain.

Work It Out!

Estimate. Then measure to the nearest centimeter.

9.

10.

11. length of your desk   12. length of a pencil

Use a centimeter ruler. Draw the line segment.

13. 10 cm   14. 1 dm   15. 24 cm   16. 13 cm   17. 3 dm

18. **Critical Thinking** What do you notice about the line segments in exercises 13 and 14?

19. **Algebraic Reasoning** Write a rule for finding the number of centimeters in any number of decimeters.

More Practice Set 9.7, p. 468

Meters and Kilometers

LESSON 8

You can measure large objects and long distances in **meters (m)** and **kilometers (km)**.

Meters and kilometers are metric units of length.
1 m = 100 cm
1 km = 1000 m

Getting Started

What You'll Need:
► tens blocks
► scissors
► tape

Vocabulary:
kilometer (km)
meter (m)
Glossary, p. 480

Activity

1 You know 1 m equals 100 cm. A tens block is 10 cm long. Use tens blocks to show how long 1 meter is.

2 Make a strip of paper 1 m long. Use your row of tens blocks to measure. You may need to tape several strips together.

• Find some things in your classroom that you think are about 1 m long.

• Use your meter strip to measure them. List the things you measured and their lengths.

3 This bridge shows about 1 km. You know 1 km equals 1000 m. List five things that could be measured in kilometers.

Show What You Know!

1. Copy and complete the table.

m	1000	?	3000	4000	?	?	7000	8000	?	?
km	1	2	3	?	5	6	?	?	9	?

2. **Critical Thinking** How many meters are in half of a kilometer?

3. How many centimeters are in half of a meter?

Write >, < , or =. Use the table that you completed if you need to.

4. 100 cm ■ 1 m   5. 10 m ■ 10 km   6. 2500 m ■ 2 km

7. 10 m ■ 1 km   8. 2000 m ■ 20 km   9. 3 km ■ 300 m

Which unit would you use to measure each? Write *meter* or *kilometer*.

10. length of your classroom   11. distance between cities

12. **Critical Thinking** When is it better to measure in kilometers rather than meters?

Choose the better estimate. Write *a* or *b*.

13. depth of a swimming pool
    a. 3 cm   b. 3 m

14. length of a table
    a. 1 m   b. 1 km

15. length of a ball field
    a. 100 m   b. 100 km

16. length of a skateboard
    a. 75 cm   b. 75 m

17. **Estimation** Estimate the perimeter of your classroom chalkboard in meters. Write your estimate. Then measure the perimeter. How close was your estimate?

18. **Create Your Own** Measure the perimeter of a room in meters. Draw and label an outline of the room.

More Practice Set 9.8, p. 469

Problem Solving
Work Backward

Suppose you bought some yarn. You used half of it to tie boxes. You gave 3 ft of it to a friend for her braids. Now you have 5 ft of yarn left. How much yarn did you buy? You can work backward to find out.

Here's A Way! Use Work Backward.

1 Understand

- What are you supposed to find out?
- How much yarn is left? How much did you use or give away?

2 Plan

- Does the diagram show what happened to the yarn?

| have 5 ft left | → | add back 3 ft
5 + 3 = 8 | → | double 8
2 x 8 = 16 | → | bought 16 ft |

3 Try It

- Use the diagram above, but work backward.

| bought ? ft | → | used half | → | gave away 3 ft | → | have 5 ft left |

- Why did you add 3 to 5?
- Why did you double 8?

4 Look Back

- You bought 16 ft of yarn. Check by working forward.

Use Work Backward to solve the problem. Make a diagram if it helps.

1. Suppose you have a strip of paper. You cut it in half. Then you cut off 6 in. You are left with 8 in. How long was the strip when you started?

2. **Critical Thinking** How did working backward help you to solve the problem?

Work It Out!

Use Work Backward or another strategy to solve the problem.

3. Read the directions from the theater to Joe's Diner. Now write the directions from the diner to the theater. Hint: You can use squared paper to draw a map before you write.

4. Two numbers that come one after the other add up to 35. What are the numbers?

5. At the Craft Shack you bought 2 of the same paintbrushes. You also bought a set of paints for $6.00. You spent $12.00. How much did each paintbrush cost?

6. **Patterns** Each figure is made from 1-in. squares. Draw Figure 4 and Figure 5. What is the perimeter of each? What would be the perimeter of Figure 9?

7. The Craft Shack is having a half-price sale on clay. You buy 1 package of clay. You pay with a $10 bill and receive $4.00 change. What is the regular price of the clay?

From the Royal Theater to Joe's Diner

1. Leave the theater, turn right, and walk 3 blocks.

2. Turn left and walk 2 blocks.

3. Turn left and walk half a block. Joe's Diner will be on your right.

From Joe's Diner to the Royal Theater

1. Leave the diner, turn left and

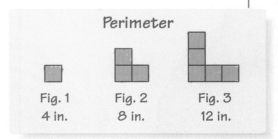

Perimeter

Fig. 1
4 in.

Fig. 2
8 in.

Fig. 3
12 in.

Share Your Thinking

8. How could you use Work Backward to solve problem 7?

Milliliter and Liter

Getting Started

What You'll Need:
► ones block
► thousands block

Vocabulary:
liter (L)
milliliter (mL)
Glossary, p. 480

You know that the amount a container can hold is its capacity. You can measure capacity in **liters (L)** and **milliliters (mL)**.

Activity

Milliliters and liters are metric units of capacity.

1 mL = about 5 drops of liquid

1 L = 1000 mL

1 Look at a ones block. Each side is 1 cm long. If the ones block were hollow, it would hold 1 mL of water.

2 There are 1000 mL in 1 L. Look at a thousands block. If it were hollow, it would hold 1 L of water.

③ Look at containers A–F on page 324. Decide if each container holds more than 1 L or less than 1 L.

④ Copy the chart. Record your results.

Container	Capacity		
	About 1 liter	Less than 1 liter	More than 1 liter
A			
B			

Show What You Know!

1. Copy and complete the table.

mL	1000	2000	?	4000	5000	?	?	8000	?	?
L	1	2	3	?	?	6	7	?	9	?

2. **Critical Thinking** How many milliliters are in half of a liter? Explain.

Write >, <, or = . Use the table you completed if you need to.

3. 1 L ■ 500 mL

4. 2000 mL ■ 2 L

5. 50 mL ■ 5 L

Which unit would you use? Write _liters_ or _milliliters_.

6.

7.

8.

Does the object hold more than or less than a liter? Write _more than_ or _less than_.

9. a sink

10. a glass

11. a pool

12. a soup can

Problem Solving

13. For a science project, you need 2 L of water. Your container holds 500 mL. How can you use it to measure 2 L?

14. Suppose you put 3 spoonfuls of honey on your cereal. A small spoon holds about 5 mL. About how many milliliters of honey will you eat?

More Practice Set 9.10, p. 469

Gram and Kilogram

Grams and kilograms are metric units of mass.
1 kg = 1000 g

You can use **grams (g)** and **kilograms (kg)** to measure how heavy an object is.

about 1 g

about 1 kg

3 kg

850 g

Which is heavier, the watermelon or the basket?

You know that 1 kg = 1000 g.
So, 3 kg = 3000 g.
3000 > 850

The watermelon is heavier.

Show What You Know!

Copy and complete the number sentence.

1. 2 kg = ■ g
2. 4000 g = ■ kg
3. $\frac{1}{2}$ kg = ■ g
4. 8 kg = ■ g

5. **Critical Thinking** Explain how multiplication patterns can help you find the number of grams in 10 kg.

Which unit would you use to measure how heavy the object is?
Write *gram* or *kilogram*.

6. eraser
7. pony
8. carrot
9. yourself
10. car

Complete the exercise. Write >, <, or =.

11. 3000 g ■ 3 kg
12. 2 kg ■ 200 g
13. 7000 g ■ 70 kg

More Practice Set 9.11, p. 470

Problem Solving
Is the Answer Reasonable?

Ready, set, go!

The soapbox derby starts on your street and ends 2 blocks away. You estimate the race route is 3 meters long. Is your estimate reasonable?

You Decide

- Think of an object that is about a meter long.

- Imagine putting 3 of those objects in a row. Would the row be about 2 blocks long?

- Decide whether your estimate is reasonable. Explain.

Work It Out!

Decide whether the measurement makes sense. Explain.

1. A student takes the bus to school. He lives 4 m from the school.

2. The top of a desk is 22 in. across and 18 in. from front to back.

3. It took two grownups to lift a rock. The rock weighed about 4 oz.

4. The principal of a school is between $1\frac{1}{2}$ m and 2 m tall.

5. During a soccer game, a player drinks 1 L of juice.

6. The hallway at school is about 5 cm wide.

Share Your Thinking

7. How did you decide if the measurement in problem 6 is reasonable?

327

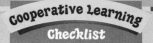
Cooperative Learning
Checklist
☑ Work alone.
☑ Work with a partner.
☑ Work with a group.

Heavier or Lighter?

Getting Started

What You'll Need:
▶ pan balance
▶ 2 small containers that match
▶ materials such as gravel, rice, beans, popcorn, cotton, counters
▶ recording sheet

You can compare how heavy two things are. First predict which material will be heavier. Then check with a pan balance.

Activity

● **Use the recording sheet or make a chart like the one below.**

1 Choose two materials to compare, such as counters and cotton. List them.

2 Fill each container with one of the materials. Predict which material will be heavier. Record your prediction.

3 Hold a container in each hand. Compare how heavy they are. Record which material feels heavier.

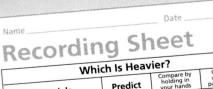

Name _____ Date _____

Recording Sheet

Which Is Heavier?				
Materials		Predict	Compare by holding in your hands	Compare using the pan balance
Cotton	Counters	Cotton	Counters	Counters

4

Now place the materials in the balance scale. Record which material is heavier.

• Repeat steps 1–4 five more times with other materials.

Show What You Know!

1. **Critical Thinking** How do you know which side of a balance has the heavier material on it? Explain.

2. **Estimation** Did you find it difficult to make predictions about any of the materials? Why?

Which is heavier? Write *a* or *b*.

3. a. Pennies b. Feathers 4. a. Ones Blocks b. Marbles

5. a. a pail of rocks
   b. a pail of leaves

6. a. 1 cup of cornflakes
   b. 1 cup of raisins

7. a. 10 apples
   b. 10 balloons

8. Is a large item always heavier than a small item? Explain.

Measuring Temperature

Cooperative Learning
Checklist

☑ Work alone.
☑ Work with a partner.
☐ Work with a group.

Getting Started

Vocabulary:
degrees
  Celsius (°C)
degrees
  Fahrenheit (°F)
temperature
Glossary, p. 480

Do you need to put on a jacket when you go outside?

Temperature is a measure of how hot or cold something is. The temperature of the air outside can be measured with a thermometer. It is measured in **degrees Fahrenheit (°F)** or **degrees Celsius (°C)**.

Degrees Fahrenheit are customary units.

Degrees Celsius are metric units.

Activity

- **Copy the chart below.**
- **Read and record the temperature.**

Read a Fahrenheit Thermometer

water boils

a warm day

a chilly day

water freezes

1 What temperature does this Fahrenheit thermometer show?

- Put your finger on the top of the red line.

- Move your finger to the right. Read the number.

2 This thermometer shows 60° Fahrenheit, or 60° F.

Find each temperature on the thermometer. Read the label. Then write the temperature in the correct place in the chart.

a. 80°F
b. 50°F
c. 32°F
d. 212°F

	Temperature of Air	
What Happens	Degrees Fahrenheit	Degrees Celsius
A warm day	?	?
A chilly day	?	?
Water freezes	?	?
Water boils	?	?

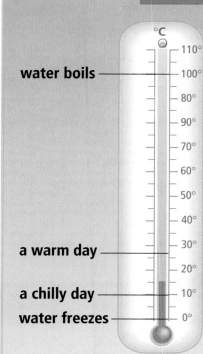

°C

water boils — 110°
— 100°
— 80°
— 90°
— 70°
— 60°
— 50°
— 40°
a warm day — 30°
— 20°
a chilly day — 10°
water freezes — 0°

1 What temperature does the Celsius thermometer show?

The top of the red line is halfway between 10 and 20.

So, the temperature is 15° Celsius, or 15°C.

2 Find each temperature on the thermometer. Then write the temperature in the correct place in the chart.

a. 27°C   b. 10°C   c. 0°C   d. 100°C

3 The red line in a thermometer is really a liquid. It can move up or down. What happens to the liquid when the weather gets warmer?

Show What You Know!

Write the temperature that the thermometer shows.

1.   °F

— 30°
— 20°
— 10°
— 0°

2.   °F
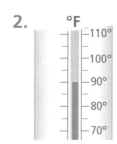
— 110°
— 100°
— 90°
— 80°
— 70°

3.   °C
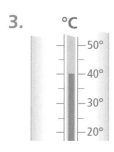
— 50°
— 40°
— 30°
— 20°

4.   °C
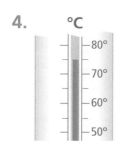
— 80°
— 70°
— 60°
— 50°

5. Critical Thinking Would you go ice skating if it were 10°C? Explain.

Use your chart to compare. Write *true* or *not true*.

6. 32°F is the same as 32°C.

7. 212°F is the same as 100°C.

8. 32°F is warmer than 27°C.

Tell what you would wear. Write *T–shirt* or *warm jacket*.

9. 0°C   10. 30°C   11. 85°F   12. 30°F

More Practice Set 9.14, p. 470

Time

Vocabulary:
day (d)
hour (h)
minute (min)
second (s)
Glossary, p. 480

You can measure time in **seconds (s)**, **minutes (min)**, **hours (h)**, and **days (d)**.

Suppose you just looked outside and saw a rainbow. You want to record the time you saw it in your journal. Look at the clock below. How will you write the time?

1 minute = 60 seconds
1 hour = 60 minutes
1 day = 24 hours

Here's A Way! Write the time.

1. The hour hand is between the 1 and the 2. So, it is after one o'clock.

2. The minute hand shows the number of minutes past one o'clock.
   - Start at the 12. Skip count by 5's to the 10.
   - Then count on by 1's. The total is 53 minutes.

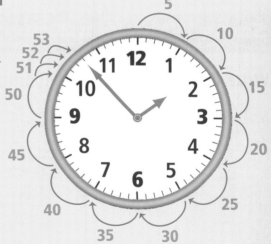

Use What You Know

A.M. the 12 hours from midnight until noon

P.M. the 12 hours from noon until midnight

3. To write the time, write the hour and then the minutes. Then write A.M. or P.M.
   - The time is 1:53 P.M.

Talk About It! Could you have seen a rainbow if the time were 1:53 A.M.? Why or why not?

Write the time shown on the clock.

1.

2.

3.

4. **Critical Thinking** Suppose it is the time shown in exercise 3. What might you be doing if the time is labeled A.M.? P.M.?

Work It Out!

Write the time shown on the clock.

5.

6.

7.

Draw a clock to show each time.

8. 3:37	9. 9:11	10. 10:41	11. 12:03	12. 2:55
13. 4:59	14. 1:43	15. 6:29	16. 11:21	17. 4:12

18. Copy and complete the table.

min	60	120	?	240	?	?	420	480	?	?
hr	1	2	3	?	5	6	?	?	9	?

19. How could you multiply to find the number of minutes in 10 hours? How could you find the number by adding?

20. **Estimation** How many letters of the alphabet can you write in order in 10 seconds? Estimate. Then have a friend time you.

21. How many letters can you write in 1 minute? Estimate. Then have a friend time you. Repeat the alphabet if you need to.

More Practice Set 9.15, p. 471

Elapsed Time

Your brother is running a 5-kilometer road race. You are timing him. The race starts at 1:45. Your brother crosses the finish line at 2:13. What was his running time?

Here's A Way!

1:45

2:13

1 Compare the two clocks.

- The first clock shows 1:45. The minute hand points to the 9.

- The second clock shows 2:13. The minute hand is between 2 and 3. The shaded part shows how much time has passed since 1:45.

2 Count the minutes by 5's and 1's.

- Skip-count by 5's to find the number of minutes between 9 and 2.

5, 10, 15, 20, 25   25 minutes

- Then, count on by 1's to find the number of minutes that have passed .

26, 27, 28   28 minutes

Your brother's running time was 28 minutes.

Talk About It! Why did you count by 5's first?

Look at the clocks. Write how much time has passed.

1.

2.

3. Look at the clock in your classroom. Write the time it shows now. What time will it show 15 minutes from now?

4. **Critical Thinking** You began reading a story at 11:20 A.M. You finished at 11:50 A.M. What fraction of an hour passed between those two times?

Work It Out!

Write how much time has passed.

5.

6.

Patterns Copy the times and complete the pattern. Describe each pattern.

7. 9:50, ■, 10:10, 10:20, ■, ■

8. 3:35, 3:45, 3:55, ■, ■

9. 6:20, 6:40, 7:00, ■, ■, ■

10. 5:15, 5:30, ■, 6:00, ■, ■

Problem Solving

11. Your friend gets off the bus at Pine Road. You get off at River Road. How much longer will you be on the bus after your friend gets off?

12. Four of your classmates get off the bus at Woods Street. How long is their ride from school?

School Bus Schedule	
Leave School	2:25 P.M.
Pine Road	2:35 P.M.
River Road	2:48 P.M.
Woods Street	3:06 P.M.

More Practice Set 9.16, p. 471

Math Journal

What time do you get up in the morning? What time do you leave for school? How much time passes between these times?

LESSON 17

Problem Solving
Using Work Backward and Other Strategies

A new water park is going to open in your town. The owners of the park want to send out flyers about the opening.

BIG SPLASH
WATER PARK
Opens May 30th

Problem Solving Process
✓ Understand
✓ Plan
✓ Try It
✓ Look Back

Choose a Strategy You Have Learned
✓ Act It Out
✓ Look for a Pattern
✓ Guess and Check
✓ Draw a Picture
✓ Make a Table
✓ Work Backward
  Make a List
  Work a Simpler Problem

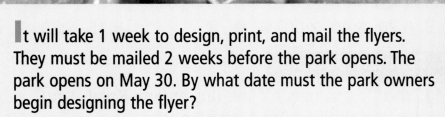

It will take 1 week to design, print, and mail the flyers. They must be mailed 2 weeks before the park opens. The park opens on May 30. By what date must the park owners begin designing the flyer?

- What problem needs to be solved?
- When does the park open?
- How many days before the opening must the flyers be mailed?
- Explain a strategy you can use to solve the problem. Then solve it.

Use any strategy to solve the problem. Show your work.

1. You have to wait in line for 8 minutes each time you want to ride the water slide. It takes 2 minutes to slide down and get back in line. How many turns on the slide can you take in $1\frac{1}{2}$ hours?

2. Every Wednesday will be half-price day at the water park. Suppose July 1 is a Wednesday. How many half-price days will there be in July and August? (Hint: Both July and August have 31 days.)

3. Workers at the water park are laying square tiles around the border of this swimming pool. How many more tiles will they need?

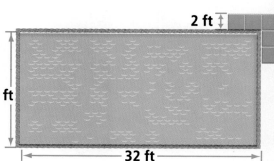

4. You are waiting to go on the water-car ride. Cars leave every 30 seconds. There are 13 people ahead of you in line. If each water-car takes 2 people, how long will you wait in line?

16 ft

32 ft

5. There are 600 inner tubes for the slides at the water park. There are twice as many blue tubes as yellow tubes. How many of each color tube are at the water park?

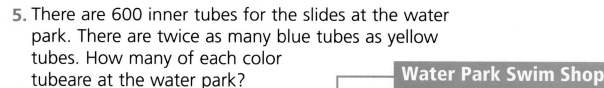

Water Park Swim Shop

Item	Cost
Swimming Tube	$8.50
Swim Cap	$3.00
Goggles	$6.00
Flippers	$12.00
Postcards	$5.00 for 10

6. Suppose you buy a swimming tube, goggles, and a pair of flippers at the water park. You also buy 5 postcards. You receive $1 change. How much money did you give the salesperson?

7. Suppose the Water Park Swim Shop is having a sale. All prices are half off. You buy the same items that are listed in problem 6. Estimate what the total cost will be.

Share Your Thinking

8. What strategy did you use to solve problem 7? Explain.

LESSON 18

Problem Solving
Using Strategies

Read more about basketball players in the pages of *Children's Digest*.

In 1993 Gheorghe Muresan (JAWRJ MYUR uh san) began playing basketball for the Washington Bullets, a team in the National Basketball Association. At 7 ft 7 in. tall, he can almost touch the basketball hoop without jumping!

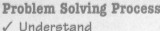

Problem Solving Process
- ✓ Understand
- ✓ Plan
- ✓ Try It
- ✓ Look Back

Choose a Strategy You Have Learned
- ✓ Act It Out
- ✓ Look for a Pattern
- ✓ Guess and Check
- ✓ Draw a Picture
- ✓ Make a Table
- ✓ Work Backward
-   Make a List
-   Work a Simpler Problem

10 ft

11 in.

11 in.

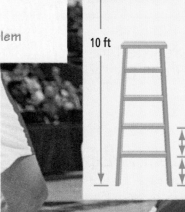

When Kate reaches straight up, she can touch something 5 ft high. If she climbs to the fourth step of this ladder, will she be able to touch the basketball hoop? Explain.

- What problem do you have to solve?
- How high is the hoop?
- How high can the student reach without a ladder?
- How high is each step of the ladder?
- Explain a strategy that can help you to solve the problem. Then solve it.

Work It Out!

Use any strategy to solve the problem. Show your work.

1. A basketball coach wants to show her players their positions. She folds a sheet of paper in half 3 times. How many sections will she have on which to draw diagrams?

In problems 2–4, player A and player B run to the end of the basketball court and back. The speed of each player does not change. Where is player B when player A finishes if…

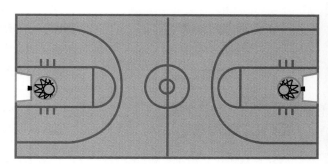

2. player A gets to the end of the court when player B is $\frac{3}{4}$ of the way there?

3. player A gets to the end of the court when player B is $\frac{1}{2}$ of the way there?

4. player A gets to the end of the court when player B is $\frac{1}{4}$ of the way there?

5. Team A scores 20 points in the first half of the game and 18 points in the second half. If team B scores 32 points during the whole game, who won? By how much?

6. Cheerleaders are planning a new cheer to use at a basketball game. They will repeat the same pattern of positions 4 times. Draw pictures to show the next three positions.

7. **Create Your Own** Use stick figures to make up a pattern for a cheer. Repeat the pattern 3 times.

8. Suppose your cousin grew 2 in. each year from his 13th birthday until his 17th birthday. On his 17th birthday he was 5 ft 7 in. tall. How tall was he on his 13th birthday?

Share Your Thinking

9. What strategy did you use to solve problem 8? Explain.

Chapter 9 Test

for Pages 302–339

Test-Taking Tips
If you have enough time, always recheck your answers. Ask yourself whether each one makes sense.

Problem Solving

Use any strategy to solve. Show your work. (pages 322, 336)

1. Suppose you have grown 2 in. every year for 4 years. If you are 51 in. now, how tall were you 4 years ago?

2. Your class has Show and Tell every other Tuesday. The calendar shows that you had Show and Tell on Tuesday, March 25. When is your next Show and Tell?

Concepts

Use paper clips to estimate the length. Write a, b, c, or d.
(pages 304, 306, 318)

3.
   a. 1 in.　　　b. 3 in.　　　c. 4 in.　　　d. 2 in.

4.
   a. 2 in.　　　b. 4 in.　　　c. 6 in.　　　d. 1 in

Which unit would you use to measure? Write a or b.
(pages 310, 312, 314, 320, 324, 326)

5. length of a hammer	a. inches	b. yards
6. distance across a lake	a. kilometers	b. decimeters
7. tea in a teapot	a. cup	b. gallon
8. gas in a gas tank	a. liter	b. milliliter
9. weight of a television set	a. ounce	b. pound
10. a crate of apples	a. ounce	b. pound
11. a slice of bread	a. gram	b. kilogram
12. weight of a comb	a. gram	b. kilogram

Find the perimeter. (page 308)

13.
5 in.   5 in.
6 in.   6 in.
7 in.

14.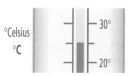
5 in.   5 in.
5 in.   5 in.
5 in.   5 in.

Complete. Write >, < , or =. (pages 310, 312, 320, 324)

15. 12 in. ● 1 yd
16. 10 mi ● 10 ft
17. 2 c ● 2 pt
18. 1 km ● 100 cm
19. 1 m ● 100 cm
20. 1000 mL ● 1000 L

Complete the number sentence. (pages 314, 326)

21. 16 oz = ■ lb
22. 4 cups = ■ oz
23. 5 kg = ■ g

Write the temperature. (page 330)

24. °Fahrenheit °F — 70° — 60° — 50°

25. °Celsius °C — 30° — 20°

Write how much time has passed. (page 334)

26.

27.

Performance Task

(pages 322, 336, 338)

Students get to choose their own activities for Field Day. Use the schedule to answer the questions.

- The film lasts 1 hour. If you go to the film, what event will you miss?

- Soccer games will last $1\frac{1}{2}$ hours. If you decide to play, what will be the next activity you can join?

- Write a new problem, using the schedule.

Keep In Mind . . .

Your work will be evaluated on the following:

☑ Steps for solving
☑ Method for checking
☑ Written problem
☑ Use of schedule information

FIELD DAY SCHEDULE			
Film: *Sports Heros*	8:30 A.M.	Soccer Games	11:00 A.M.
Tour of New Gym	9:00 A.M.	Long Jump	11:30 A.M.
100-Meter Run	9:30 A.M.	Squirt Gun Fun	12:00 A.M.
Snowcone Snack	10:00 A.M.	Volleyball	12:30 A.M.
Team Relays	10:30 A.M.	Picnic Lunch	1:00 A.M.

Cumulative Review

Coins (Chapter 2)
What is the value of the coins?

> ### Here's A Way!
>
> Skip-count by 10's.
> Skip-count by 5's.
>
>
>
> **10, 20, 30, 40, 45 cents**

Write the value of the coins.

1.

2.

3.

4. Write the value in exercise 3 in words.

Estimating Sums (Chapter 3)
Estimate 457 + 307.

> ### Here's A Way!
>
> Use front-end estimation.
> 457 + 307
>
> 4 hundreds + 3 hundreds
> **The sum is about 700.**

Use front-end estimation to estimate.

5. 321 + 164   6. 516 + 373

7. 759 + 102   8. $286 + $367

9. $427   10. $785
   + 160   + 562

11. To estimate 89 + 92 using front-end estimation, what would you do?

Division Facts (Chapter 5)
Divide 20 by 5.

> ### Here's A Way!
>
> You can draw a picture.
> You can skip-count by 5's:
> 5, 10, 15, 20;
> 20 ÷ 5 = 4
>
>

Find the quotients.

12. 30 ÷ 5

13. 25 ÷ 5

14. 15 ÷ 5

15. 35 ÷ 5

16. 45 ÷ 5

17. 40 ÷ 5

18. How can you use skip-counting to find out how many nickels are in 40¢?

Angles (Chapter 7)

Which figure has a right angle?

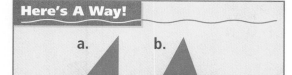

a. b.

Check each figure to see if any angle is like a corner in a square. **Figure a has a square corner, so it has a right angle.**

Write the number of square corners in each figure.

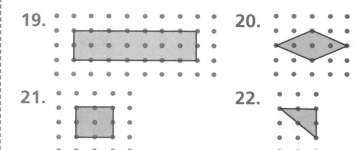

19.   20.

21.   22.

23. Look at exercise 21. What is true about the sides and corners of any square?

Writing Fractions (Chapter 8)

What fraction of this figure is shaded?

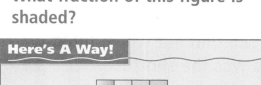

One part out of 4 parts is shaded.

So, $\frac{1}{4}$ is shaded.

What fraction names the shaded part.

24.   25.

Write the fraction for the unshaded part.

26.   27.

28. What does the top number in a fraction tell? What does the bottom number tell?

Problem Solving

Problem Solving Process
- ✓ Understand
- ✓ Plan
- ✓ Try It
- ✓ Look Back

Choose a Strategy You Have Learned
- ✓ Act It Out
- ✓ Look for a Pattern
- ✓ Guess and Check
- ✓ Draw a Picture
- ✓ Make a Table
- ✓ Work Backward
-   Make a List
-   Work a Simpler Problem

Solve using any strategy. Show your work.

29. You need to plant seeds 2 inches apart in your garden. Your rows are 36 inches long. The first and last seeds must be 2 inches from the edge. How many seeds can you plant in 1 row?

30. You see a blanket that is made with stripes. It has 1 white stripe, 2 blue stripes, 3 red stripes, then 4 white stripes, 5 blue stripes, 6 red stripes. Describe the pattern.

Up and Away!

Science Connection · **With Your Group**

Your challenge will be to build an airplane using paper and a straw. Then, test how far it will fly! Measure and record the distance flown to the nearest half inch. Then, turn the plane around and test it again. You will find out which flight was the longest and which was the shortest.

Materials:
construction paper
a straw
regular tape
masking tape

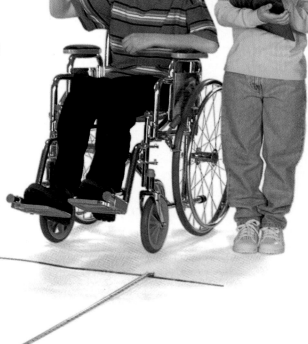

1

Plan It

- With your group, measure and cut a strip of paper $\frac{1}{2}$-in. wide and $3\frac{1}{2}$-in. long.
- Measure and cut a second strip of paper $\frac{3}{4}$-in. wide and $4\frac{3}{4}$-in. long.
- Make a loop with each strip of paper. Overlap the ends and tape them together.
- Tape the straw inside the loops.

Loop in front	Distance
big loop	$11\frac{1}{2}$ ft
small loop	

2

Put It Together

- Tape a line on the floor. Stand there to launch your plane.
- Aim your plane toward a wall and toss it.
- Measure the distance the plane flies to the nearest half inch.
- Let everyone in your group fly the plane. Make the chart above to record the distances flown.

3

Wrap It Up

- Turn the plane around so the loops are at different ends. Repeat step 2.
- Record on your chart the distances flown. Also record the new position of the loops.

4

Discuss Your Results

- Did you meet all of the goals in Keep In Mind?
- Does changing the position of the loops change the distance the plane flies?

Internet

> Visit the **Math Center** at **Houghton Mifflin Education Place.** http://www.eduplace.com

Decimals

Math Power

Use What You Know

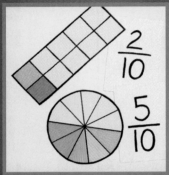

$\frac{2}{10}$

$\frac{5}{10}$

- how to write fractions

$1.25

- about decimal points

four tenths

- words to name fractions

Try This!

Use play money to write decimals.

What You'll Need

10 dimes, pencil, paper

1

Make a set of 10 dimes. You already know that there are 10 dimes in 1 dollar. So, each dime is $\frac{1}{10}$ of a dollar.

2

Take 3 dimes, or $\frac{3}{10}$ of the set. Write the money amount that tells how much you took. Use a dollar sign and a decimal point.

$$\frac{3}{10}$$
$$\$.30$$

3

Make a set of ten dimes again. Now take away one tenth of the set. Write the fraction for the part of the set that you took away. Write the money amount.

How would you write the money amount for 10 dimes?

$$\frac{10}{10} = ?$$

How are fractions different from decimals? How are they alike?

Ready to Go!

347

Exploring Tenths

Cooperative Learning Checklist

☑ Work alone.

☑ Work with a partner.

☑ Work with a group.

Getting Started

What You'll Need:
▶ 10 tenths squares
▶ paper

Vocabulary:
tenths
decimal
Glossary, p. 480

In this lesson, you will explore a new way to write tenths.

Activity

Using Tenths

This square is divided into 10 equal parts.

One of 10 parts is red. So, $\frac{1}{10}$ is red.

1 You can say: One tenth of the square is red.

2 You can write a fraction: $\frac{1}{10}$ of the square is red.

3 You can write a decimal: 0.1 of the square is red.

Making a Decimal Chart

Shade	Fraction	Decimal
1 of 10	$\frac{1}{10}$	0.1
2 of 10		
3 of 10		
4 of 10		
5 of 10		
6 of 10		
7 of 10		
8 of 10		
9 of 10		
10 of 10		

1.0

1 Use tenths squares to make 9 decimal cards. Shade 1 part on the first square, 2 parts on the second, and so on, up to 9 parts.

2 Copy this chart onto paper. Fill in the spaces with information about your decimal cards.

3 Now shade all of the parts on another card. To show this number, you can write the whole number 1, a fraction $\frac{10}{10}$, or the decimal 1.0.

Show What You Know!

Use the tenths squares you made.

1. On the back of each tenths square you shaded, write the fraction and the decimal it shows.

2. Put your tenths squares in order from least to greatest. Write the fractions and decimals in order on a sheet of paper.

Estimation Is the decimal closer to 0 or to 1.0? Write *0* or *1*.

3. 0.3   4. 0.6   5. 0.1

6. You know that $\frac{1}{2}$ and $\frac{5}{10}$ are equivalent fractions. Find the decimal card that shows half of the tenths shaded. What do you notice?

Shade parts to show each decimal. Use a tenths square or the recording sheet.

7. 0.3   8. 0.9   9. 0.6

10. **Critical Thinking** How are decimals and fractions alike?

11. **Critical Thinking** How do decimals and fractions differ?

Copy the chart or use the recording sheet. Use your decimal cards to complete the chart.

Decimal	Words	Greater Than or Less Than One Half
12. 0.2	two tenths	?
13. 0.7	seven tenths	?
14. 0.5	?	?
15. ?	four tenths	?
16. 0.6	?	?

Copy the chart or use your recording sheet. Use your decimal models to find the greater decimal.

Find These Decimal Squares	Compare
0.6 and 0.3	0.6 > 0.3
17. 0.6 and 0.7	
18. 0.1 and 0.4	
19. 0.9 and 0.8	

Decimals Greater Than 1

This comic book shows more than one page filled in. Use what you know about decimal models to write the amount in the decimal form.

Getting Started

What You'll Need:
▶ recording sheet

Use What You Know

$1\frac{3}{10}$

A mixed number has a whole number and a fraction.

Activity

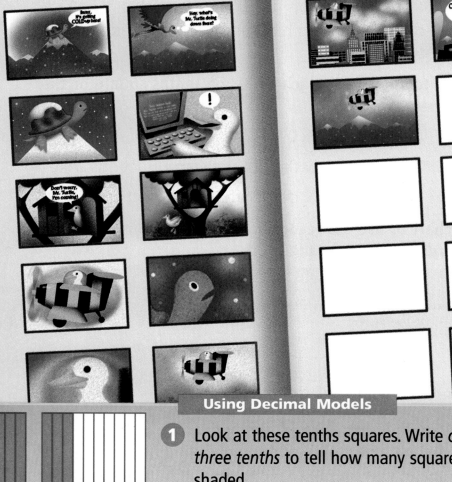

Using Decimal Models

1. Look at these tenths squares. Write *one and three tenths* to tell how many squares are shaded.

2. You can use the tenths squares and the words to help you write the decimal.

one and three tenths ⟶ 1.3

1 On your recording sheet, shade the tenths squares to show two and five tenths.

You can write a mixed number to help you : $2\frac{5}{10}$.

Then you can write a decimal: 2.5

2 Shade three and three tenths. Write the mixed number. Write the decimal.

   a. How do you know the decimal and the mixed number name the same amount?

Show What You Know!

On your recording sheet, use shading to show the decimal.

  1. 1.9   **2.** 4.2   **3.** 2.4

  4. Number Sense Look at your shaded squares. Which is greater, 1.9 or 4.2? How do you know?

  5. Critical Thinking Where else have you seen decimals used besides in your math book?

Write the decimal.

  6. 6 and 1 tenth   **7.** 1 and 5 tenths   **8.** 3 and 0 tenths

Write the words, mixed number, and decimal that names how many squares are shaded.

  9.

  10.

  11. Write About It Without drawing pictures, explain how you can tell that 1.2 is greater than 0.9.

Tenths

You have about two and four tenths liters of blood in your system. How can you show this number in different ways?

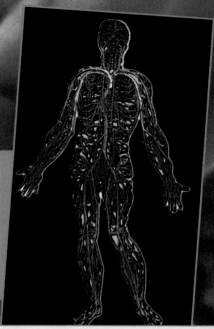

Here's A Way! Show a number with tenths.

1 Show the number with tenths squares and as a mixed number. Both ways show a whole and tenths.

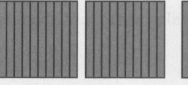

2          $\frac{4}{10}$

2 Write the number in a place-value chart and as a decimal. Both of these ways also show a whole and tenths.

Ones	Tenths
2	4

2.4

3 When you write a decimal, use a decimal point to separate the whole from the tenths.

Talk About It!

Does the tenths part of the mixed number show the same amount as the tenths part of the decimal? Explain.

Other Examples

You have about three tenths liters of blood when you are born. How can you show this amount?

Ones	Tenths
0	3

0.3

Show What You Know!

Write the decimal.

1.

2.

3.

4.
Ones		Tenths
0	•	7

5.
Ones		Tenths
7	•	5

6.
Ones		Tenths
1	•	0

7. **Critical Thinking** What does the zero mean in 0.3? In 2.0?

Work It Out!

Write the decimal.

8.
Ones		Tenths
0	•	8

9.
Ones		Tenths
0	•	1

10.
Ones		Tenths
9	•	2

11. $\frac{3}{10}$

12. $5\frac{2}{10}$

13. 10 tenths

14. 3 tenths

15. four tenths

16. two and five tenths

17. six and zero tenths

18. three and three tenths

19. $\frac{5}{10}$

20. 2 and 3 tenths

Patterns Write the next three numbers in the pattern.

21. 0.3, 0.5, 0.7, 0.9 ■ ■ ■

22. 1.5, 1.4, 1.3, 1.2 ■ ■ ■

23. 0.2, 0.4, 0.6, 0.8 ■ ■ ■

24. 2.5, 3.0, 3.5, 4.0 ■ ■ ■

Problem Solving

25. A ranger drove 20.8 mi. If she drives 0.1 mi farther, how many miles will she have driven?

26. You hiked 4.9 mi one day and 3.3 mi the next day. Did you walk more than 10 mi?

More Practice Set 10.3, p. 472

Math Journal

Which is greater, 0.4 of a mile or 0.7 of a mile? Explain.

Problem Solving
Make a List

Getting Started

What You'll Need:
► 4 index cards or slips of paper

Your class is playing a sorting game. Using two digits, you must make as many decimals greater than 1 as possible using the digits 2, 3, and 5. How can you be sure that you find all the possible combinations? You can make a list of the numbers.

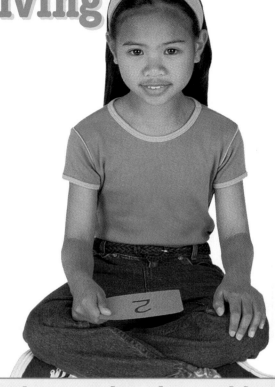

Here's A Way! Use Make a List to solve the problem.

1 Understand

• You can make a list to help you find the decimals.

2 Plan

• Use cards to make decimals.

• List the decimals that you make.

3 Try It

• Write one digit on each of 3 cards. Use a fourth card to show a decimal point.

• List all the decimals you make.

4 Look Back

• There are 6 decimals greater than 1: 2.3, 2.5, 3.2, 3.5, 5.2, 5.3. How did making a list help you to solve the problem?

Use Make a List to solve this problem.

1. Using two digits, how many decimals greater than 1 can you make with the digits 1, 6, 8, and 3?

2. **Critical Thinking** Once your list is complete, predict how many 2-digit decimals you can make with a fifth card.

Work It Out!

Use Make a List or any other strategy to solve the problem.

3. How many different ways can you shade 0.1 of a tenths square? This picture shows one way.

4. How many different ways can you shade 0.9 of a tenths square? This picture shows one way.

5. You and 3 classmates form pairs to do a class project. How many different pairs of partners can the four of you make?

6. You and a friend each choose a tenths square. Yours shows 0.8. Your friend's shows 0.4. Count up from your partner's number to your number. You get 1 point for each tenth. How many points do you get?

7. You have a spinner that is divided into tenths. You want to color 0.2 of the spinner blue and the rest of it red. Show 5 different ways to do it.

8. You have 2 equal piles of pennies. To buy a cookie, you use one of your piles plus 1 penny more. After you buy the cookie, you have 4 pennies left. How much money did you have before you bought the cookie?

Share Your Thinking

9. Which problems did you solve by making a list?

LESSON 5

Comparing and Ordering Decimals

You help your neighbors take their pets to the veterinarian. You learn that the hamster is 0.3 kg, the kitten is 0.9 kg, and the puppy is 1.2 kg. You can use a number line to compare the decimals.

Here's A Way! Use a number line.

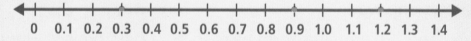

0   0.1   0.2   0.3   0.4   0.5   0.6   0.7   0.8   0.9   1.0   1.1   1.2   1.3   1.4

1 Put your finger at 0 on the number line.

As you move your finger to the right, the decimals are greater.

2 Compare the decimals on the number line.

0.9 is to the right of 0.3   0.9 > 0.3
1.2 is to the right of 0.9   1.2 > 0.9

The kitten is heavier than the hamster.
The puppy is heavier than the kitten.

3 Write the decimals in order from least to greatest.

0.3, 0.9, 1.2

The hamster is lightest, the kitten is heavier, and the puppy is heaviest.

Talk About It!

Name a decimal greater than 1.2. Explain how you know.

Show What You Know!

Write <, >, or =. Use a number line.

1.

```
<——+—+—+—+—+—+—+—+—+—+—+——>
  0  0.1 0.2 0.3 0.4 0.5 0.6 0.7 0.8 0.9 1.0
```

0.6 ● 0.8

2.

```
<——+—+—+—+—+—+—+—+—+—+—+——>
  0  0.1 0.2 0.3 0.4 0.5 0.6 0.7 0.8 0.9 1.0
```

0.9 ● 0.5

3. 2.5 ● 2.2   **4.** 2.0 ● 2   **5.** 3.8 ● 4.2   **6.** 3.4 ● 2.4

7. Critical Thinking For exercise 6, how did you decide which decimal was greater?

Work It Out!

Write <, >, or =. Use a number line if you wish.

8. 1.7 ● 2.3   **9.** 0.6 ● 0.2   **10.** 1.3 ● 1.4

11. 3.7 ● 3.5   **12.** 3 ● 3.0   **13.** 7.0 ● 0.7

Write the decimals in order from least to greatest.

14. 0.5, 0.2, 0.7   **15.** 2.0, 2.2, 0.2

16. 2.3, 2.8, 2.4   **17.** 8.2, 5.2, 3.2

Use the pictures to write your answer.

18. Order the weights of the pets from least to greatest.

19. Which animals are less than 3.5 kg? Explain.

Problem Solving

20. Calculator Make your calculator count by tenths. Press ⓪ ➕ ⓪ ● ① ＝. Keep pressing ＝ and see what happens. Use your calculator to find the missing numbers. 1.5, 1.6, ■, 1.8, ■, 2.0, ■.

duck
9.9 kg

turtle
3.2 kg

dachshund
7.9 kg

More Practice Set 10.5, p. 672

357

LESSON 6

Hundredths

Getting Started

What You'll Need:
► hundredths squares

Quilting is a popular tradition in many parts of the world. Skilled quilters, like the women in the picture, make these large covers for the cold winters.

Activity

Make a Decimal Model

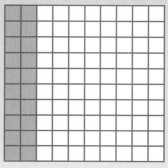

- This quilt is divided into 100 equal parts

- Of the 100 parts, only 20 parts are yellow. So, $\frac{20}{100}$ of the quilt is yellow.

- You can write this fraction as a decimal.

$$\frac{20}{100} = 0.20$$

- Read this decimal as twenty hundredths.

- Color in a hundredths square to show 0.20. Shade 20 parts.

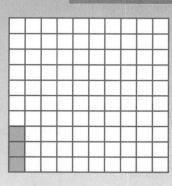

- Suppose only 3 parts are yellow. Write this amount as $\frac{3}{100}$ or 0.03.

- Make a place-value chart to show three hundredths. Write 3 in the hundredths place.

Ones		Tenths	Hundredths
0	•	0	3

Show What You Know!

Write the decimal.

1. 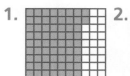 2. 3. 4.

5. $\frac{70}{100}$ 6. $\frac{12}{100}$ 7. $\frac{56}{100}$ 8. $\frac{5}{100}$

9. four hundredths

10. fifty hundredths

Color in a hundredths square to show each decimal.

11. 0.12   12. 0.32   13. 0.67   14. 0.06

15. Suppose you shaded 24 parts of a hundredths square. Write a decimal for the number of parts you shaded.

16. **Critical Thinking** Suppose you shaded 5 columns of a hundredths square. How many hundredths of the whole did you shade?

Estimation Is the number closer to 0.01 or to 0.99? How do you know?

17. 0.03   18. 0.87   19. 0.12   20. 0.45

Mixed Review Write the fraction or mixed number

21. seven tenths   22. five eighths   23. one and three fourths

Problem Solving
Is the Answer Reasonable?

You want to compare the wingspans of the airplane and the stork. Which wingspan is greater?

1.7 m

Bumblebee Two

4 m

You Decide

• There are more digits in the airplane's measurement than in the stork's. Does that mean the airplane's wingspan is greater? Why or why not?

• Can you use what you know about comparing decimals to help answer the question? Explain.

Is the Answer Reasonable

Ask Yourself:

Did I answer the question?

Did I calculate correctly?

Is the answer labeled with the right units?

Does my answer need to be rounded to a whole number to make sense?

Work It Out!

Decide if the answer is reasonable. Explain.

1. *Silver Bullet*, the world's smallest jet, has a wing span of 5.2 m. The large albatross has a wingspan of 3.7 m. Which has the greater wingspan? (Answer: The jet has the greater wingspan.)

2. *Baby Bird* is a small airplane with a wingspan of about 190 cm. Is it greater than or less than the 1.7-m wingspan of *Bumble Bee Two*? (Answer: Baby Bird's wingspan is greater than Bumblebee Two's.)

Share Your Thinking

3. What can you do to make sure that your answers are reasonable?

Midchapter Review

for Pages 346–360

(page 354)

Problem Solving

Use any strategy to solve the problem. Show your work. (page 354)

1. For a trip, you pack a red shirt, a blue shirt, jeans, tan pants, a black hat, and a white hat. How many outfits can you make?

2. You have grape juice, apple juice, cherry, and peach. If you mix 3 juices in equal amounts, how many combinations can you make?

Concepts

Fill in the chart. Use tenths squares to help you. (page 348)

	Fraction	Decimal	Word Form	Is it closer to 0 or 1?
3.	?	?	four-tenths	0
4.	?	0.8	?	?
5.	?	?	one-tenth	?

Write the decimal. (page 350)

6. $4\frac{9}{10}$　　7. 　　8.

Skills

Write the decimal. (page 352)

9.
Ones	Tenths
2 •	9

10.
Ones	Tenths
0 •	4

11. five and six tenths　　12. 7 tenths　　13. $\frac{9}{10}$　　14. $\frac{6}{10}$

Write >, <, or =. (pages 356, 358)

15. 0.8 ● 0.3　　16. 6.1 ● 6.2　　17. 0.29 ● 0.92　　18. 0.41 ● 0.28

Write the decimals in order from least to greatest. (pages 356, 358)

19. 1.5, 1.0, 1.1　　　20. 6.5, 5.6, 0.6

Math World

Learn about early number systems, math on the radio, and how decimals can be used to organize information.

Why 10?

We use a number system with 10 digits. All of our numbers are made from 0, 1, 2, 3, 4, 5, 6, 7, 8, and 9. The first number systems only had two digits. Later systems had 5, 12, and 20 digits.

The Babylonians used a system with 60 symbols! But, a system with 10 digits seems best for counting. Why do you think this is true?

Tune In to Decimals

People all over the world use decimals every time they turn on the radio. In most countries, the radio dial for FM stations uses numbers with tenths. Does this radio dial use decimals? Are they in order on the number line?

| FM | 88.1 | 91.3 | 94 | 103 | 104.5 | 108 | FM |
| AM | 1000 | 1020.2 | 1100 | 1250 | 1300 | AM |

Try This!

This map shows the Central American countries of Belize, Costa Rica, El Salvador, Guatemala, Honduras, Nicaragua, and Panama. The numbers on the map tell how many millions of people live in each country. You can make a chart to organize the data from this map.

1 List the decimals from the map on a sheet of paper.

2 Arrange the decimals you listed from greatest to least. If you need help, use tenths squares or a number line.

3 Copy this list onto a chart.

4 Write the decimals in the right column. Write *million* after each decimal. Write the names of the countries in the left column.

Belize
0.2

Guatemala
10.6

Honduras
5.5

El Salvador
5.9

Nicaragua
4.4

Panama
2.4

Costa Rica
3.3

Population Chart

Country — Population

Guatemala — 10.6 million

KEY: Each decimal is in millions. So, 2.4 on the map means 2.4 million.

Comma Sense

What do you notice about this radio station logo? It has a decimal comma instead of a decimal point. In many parts of South America, this is how people write all decimals.

105,8
BRAZIL RADIO

Respond

Work with a partner . . .
to find decimals in other places.

Internet: Education Place
http://www.eduplace.com
Explore Houghton Mifflin's *Education Place Math Center*.

Adding and Subtracting Tenths

What You'll Need:
► grid paper or number line paper

Cooperative Learning
Checklist

☑ Work alone.
☑ Work with a partner.
☑ Work with a group.

You can use number lines to add and subtract decimals.

Activity

• Jump ahead on the number line to add. Jump back to subtract.

Find 0.7 + 0.4.

0   0.1 0.2 0.3 0.4 0.5 0.6 0.7 0.8 0.9 1.0 1.1 1.2 1.3 1.4 1.5

1. Make a number line that shows 0 to 1.5. Mark the number line in tenths.

2. Mark 0.7 on the line. To add 0.4, count on 4 tenths. Draw 4 arrows to show each tenth as you count. Where do you end?

3. Write an addition sentence to show the sum.

4. Use a number line to find the sum. Write the addition sentence.
   a. 0.9 + 0.5   b. 0.2 + 0.8   c. 0.4 + 1.0   d. 0.5 + 0.5

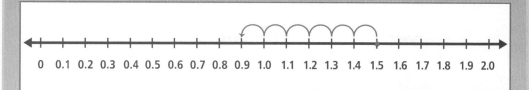

0   0.1 0.2 0.3 0.4 0.5 0.6 0.7 0.8 0.9 1.0 1.1 1.2 1.3 1.4 1.5 1.6 1.7 1.8 1.9 2.0

1 Make a number line that shows 0 to 2. Mark the number line in tenths.

2 Mark 1.5 on the line. To subtract 0.6, count back 6 tenths. Draw 6 arrows to show each tenth that you count. Where do you end?

3 Write a subtraction sentence to show the difference.

4 Make a number line to find the difference. Write the number sentence for each.

    a. 1.3 − 0.7   **b.** 1.0 − 0.9   **c.** 0.8 − 0.7   **d.** 1.1 − 0.9

Show What You Know!

Find the sum or difference. Then write a number sentence.

1.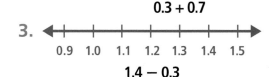

0.2 0.3 0.4 0.5 0.6 0.7 0.8 0.9 1.0

0.3 + 0.7

2.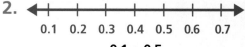

0.1 0.2 0.3 0.4 0.5 0.6 0.7

0.1 + 0.5

3.

0.9 1.0 1.1 1.2 1.3 1.4 1.5

1.4 − 0.3

4.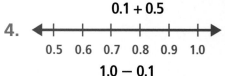

0.5 0.6 0.7 0.8 0.9 1.0

1.0 − 0.1

5. Critical Thinking How is adding and subtracting decimals on a number line like adding and subtracting whole numbers on a number line? How is it different?

Find each sum. Use a number line if needed.

  6. 0.8 + 0.1   **7.** 0.5 + 0.7   **8.** 0.4 + 0.1   **9.** 1.0 + 0.2

10. 0.6 + 0.7   **11.** 0.2 + 0.1   **12.** 0.5 + 0.2   **13.** 0.4 + 0.6

Find each difference. Use a number line if you need to.

14. 1.2 − 0.1   **15.** 1.5 − 0.8   **16.** 1.3 − 0.9   **17.** 0.3 − 0.2

18. 0.1 − 0.1   **19.** 0.8 − 0.6   **20.** 1.5 − 1.4   **21.** 0.6 − 0.3

 22. Calculator Enter 0.7 + 0.6 = . Write and say the result.

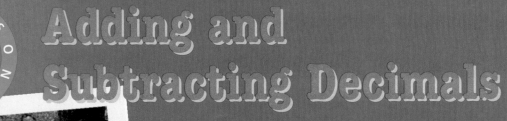

Adding and Subtracting Decimals

You want to build a tree house. You can ask addition and subtraction questions about the materials you will need.

0.7 m

1.5 m

Here's A Way! — Add and subtract tenths.

Add

How wide is the tree house? Find 1.5 m + 0.7 m.

1 Line up the digits by place value.

Ones	Tenths
1	5
+ 0	7

2 Add the tenths. Regroup if you need to.

Ones	Tenths
1	
1	5
+ 0	7
	2

3 Add the ones. Write the decimal point.

Ones	Tenths
1	
1	5
+ 0	7
2	2

The tree house is 2.2 m wide.

Subtract

A piece of rope is 4.2 m long. You cut a piece that is 3.5 m long. How much is left? Find 4.2 m − 3.5 m.

1 Line up the digits by place value.

Ones	Tenths
4	2
− 3	5

2 Subtract the tenths. Regroup if you need to.

Ones	Tenths
3	12
4	2
− 3	5
	7

3 Subtract the ones. Write the decimal point.

Ones	Tenths
3	12
4	2
− 3	5
0	7

There is 0.7 m left.

Talk About It! How is regrouping a decimal like regrouping a whole number?

Show What You Know!

Add or subtract. Use a place-value chart to help you.

1.
Ones	Tenths
0	9
− 0	7

2.
Ones	Tenths
1	9
+ 0	4

3.
Ones	Tenths
3	4
− 2	9

4. $0.7 + 0$ 5. $2.3 + 1.4$ 6. $2.6 - 1.8$ 7. $0.9 - 0$

8. **Mental Math** What do you know about zero that helped you find the answer for exercises 4 and 7?

Work It Out!

Add or subtract. You may use a place-value chart to help you.

9.
$$4.7$$
$$+ 4.8$$

10.
$$2.7$$
$$- 1.4$$

11.
$$0.4$$
$$+ 0.5$$

12.
$$1.6 \text{ cm}$$
$$+ 0.5 \text{ cm}$$

13.
$$7.0 \text{ m}$$
$$- 1.4 \text{ m}$$

14. $4.5 + 2.8$ 15. $3.0 + 0.6$ 16. $1.9 - 0.6$ 17. $7.9 - 3.9$

18. **Algebraic Reasoning** Copy and complete the tables.

a.
Number	Number + 0.5
1.0	1.5
1.5	?
2.0	?
?	3.0
3.5	?

b.
Number	Number − 1.3
6.6	5.3
5.6	?
?	3.3
2.6	1.3
?	0.3

Problem Solving

19. You have some fabric that is 3.2 m long. How much should be cut off the fabric to make it 2.5 m long?

20. You have ropes that are 1.6 m 1.9 m, and 2.6 m long. Which two ropes would you tie together to make a rope between 3 and 4 meters long? Explain.

Problem Solving
Using Make a List and Other Strategies

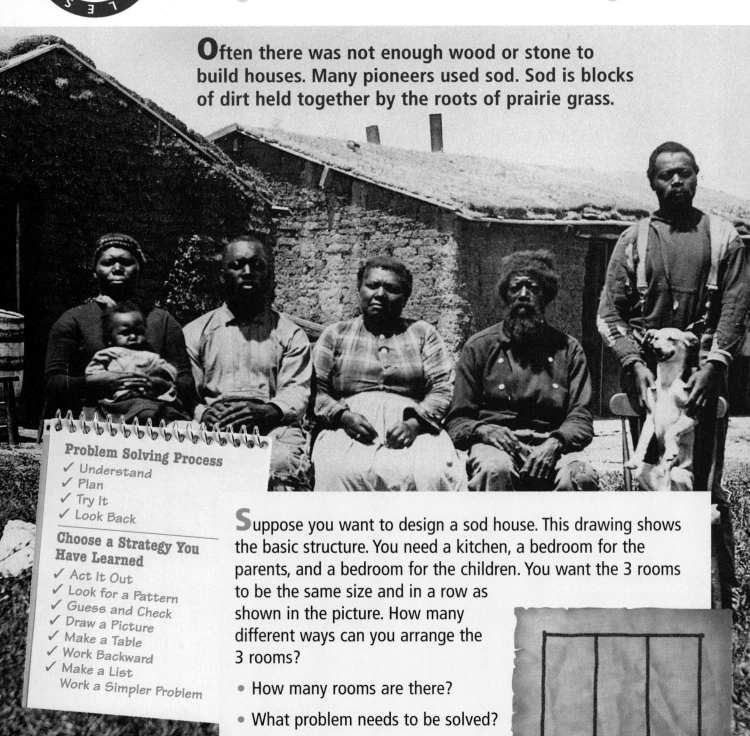

Often there was not enough wood or stone to build houses. Many pioneers used sod. Sod is blocks of dirt held together by the roots of prairie grass.

Problem Solving Process
✓ Understand
✓ Plan
✓ Try It
✓ Look Back

Choose a Strategy You Have Learned
✓ Act It Out
✓ Look for a Pattern
✓ Guess and Check
✓ Draw a Picture
✓ Make a Table
✓ Work Backward
✓ Make a List
  Work a Simpler Problem

Suppose you want to design a sod house. This drawing shows the basic structure. You need a kitchen, a bedroom for the parents, and a bedroom for the children. You want the 3 rooms to be the same size and in a row as shown in the picture. How many different ways can you arrange the 3 rooms?

- How many rooms are there?

- What problem needs to be solved?

- Explain a strategy you can use to solve the problem. Then solve it.

Use any strategy to solve the problem. Show your work.

1. Suppose each block of sod is 0.9 m long. Would 50 blocks be enough to build a row 50 m long? Explain.

2. **Create Your Own** How many different 4-sided houses can you design? Each house should have a perimeter of 16 m.

3. Many pioneers moved west in covered wagons. The wagon trains traveled an average of 29 km every day. At that rate, how many kilometers could a wagon train travel in 1 week?

Use the map to solve the following problems.

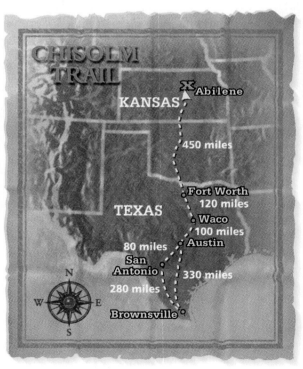

4. Your family wants to follow the Chisholm Trail, an old route for cattle drives. The first leg is from Brownsville to Austin. About how many extra miles will it take if you visit San Antonio on the way? Use one or more strategies to hep you to decide. Explain your thinking.

5. Your family decide to drive close to 300 miles on one day of your trip on the Chisholm Trail. You plan to visit as many cities as you can that day. What route should you take? Explain.

6. In Abilene, cowboys sold their cattle for $40 each. How many different combinations of $5, $10, and $20 bills would make that amount?

Share Your Thinking

7. For which problems did you use Make a List? How did it help you?

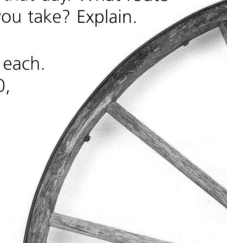

· LESSON · 11 ·

Problem Solving
Using Strategies

Read more about baseball in the pages of *Junior League Baseball*.

Problem Solving Process
✓ Understand
✓ Plan
✓ Try It
✓ Look Back

Choose a Strategy You Have Learned
✓ Act It Out
✓ Look for a Pattern
✓ Guess and Check
✓ Draw a Picture
✓ Make a Table
✓ Work Backward
✓ Make a List
   Work a Simpler Problem

The first U.S. baseball game between two organized teams was played in Hoboken, New Jersey, in 1846. Perhaps you or some of your friends play Little League baseball.

It takes 10.8 seconds for a player to run 360 feet in a straight line. Why might it take the player more than 11 seconds to run around the bases?

- What is the question you have to answer?

- What materials might help you to solve it?

- How might this diagram of a baseball diamond help you?

- Choose one or more strategies to use to solve the problem. Then solve it.

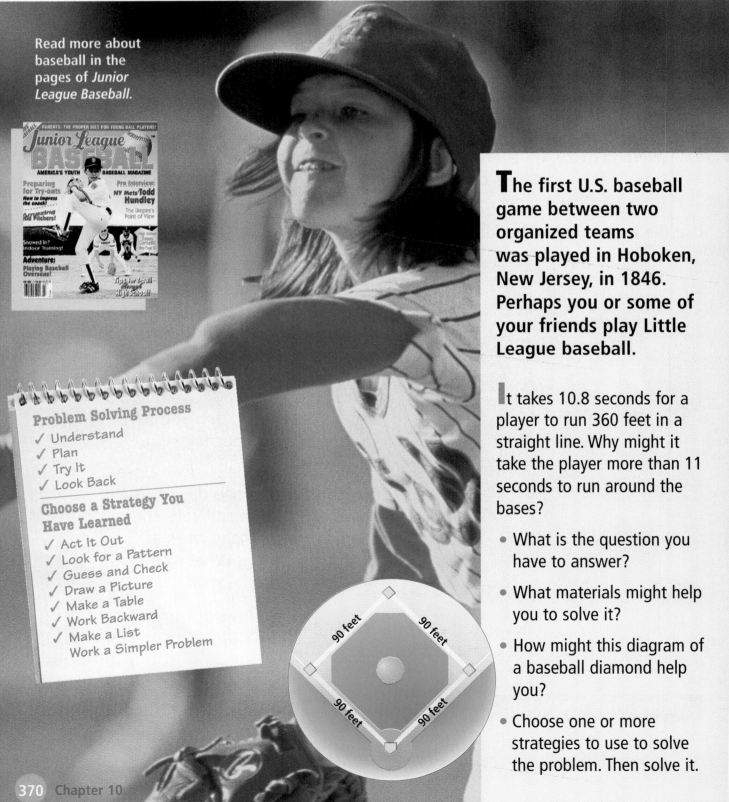

90 feet
90 feet
90 feet
90 feet

Use any strategy to solve the problem. Show your work.

1. You have 30 baseball cards to trade. You give one-third of the cards to your sister. How many baseball cards do you have left?

2. You have $8.50. You want to buy 3 baseball cards. The cards cost $4.50, $3.25, or $1.75. How many different combinations of cards can you buy?

3. A game lasts about 3 hours. Each team gets 3 outs in an inning. How many outs does each team get in 9 innings?

4. Sometimes a game lasts more than 9 innings. This scoreboard shows a game that lasted for 18 innings. It was twice as long as a normal game. How many outs did each team get in the game? How long do you think it took to finish the game? Explain.

INNING	1	2	3	4	5	6	7	8	9	10	11	12	13	14	15	16	17	18	
VISITOR	0	1	1	0	2	0	1	2	0	0	0	1	0	0	0	2	0	1	11
HOME	0	0	0	0	1	0	0	4	2	0	0	1	0	0	0	2	0	0	10

5. You are setting up a ticket booth, a snack booth, and a souvenir booth for the school Little League final. How many ways can you arrange the booths in a row?

6. Suppose every player in Little League wears red or white caps, blue or red shirts, and white or black pants. How many different combinations of outfits are possible?

Share Your Thinking

7. Choose one of the problems above. Explain the strategy or strategies you used and how they helped you to solve the problem.

Chapter 10 Test

for Pages 346-371

Test-Taking Tips
Sometimes it helps to estimate an answer before looking at the multiple-choice options.

Problem Solving

Solve using any strategy. Show your work. (pages 354, 368)

1. Suppose you are making 2 valentine cards. You have 12 identical heart stickers. You could put 9 stickers on one card and 3 stickers on the other. How many other ways can you use all the stickers so each card has at least 1 sticker?

2. A mystery number is between 8 and 23. The sum of the ones digit and the tens digit is 6. What is the mystery number?

Concepts

Which decimal is greater? Use tenths squares to help you decide.
(page 348)

3. 0.2 or 0.5   4. 0.7 or 0.6   5. 0.3 or 0.1   6. 0.8 or 0.9

Write a decimal to show the number. (pages 350, 352)

7. four and five tenths   8. nine and two tenths

9. five hundredths

How is the number written as a decimal? Write *a*, *b*, *c*, or *d*.
(page 352)

10. six and seven tenths   a. 7.6   b. 06.07   c. 6.07   d. 6.7

11.

Ones	Tenths
8 •	3

a. 0.83   b. 8.3   c. 38.0   d. 8.03

12. five and zero tenths   a. 5.0   b. 5.5   c. 0.5   d. 50

Compare the numbers. Write > or <. (pages 356, 358)

13. 4.0 ● 5   14. 5.4 ● 5.6   15. 0.12 ● 11   16. 0.78 ● 69

Write the decimals in order from least to greatest. (pages 356, 358)

17. 3.4, 2.4, 4.1   18. 5.1, 5.0, 0.5

19. 0.82, 0.1, 0.8   20. 0.7, 0.07, 0.71

Choose the correct sum. Write *a, b, c,* or *d*. (pages 364, 366)

21. 0.3 + 0.5   a. 0.6   b. 0.7   c. 0.8   d. 0.08

22. 0.4 + 1.0   a. 0.5   b. 1.4   c. 4.1   d. 1.04

23. 2.8   a. 8.1   b. 8.5   c. 9.1   d. 7.1
    + 6.3

24. 1.7   a. 2.4   b. 2.7   c. 2.9   d. 1.4
    + 0.7

Choose the correct difference. Write *a, b, c,* or *d*. (pages 364, 366)

25. 1.7 − 0.8   a. 0.5   b. 0.9   c. 1.0   d. 1.5

26. 0.9 − 0.7   a. 0.2   b. 1.0   c. 1.2   d. 2.0

27. 3.6   a. 0.3   b. 0.6   c. 1.3   d. 1.6
    − 2.3

28. 5.0   a. 4.1   b. 0.31   c. 3.01   d. 3.1
    − 1.9

 Performance Task

Keep in Mind . . .
Your work will be evaluated on the following:
☑ Complete number line
☑ Correct number placement
☑ Clear and correct labels
☑ Clear written explanation

(pages 350, 356)

- Copy the number line. Write the decimal number that belongs in each box. Explain how you decided which numbers to write.

- Draw the number line again and use fractions instead of decimals.

Cumulative Review

Addition Properties (Chapter 1)
Find 6 + 5, 0 + 28, and
10 + 15 + 20.

> **Here's A Way!**
>
> Order property with doubles:
> 5 + 6 = 5 + 5 + 1 = 10 + 1
> = 11
> Zero property: 0 + 28 = 28
> Grouping property:
> 10 + 15 + 20 = 45;
> 10 + 15 + 20 = 45

Find the sum. Tell how you found it.

1. 21 + 0
2. 8 + 6 + 2
3. 5 + 7
4. 9 + 4 + 11
5. 0 + 38
6. 4 + 6
7. Which property of addition did you find most helpful? Explain your choice.

Telling Time (Chapter 2)
What time is it?

> **Here's A Way!**
>
> The short hand points to the hour, **10.**
> Then, count by 5's up to the minute hand.
>
>
>
> It is **10:35.**

Write the time.

8.

9.

10.

11.

12.

13.

14. Divide an hour into 4 equal parts. How many minutes are in each part?

Division (Chapter 6)
Find 18 ÷ 6.

> **Here's A Way!**
>
> Use an array.
> 18 ÷ 6 = 3
>

Find the quotient. Use arrays or other models to help you.

15. 72 ÷ 9   16. 63 ÷ 7   17. 42 ÷ 6
18. 56 ÷ 7   19. 48 ÷ 8   20. 64 ÷ 8
21. How could you check your answer to exercise 19?

Comparing Fractions (Chapter 8)

Which is greater, $\frac{2}{3}$ or $\frac{3}{6}$?

Use fraction models. Which has a greater unshaded part?

 $\frac{2}{3} > \frac{3}{6}$.

Compare the fractions. Write >, <, or =.

22. $\frac{4}{6}$ ● $\frac{1}{6}$

23. $\frac{2}{8}$ ● $\frac{7}{8}$

24. $\frac{1}{5}$ ● $\frac{1}{2}$

25. $\frac{1}{6}$ ● $\frac{1}{8}$

26. $\frac{2}{4}$ ● $\frac{4}{8}$

27. $\frac{1}{3}$ ● $\frac{3}{5}$

28. Two apple pies are the same size. One is sliced into eighths. Another is sliced into sixths. Which is sliced into larger pieces?

Measuring Perimeter (Chapter 9)

Find the perimeter.

Add the side lengths.
2 in. + 4 in. + 2 in. + 4 in. = 12 in.
The perimeter is 12 in.

Write the perimeter.

29.

30.

31.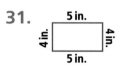

32.

33.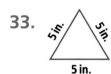

34.

Problem Solving

Problem Solving Process

✓ Understand
✓ Plan
✓ Try It
✓ Look Back

Choose a Strategy You Have Learned

✓ Act It Out
✓ Look for a Pattern
✓ Guess and Check
✓ Draw a Picture
✓ Make a Table
✓ Work Backward
✓ Make a List
  Work a Simpler Problem

Solve the problem. Show your work.

35. You and 2 friends are going to blow up 16 balloons. Suppose one friend takes 6 balloons. You and the other friend each blow up half of the rest. Who would blow up the most balloons?

36. Your scout leader buys 3 packs of hot dogs and 3 packs of buns. The hot dogs cost $2.95 a pack. The buns cost $.95 a pack. Your scout leader gets $.30 change. How much did she give the cashier?

CHAPTER
10
INVESTIGATION

Lickety-Split!

Health Connection

With Your Group

Have you ever been in a race or watched one? Here is your chance to design a race of your own. Decide how people will move in each different part, or leg, of the race. Have teams race. Use a stopwatch to time how long it takes them to complete each leg. Then, make a chart showing the times for each leg and for the whole race.

Keep In Mind . . .

Your work will be evaluated on the following:

☑ How well you add the decimals

☑ How clearly you lay out the race course

☑ How complete your chart is

☑ How well your group works together

1

Plan It

- Write a list of ways to move from one place to another. Include many ideas like dancing, rolling, and crawling. Be sure to include a way of moving that everyone in the class can do.
- Decide how many legs your race will have and what activity people do for each leg.

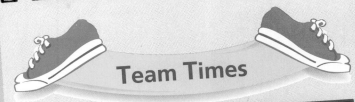

Team Times

Leg	Name	Time	Name	Time
dance	David	20.8	José	22.1
hop	Jamal	19.3	Maria	17.5
crawl	Lisa	26.7	Lee	30.2
Team Total	Team A	66.8	Team B	69.8

2

Put It Together

- Lay out the race course. Where will each leg begin and end? Where will the race take place?
- Make a chart like the one above. Record the times of each leg as the teams race.

4

Discuss Your Results

- Did you meet the goals in Keep In Mind?
- What was each team's total time?

3

Wrap It Up

- Hold the race. Each team should let team members choose which leg they want to race.
- Time each leg with a digital stopwatch. Record the times.
- Add up the results and compare.

Internet

> Visit the Math Center at **Houghton Mifflin Education Place.** http://www.eduplace.com

Math Power

Use What You Know

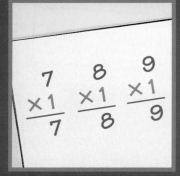

- how to multiply ten

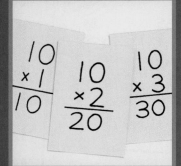

- how to find multiplication patterns

- factor
- product

- vocabulary

Multiplying by 1-Digit Numbers

Try This!

Find a pattern for multiplying by 3.

What You'll Need

notebook paper, pencil, calculator

1

List the numbers 11–20 on a piece of notebook paper.

Multiply each number by 3. Use a calculator if you wish.

$$\begin{array}{r} 11 \\ \times 3 \\ \hline 33 \end{array} \qquad \begin{array}{r} 12 \\ \times 3 \\ \hline 36 \end{array} \qquad \begin{array}{r} 13 \\ \times 3 \\ \hline \end{array} \qquad \begin{array}{r} 14 \\ \times 3 \\ \hline \end{array} \qquad \begin{array}{r} 15 \\ \times 3 \\ \hline \end{array}$$

$3+3=6 \qquad 3+6=9$

6	9			

Pattern

Add the digits in each product together. What pattern do you see?

Do you think the pattern continues? Try it.

How might you find other patterns in multiplication?

Ready to Go!

Exploring Multiplication

How would you find the product of 3 × 40? What about 4 × 15? Use your place-value blocks to try this activity.

Getting Started

What You'll Need:
▶ place-value blocks

Use What You Know

To multiply, you can use counters to make an array.

3 × 6 = 18

Activity

• **Use your place-value blocks to multiply.**

Multiplying Tens

1. Use your place-value blocks. Show 1 row of 4 tens with tens blocks.

2. Show 2 more rows of 4 tens.
   a. How many rows of 4 tens do you have in all?
   b. How many tens do you have in all?
   c. How do you write 12 tens as a number?

3. To show the total, you can write a multiplication sentence.
   3 × 40 = 120

Multiplying Tens and Ones

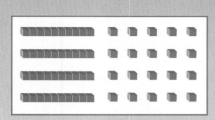

1. Use tens and ones to show 1 row of 15.
   a. How many ones are there?
   b. How many tens?

2. Show 3 more rows of 15.
   a. How many rows of 15 are there in all?
   b. How many ones are there?
   c. How many tens are there?
   d. How do you write 4 tens as a number?

3. What is the product of 4 × 15?
   Write the multiplication sentence.

   4 × 15 = 60
   a. How did you get your answer?

Show What You Know!

Use your blocks. Find the product.

1. 3 × 29	2. 3 × 17	3. 4 × 14	4. 2 × 25
5. 5 × 21	6. 8 × 11	7. 5 × 29	8. 4 × 34
9. 7 × 27	10. 2 × 43	11. 9 × 16	12. 6 × 12

Use your blocks. Write a multiplication sentence about the arrays.

13. 6 rows of 45   14. 5 rows of 31   15. 8 rows of 19

Complete the multiplication sentence. Use blocks.

16. 5 × 12 = ▨   17. 5 × 31 = ▨   18. 7 × 16 = ▨

19. **Critical Thinking** How is multiplying with an array of place-value blocks like multiplying with counters? How is it different?

20. **Write About It** What are three ways you can find the product of 5 × 95?

Mixed Review Write the quotient.

21. 24 ÷ 6   22. 15 ÷ 3   23. 3)‾21‾   24. 2)‾8‾   25. 9)‾36‾

Estimating Products

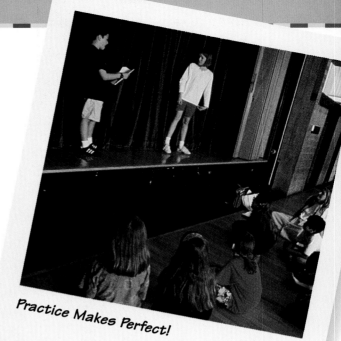

You are making programs for a play. There will be 3 shows. Up to 64 people can come to each show. You have made 175 programs. Will that be enough?

Estimate to find out.

Practice Makes Perfect!

Here's A Way! Estimate 3 × 64.

1 Use rounding to estimate. Round one of the factors.

3 × 64 ➡ 3 × 60

2 Multiply.

3 × 60 = 180

So, 3 × 64 is about 180.

3 Think about the actual product.

64 > 60   So, 3 × 64 > 3 × 60.

So, the actual product will be greater than 180. More than 180 people can come to the shows. You do not have enough programs.

Talk About It! How do you know that 3 × 64 is greater than 180?

Other Examples Estimate 5 × $4.65.

Front-end estimation: 5 × $4 = $20

Rounding: 5 × $5 = $25

The product of 5 × $4.65 is between $20 and $25.

Estimate the product.

1. 3 × 67
2. 4 × 62
3. 7 × 82
4. 5 × $7.15
5. 9 × $5.43
6. 5 × 34
7. 6 × 273
8. 6 × 216

Estimate. Write < or > to make the number sentence true. Show your work.

9. 3 × 49 ● 4 × 32
10. 6 × 379 ● 5 × 514
11. 2 × 5079 ● 3 × 2895
12. 3 × 124 ● 2 × 225

13. **Critical Thinking** You know that one quarter is 25¢. Now estimate 2 × 23¢, 3 × 24¢, and 4 × 26¢. Explain how thinking about a quarter can help you estimate.

Work It Out!

Estimate the product.

14. 3 × 241
15. 6 × 83
16. 8 × 293
17. 9 × 63

Estimate. Write < or > to complete the number sentence.

18. 6 × 30 ● 3 × 50
19. 4 × 59 ● 8 × 24
20. 9 × 19 ● 8 × 21
21. 4 × 12 ● 2 × 29

22. **Critical Thinking** Explain your answer to exercise 21.

Problem Solving Using Data

Estimate to solve the problem. Show how you estimated.

23. Which costs more, 7 pairs of shoes or 5 pirate shirts?

24. Your school play has 8 pirates. Will $200 be enough to buy each actor a pirate mask, a pirate hat, and a scarf?

Costumes

Item	Cost
Pirate Mask	$4
Pirate Hat	$7
Shoes	$28
Scarf	$13
Pirate Shirt	$36

More Practice Set 11.2, p. 474

Problem Solving: Strategy

Problem Solving
Work a Simpler Problem

Architect Frank Lloyd Wright designed this window for a ceiling. Each wide section has 82 pieces of glass. How many pieces of glass would replace 3 wide sections?

Here's A Way! Use Work a Simpler Problem.

1 **Understand**

- How many pieces are in each wide section?

- How many sections do you need to replace?

2 **Plan**

- Use a simpler problem to solve this problem.

3 **Try It**

- Choose numbers that are easy to work with.

- What if there were 4 pieces in each section? Would there be 3 × 4 pieces altogether?

4 **Look Back**

- You would need 3 × 82, or 246, pieces of glass. How did the simpler problem help you to solve this problem?

Pieces in 1 section	Pieces in 3 sections
4	3 × 4
82	

Use Work a Simpler Problem to solve the problem.

1. You buy 3 cans of soup for 45¢ each and 7 boxes of macaroni and cheese for 39¢ each. You pay the clerk $5.00. How much change should you receive?

2. **Critical Thinking** How did simpler numbers help you make a plan for solving the problem?

Work It Out!

Use Work a Simpler Problem or any strategy to solve.

3. A school is holding a walkathon. People will pay $1.00 for every lap walked. There are 53 walkers. If each one walks 8 laps, will students reach their goal of $400?

4. The school bought 2 computer programs, 5 packs of disks, 2 mice, 3 mouse pads, and 2 keyboards. How much of the $400 is left?

Item	Price
Keyboard	$49.00
Program	$89.00
Disk 10 pack	$5.00
Mouse	$24.00
Mouse pad	$12.00

5. A fruitcake recipe needs 6 c dried fruit and nuts. You have $1\frac{1}{4}$ c cherries, $1\frac{1}{4}$ c apricots, $\frac{1}{2}$ c raisins, and $\frac{1}{2}$ c pecans. Do you have enough for the recipe? If not, how much more do you need?

6. Exactly half of the people at a party wore red. The other 87 wore different colors. How many people were at the party?

7. A straight fence will have posts 6 ft apart. If 31 posts are used, how long will the fence be?

Share Your Thinking

8. When did you decide to use a simpler problem?

9. Does everyone have to use the same simpler problem? Explain.

LESSON 4

Multiplying with an Array

Suppose you have 6 rolls of film. You can take 12 pictures with each roll. If you use all 6 rolls, how many pictures will you take?

You can use an array or an array diagram to find out.

Here's A Way! Find 6 × 12.

1 Multiply the ones.

$$\begin{array}{r} 12 \\ \times\ 6 \\ \hline 12 \end{array}$$ 6 × 2

2 Multiply the tens.

$$\begin{array}{r} 12 \\ \times\ 6 \\ \hline 12 \\ 60 \end{array}$$ 6 × 10

3 Add to find the product.

$$\begin{array}{r} 12 \\ \times\ 6 \\ \hline 12 \\ 60 \\ \hline 72 \end{array}$$

4 Explain what the answer means.

You will take 72 pictures.

Talk About It! How does putting the blocks into a ones and tens array help you find 6 × 12?

Use the array to answer the question.

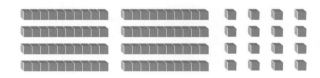

1. Write a multiplication sentence for the array of blocks.

2. **Estimation** Is the product less than 100? How can you tell?

3. Draw a diagram of the array of blocks. Find the product.

Find the product. Use blocks or draw a diagram.

4. 3 × 16   5. 5 × 25   6. 9 × 13   7. 3 × 50   8. 4 × 25

9. **Critical Thinking** Do you need to use an array to find all of the products in exercises 4–8? Why or why not?

10. **Create Your Own** Write a multiplication problem for a friend to solve.

Find the product.

11.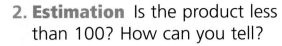

12.
```
        20        6
   ┌─────────┬───────┐
 3 │         │       │
   └─────────┴───────┘
```

Find the product. Use a diagram, blocks, or mental math.

13. 3 × 19   14. 6 × 50   15. 7 × 12   16. 8 × 24

17. 6 × 20   18. 5 × 23   19. 8 × 10   20. 4 × 30

21. **Mental Math** In exercises 13–20, which products did you find by using mental math? Explain how you found them.

22. **Problem Solving** You used 4 rolls of film. Two rolls had 36 pictures each. The rest had 24 pictures each. How many pictures did you take?

Mixed Review

Compare the two amounts. Write >, <, or =.

23. 2 c ● 1 qt   24. 2 ft ● 18 in.   25. 985 m ● 1 km   26. 6 pt ● 3 qt

More Practice Set 11.4, p. 474

Multiplying 2-Digit Numbers

You have 3 checkerboards. You need 24 checkers to go with each board. How many checkers do you need to get?

You can multiply to find out. Estimate first to help you check your answer.

Here's A Way! Find 3 × 24.

1 Estimate. Round one of the factors and multiply.

$3 \times 24 \implies 3 \times 20$

$3 \times 20 = 60$

You need about 60 checkers.

2 Multiply the ones. Regroup the 12 ones as 1 ten and 2 ones.

$$\begin{array}{r} \overset{1}{2}4 \\ \times\ \ 3 \\ \hline 2 \end{array}$$

3 × 4 ones = 12 ones

3 Multiply the tens.

$$\begin{array}{r} \overset{1}{2}4 \\ \times\ \ 3 \\ \hline 2 \end{array}$$

3 × 2 tens = 6 tens

4 Add the regrouped ten. Write the total number of tens.

$$\begin{array}{r} \overset{1}{2}4 \\ \times\ \ 3 \\ \hline 72 \end{array}$$

6 tens + 1 ten = 7 tens

You need to get 72 checkers.

Talk About It! Why is a *1* written above the tens column?

Show What You Know!

Find the product.

1. 34
   × 3

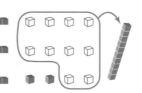

2. 4 × 12   3. 6 × 40   4. 2 × 35   5. 6 × 28   6. 3 × 42

7. **Critical Thinking** What method would you use to find 9 × 99? Explain.

Work It Out!

Multiply. Use any method you like.

8. 8 × 26   9. 7 × 39   10. 5 × 20   11. 6 × 17   12. 4 × 29

13. 45
    × 7

14. 16
    × 6

15. 84
    × 4

16. 39
    × 5

17. 25
    × 6

18. 25
    × 3

19. 25
    × 9

20. 34
    × 2

21. 44
    × 3

22. 34
    × 4

23. **Patterns** How can you use 3 × 15 and 6 × 15 to help you find 9 × 15?

24. **Algebraic Reasoning** Copy and complete the table.

Checkerboards	1	2	?	?	5	6	?	8
Checkers	24	48	72	?	?	?	168	?

25. **Problem Solving** A checkerboard is 8 squares by 8 squares. When all 24 checkers are on the board, are more than half the squares covered? Explain.

More Practice Set 11.5, p. 475

Math Journal

Describe three ways to find 5 × 35.

LESSON 6

Problem Solving
Choose a Computation Method

A Ranger at Work

Choose a Computation Method

Ask Yourself:

Do I need an exact answer or an estimate?

Should I use a model, paper and pencil, mental math, or a calculator?

What operation should I use?

Forest rangers keep track of plants and animals that live near them. You could keep track where you live. How could you find out how many fish live in a lake?

You Decide

- Could you count all the fish? Explain.

- Must you have an exact number, or could you use an estimate? Explain your decision.

Work It Out!

Decide whether to estimate or find an exact answer. Explain.

1. You are making rice pudding from a recipe. You need to know how much sugar to add.

2. You want to buy a package of stickers and a drink. The stickers cost $1.98 and the drink costs $.75. Is $5.00 enough money?

3. You are inviting friends to your birthday party. You want to know how many invitations you will need.

4. **Create Your Own** Write a problem for a friend to solve by estimating or finding an exact answer.

Share Your Thinking

5. How do you know when to estimate?

Midchapter Review
for Pages 378–390

for Pages 378–390

Problem Solving

Use any strategy to solve the problem. Show your work. (page 384)

1. Suppose you want to buy 6 colored markers that cost 79¢ each and 2 black markers that cost 98¢ each. You have $4.00. About how much more do you need to buy the markers?

2. Some students from your school are going to the art museum. You fill 3 buses and half of another bus. There are 46 seats on each bus. How many people from your school are going on the trip?

Concepts

Write a multiplication sentence for the array. (page 380)

3.

4.

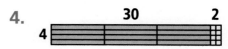

Find the product. You may use arrays to help. (page 380)

5. 8 groups of 24

6. 19 × 3

Estimate. Write > or < to complete the number sentence. (page 382)

7. 21 × 3 ● 37 × 2

8. 8 × 50 ● 70 × 4

9. 9 × 31 ● 42 × 8

10. 69 × 4 ● 51 × 5

Skills

Find the product. (page 388)

11. 70 × 9   12. 8 × 13   13. 54 × 3   14. 5 × 99   15. 32 × 2

16. 76   17. 51   18. 69   19. 28   20. 17
   × 6   × 8   × 4   × 3   × 2

Math *World*

Learn about different kinds of multiplication problems, dollars, and calculators.

Get Your Money's Worth

Barbados (bahr BAY dohz) is an island in the Caribbean Sea. Barbados has its own money, but many stores, hotels, and restaurants also accept U.S. money. U.S. dollars are worth about twice as much as Barbados dollars. Suppose a hat costs $6.00 in Barbados money. You have $3.65 in U.S. money. Will this be enough to buy the hat? (Hint: How can you estimate 2 × $3.65?)

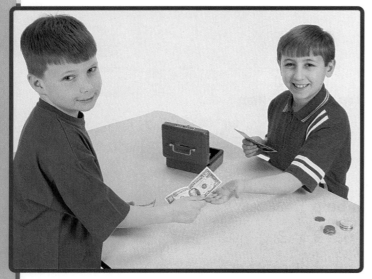

Writing Multiplication

Mathematics is a language that people all over the world can read and understand. Students in different parts of the world do not always write math problems exactly the same way. For example, someone who goes to school in Iran might write a multiplication problem with the multiplication sign to the right of the top number.

$$214 \times$$
$$3$$

Try This! NAPIER'S BONES

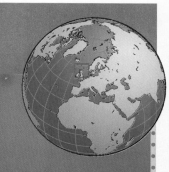

About 400 years ago, John Napier of Scotland showed how to use a set of rods, or bones, to solve multiplication problems. Follow these steps to make your own set of Napier's bones to multiply 12 × 4.

1 Draw a square and divide it in half. Write 1 and 2 across the top. Write 4 on the right side.

2 Divide each small square in half by drawing a line from the top right corner to the bottom left corner.

3 Multiply the 2 by the 4. Write the ones in the bottom triangle and the tens in the top triangle. Repeat for the 1 and 4.

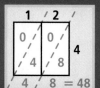

4 To find the product of 12 × 4, add the blue numbers along the dotted lines. The number of ones is 8. The number of tens is 4. So, 12 × 4 = 48.

Try: 13 × 3

Respond

Work with a partner . . .

to write some multiplication problems like students in Iran.

Internet:
Houghton Mifflin Education Place
Explore the Math Center at
http://www.eduplace.com

LESSON 7

Multiplying 3-Digit Numbers

Use What You Know

You know that
1 week = 7 days.

An elephant at a zoo eats 225 lb of hay every day. How much hay does the elephant eat in 1 week?

You can multiply 225 by 7 to find out.

Here's A Way! Find 7 × 225.

1 Estimate by rounding to the nearest hundred.
Since 7 × 200 = 1400, the elephant eats about 1400 lb.

2 Multiply the ones.

Regroup if needed.

$$\begin{array}{r} \overset{3}{2}\overset{}{2}5 \\ \times \quad 7 \\ \hline 5 \end{array}$$

7 × 5 ones = 35 ones

35 ones = 3 tens, 5 ones

3 Multiply the tens.

Add the regrouped tens.

Regroup the tens if needed.

$$\begin{array}{r} \overset{1\,3}{2}25 \\ \times \quad 7 \\ \hline 75 \end{array}$$

7 × 2 tens = 14 tens

14 tens + 3 tens = 17 tens

17 tens = 1 hundred, 7 tens

4 Multiply the hundreds.

Add the regrouped hundred.

Regroup the hundreds if needed.

$$\begin{array}{r} \overset{1\,3}{2}25 \\ \times \quad 7 \\ \hline 1575 \end{array}$$

7 × 2 hundreds = 14 hundreds

14 hundreds + 1 hundred
15 hundreds
1 thousand, 5 hundreds

The elephant eats 1575 lb of hay in 1 week.

Talk About It! Compare the answer to your estimate.

Find the product. Use mental math if you can.

1. 434
    × 4

2. 111
    × 5

3. 868
    × 2

4. 256
    × 6

5. 222
    × 5

6. **Critical Thinking** When do you need to regroup hundreds when you multiply?

Work It Out!

Estimate first. Then find the product.

7. 419
    × 2

8. 423
    × 2

9. 263
    × 6

10. 363
     × 3

11. 421
     × 4

12. 129
     × 6

13. 324
     × 5

14. 193
     × 4

15. 100
     × 7

16. 221
     × 2

17. 518
     × 4

18. 197
     × 2

19. 132
     × 5

20. 513
     × 2

21. 345
     × 3

Find the missing digit. Show your work.

22. 134
     × 2
     ────
     26■

23. 154
     × 3
     ────
     ■62

24. 235
     × 2
     ────
     47■

25. 148
     × 6
     ────
     8■8

26. 224
     × 8
     ────
     ■792

Problem Solving

27. An elephant eats 24 lb of grain, 15 lb of fruit and vegetables, and 225 lb of hay each day. How many days will it take the elephant to eat 1 ton of food? (Hint: 1 ton = 2000 lb)

28. **Calculator** Each of the 7 keepers at a zoo needs hay to feed animals. One gets 450 lb. The others get 900 lb each. How much hay do the 7 keepers get?

29. A zoo gets 8 bales of hay. Each bale weighs 125 lb. Will the hay feed an elephant for more than 1 week? Explain.

More Practice Set 11.7, p. 475

Problem Solving
Using Work a Simpler Problem and Other Strategies

The Special Olympics World Games bring together athletes with disabilities from all over the world. They compete in 22 different events, including soccer, swimming, and track and field.

Problem Solving Process
- ✓ Understand
- ✓ Plan
- ✓ Try It
- ✓ Look Back

Choose a Strategy You Have Learned
- ✓ Act It Out
- ✓ Look for a Pattern
- ✓ Guess and Check
- ✓ Draw a Picture
- ✓ Make a Table
- ✓ Work Backward
- ✓ Make a List
- ✓ Work a Simpler Problem

At the 1995 World Games, 7 teams from Central and South America played with 11 players on the field for each team. Two teams had 15 players each (including substitutes). The rest had 14 players. How many soccer players were there?

- What problem needs to be solved?

- How many teams are there?

- Can you make a simpler problem to help you solve the larger problem?

- What operations would you use to solve the simpler problem?

- Explain a strategy you can use to solve the problem. Then, solve it.

Work It Out!

Use any strategy to solve the problem. Show your work.

1. Special Olympics World Games are held every two years. They alternate between Summer and Winter Sports. World Games for Summer Sports took place in 1995 and for Winter Sports in 1997. Will there be a World Games in the year you turn 13? Explain.

2. Will the Special Olympics World Games ever happen in an even year? Explain.

3. In Unified Sports, people with and without disabilities compete on the same teams. In Unified soccer, 5 people can play on a team at one time. In 1995, 210 people played Unified soccer. Thirty of those were extra players. How many teams of 5 were there?

4. There were 40 athletes from Jamaica at the 1995 World Games. Suppose half won 1 gold medal each. If half of the rest won 1 silver medal each and the others won 2 bronze medals each, how many medals did the team win?

Track and Field Athletes, 1995

Place	Number of Athletes
Africa	145
Asia	183
Europe	311
Central and South America	259
North America	469

5. One track and field event is the 4 × 100 relay. In it, 4 athletes on a team each run 100 yards. If 8 teams compete, how long is the race?

6. **Estimation** Use the chart. Were there more than 1000 track and field athletes at the World Games in 1995? Explain.

7. **Create Your Own** Make up a problem about a Special Olympics sport. Ask a classmate to solve your problem.

Share Your Thinking

8. What strategy did you use for problem 6? Explain why.

Multiplying with Zeros

This picture from the 1300s shows people carrying silk across Asia. One roll of silk was 380 grams. How heavy were 7 rolls?

You can multiply to find out.

Here's A Way! Find 7 × 380.

1 Estimate by rounding to the nearest hundred.

$$380 \longrightarrow 400$$

$$7 \times 400 = 2800$$

The rolls were about 2800 g.

2 Multiply the ones. Do you need to regroup?

$$\begin{array}{r} 380 \\ \times\quad 7 \\ \hline 0 \end{array}$$

3 Multiply the tens. Do you need to regroup?

$$\begin{array}{r} {\overset{5}{}} \\ 380 \\ \times\quad 7 \\ \hline 60 \end{array}$$

4 Multiply the hundreds. Add the regrouped hundreds. Regroup.

$$\begin{array}{r} {\overset{5}{}} \\ 380 \\ \times\quad 7 \\ \hline 2660 \end{array}$$

The rolls were 2660 g.

Talk About It! Why is it important to record the zero?

Other Examples

There are 0 tens in 309. Why are there 2 tens in the product?

$$\begin{array}{r} {\overset{2}{}} \\ 309 \\ \times\quad 3 \\ \hline 927 \end{array}$$

1. **Estimation** How can estimating the product first help you multiply greater numbers with zeros?

Estimate. Then find the product.

2.	140	3.	508	4.	209	5.	610	6.	290
	× 7		× 4		× 6		× 3		× 5

7. **Critical Thinking** If a 0 is in the ones place of a number, what will be in the ones place of the product? Explain.

Work It Out!

Estimate. Then find the product. Compare the estimate to the product.

8.	609	9.	302	10.	230	11.	209	12.	797
	× 4		× 1		× 7		× 2		× 9

13.	545	14.	201	15.	410	16.	680	17.	924
	× 2		× 5		× 3		× 8		× 6

18.	729	19.	609	20.	107	21.	209	22.	330
	× 3		× 2		× 6		× 6		× 9

Estimate the product. Write *a*, *b*, or *c*.

23. 5 × 102	24. 4 × 510	25. 2 × 190	26. 2 × 509
a. 50	a. 20	a. 40	a. 10
b. 500	b. 200	b. 400	b. 100
c. 5000	c. 2000	c. 4000	c. 1000

27. **Number Sense** Is the product of 3 × 409 closer to 1100 or to 1300? Explain.

28. **Problem Solving** Marco Polo was an Italian explorer who visited China. He could buy 1 pair of geese and 2 pairs of ducks for 1 piece of silver. How many pairs of ducks and geese could he buy for 150 pieces of silver?

Multiplying Money

Getting Started

What You'll Need:
▶ calculator

How much would 6 boxes of crayons cost?

You can estimate to get an idea of what the amount would be. You can also use a calculator to find the exact cost.

Artist Supplies

Crayons $2.25

Paint Set $8.99

Here's A Way! Find 6 × $2.25.

1 Round to the nearest dollar to estimate.

$2.25 ➡ $2.00

6 × $2.00 = $12.00

You would need about $12.00.

2 Press these keys: `6` `×` `2` `.` `2` `5` `=`

Remember, a calculator does not have a $ key.

3 Write the product shown on the calculator as dollars and cents.

The crayons would cost exactly $13.50. `13.5`

Talk About It! How can you use estimation to find out if you pressed the correct keys on the calculator?

Other Examples

Compare the products. How is the calculator display like the written amount? How is it different?

a. $.75
    ×   3 `2.25`
    ─────
    $2.25

b. $8.90
    ×   3 `26.7`
    ─────
    $26.70

Show What You Know!

 Write an estimate. Then use a calculator to find the product.

1. $1.27	2. $2.00	3. $.80	4. $1.70	5. $3.12
× 3	× 5	× 9	× 3	× 4

6. 7 × $8.33   7. 5 × $8.65   8. 9 × $5.96   9. 4 × $6.28

10. **Critical Thinking** Describe how you estimated the product in exercises 8 and 9.

Work It Out!

 Estimate the product. Record your estimate. Then use a calculator to find the product.

11. $2.75	12. $.25	13. $3.68	14. $2.50	15. $1.19
× 3	× 8	× 3	× 8	× 5

16. 4 × $8.90   17. 7 × $1.00   18. 6 × $3.01   19. 5 × $5.99

Read the calculator display. Write the product.

20. 4 × $6.51   `26.04`   21. 2 × $8.90   `17.8`

Problem Solving   Using Data

Use the prices shown on page 400.

22. Suppose you have $7.00. Can you buy 3 boxes of crayons? How do you know?

23. Which costs more, 1 paint set or 4 boxes of crayons? Explain.

Mixed Review

Write the decimal.

24.

25. fifty hundredths   26. $3\frac{2}{10}$

Write < or >.

27. 12.5 ● 21.2   28. 5.0 ● 4.9   29. 1.2 ● 1.9   30. 0.3 ● 0.1

More Practice Set 11.10, p. 476

Problem Solving
Using Strategies

LESSON 11

You can read more about weather in the pages of *Weatherwise*.

The Museum of American Weather in Haverhill, New Hampshire, has exhibits about all kinds of weather. One exhibit shows the Tri-State Tornado that tore through Missouri, Illinois, and Indiana in 1925.

Problem Solving Process
✓ Understand
✓ Plan
✓ Try It
✓ Look Back

Choose a Strategy You Have Learned
✓ Act It Out
✓ Look for a Pattern
✓ Guess and Check
✓ Draw a Picture
✓ Make a Table
✓ Work Backward
✓ Make a List
✓ Work a Simpler Problem

The Tri-State Tornado lasted $3\frac{1}{2}$ hours. If the tornado traveled about 1 mile every minute, about how far did it travel?

• What problem do you need to solve?

• How many minutes are in 1 hour?

• How far would the tornado travel in 1 hour?

• Explain a strategy you could use to solve the problem. Then solve it.

Work It Out!

Use any strategy to solve the problem. Show your work.

1. The chart shows the high temperature for 6 cities in January and July. Which city's temperature changes the most between January and July?

2. St. Louis, Missouri, has a higher July temperature than Honolulu and a lower January temperature than Washington. Does the temperature change more in St. Louis than in Washington? Explain.

High Temperatures		
City	In Jan.	In July
Bismarck	20°F	84°F
Chicago	29°F	84°F
Honolulu	80°F	88°F
Miami	75°F	89°F
Detroit	30°F	83°F
Washington D.C.	42°F	89°F

3. The Great New England Hurricane of 1938 had winds that blew 100 miles in an hour. It hit Connecticut at 4:10 P.M. one day and ended the same day at 4:55 P.M. How long did it last?

4. Winds in Category 1 hurricanes blow between 74 and 95 miles in an hour. Winds in Category 3 hurricanes blow between 111 and 130 miles in an hour. How fast do the winds in Category 2 hurricanes blow?

5. You can tell how far away lightning is. Count the seconds between the lightning and the thunder. Lightning is 1 mile away for every 5 seconds. If you count 15 seconds, how far away is the lightning?

6. One inch of rain has as much water as 10 inches of snow. Which has more water, 2 feet of snow or 3 inches of rain?

Share Your Thinking

7. Compare your solution to problem 6 to a partner's. Did you use the same strategy?

8. Explain how you could use a different strategy to solve problem 6.

Chapter 11 Test

for Pages 378–403

Problem Solving

Use any strategy to solve. Show your work. (pages 384, 396)

1. Your class puts on a play. You want to raise a total of $500.00 You sell 96 tickets the first night and 89 tickets the second night. Tickets are $2.00 each. How much more money does your class need?

2. You and 3 friends play each other in a one-on-one basketball tournament. Each person plays one game with every other person. How many games take place?

Concepts

Find the product. Use an array if you wish. (page 380)

3. 4 × 33   4. 5 × 19   5. 6 groups of 28

6. How could you use mental math to find 2 × 9 × 5?

Estimate. Write > or < to make the number sentence true.
(page 382)

7. 32 × 6 ● 49 × 2   8. 6 × 61 ● 5 × 78

9. 412 × 4 ● 3 × 595   10. 188 × 2 ● 3 × 167

Find the product. Circle the product if you used mental math.
(pages 388, 394)

11. 41	12. 637	13. 80	14. 70	15. 294
× 4	× 3	× 2	× 9	× 2

Decide which statement is true. Write *a*, *b*, *c*, or *d*. (page 400)

16. You have $20. Magazines cost $3.85.
    a. You have enough to buy 6 magazines.
    b. You have enough to buy 5 magazines.
    c. You need more money to buy 4 magazines.
    d. You don't have enough money to buy 5 magazines.

17. You have $20. Large pizzas cost $9.05.
    a. You have enough money for 3 large pizzas.
    b. You have enough money for 4 large pizzas.
    c. You don't have enough money for more than 1 pizza.
    d. You have enough to buy 2 large pizzas.

18. You have $20. Ice cream cones cost $1.98.
    a. You can buy ice cream cones for 12 friends.
    b. You can buy ice cream cones for 17 friends.
    c. You need more money to buy ice cream for 12 friends.
    d. You will get change if you buy cones for 12 friends.

Find the product. (pages 388, 394, 400)

19. 7×62 20. 86×8 21. 112×5 22. 341×4

23. $3 \times \$7.00$ 24. 6×19 25. 509×3 26. $4 \times \$2.99$

Performance Task

(page 380)

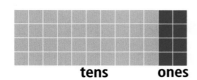

tens   ones

- Write a number sentence for the array.

- Explain the steps used in multiplying with an array.

Keep In Mind . . .

Your work will be evaluated on the following:

☑ Clearly written explanation

☑ Easy-to-follow steps

☑ True number sentence

☑ Number sentence that relates to the array

Cumulative Review

Subtracting with Zeros (Chapter 3)
Subtract 372 from 602.

Here's A Way!

Subtract the ones.
To subtract the tens, regroup the hundreds.
Subtract the hundreds.

$$\begin{array}{r} \overset{510}{6\cancel{0}2} \\ -\ 372 \\ \hline 230 \end{array}$$

Find the difference.

1. $\begin{array}{r} 109 \\ -\ 36 \\ \hline \end{array}$
2. $\begin{array}{r} 213 \\ -\ 85 \\ \hline \end{array}$
3. $\begin{array}{r} 484 \\ -\ 296 \\ \hline \end{array}$

4. $\begin{array}{r} \$8.02 \\ -\ 3.48 \\ \hline \end{array}$
5. $\begin{array}{r} \$6.13 \\ -\ 4.75 \\ \hline \end{array}$
6. $\begin{array}{r} \$5.27 \\ -\ 1.89 \\ \hline \end{array}$

7. How is subtracting money different from subtracting whole numbers? Explain.

Patterns in Basic Facts (Chapter 5)
Skip-count to find each answer.
3×5 and $20 \div 5$

Here's A Way!

Skip-count by fives 3 times:
5, 10, 15; 3 × 5 = 15
Skip-count by fives to 20:
5, 10, 15, 20
You said 4 numbers.
20 ÷ 5 = 4

Find the answer.

8. 4×3 9. 5×3

10. 6×3 11. $12 \div 3$

12. $15 \div 3$ 13. $18 \div 3$

14. What number do you skip-count by in all of exercises 8–13?

Fact Families (Chapter 6)
Solve $8 \times \blacksquare = 24$.

Here's A Way!

Use a fact family.
    $24 \div 3 = 8$
    $24 \div 8 = 3$
      $3 \times 8 = 24$
So, $8 \times 3 = 24$.

Find the missing factor.

15. $\blacksquare \times 6 = 18$ 16. $18 \div 3 = \blacksquare$

17. $7 \times \blacksquare = 21$ 18. $21 \div 3 = \blacksquare$

19. $5 \times \blacksquare = 30$ 20. $30 \div 6 = \blacksquare$

21. Subtraction is the inverse of addition. What is the inverse of multiplication?

Measurement (Chapter 9)

How many ounces are in 2 lb?

Here's A Way!

Rename pounds as ounces.

Customary Measures	Metric Measures
1 lb = 16 oz	1 kg = 100 g
1 ft = 12 in.	1 dm = 10 cm
1 yd = 3 ft	1 m = 100 cm

2 lb = 16 oz + 16 oz = 32 oz

Complete. Use the data on the charts.

22. 3 lb = ■ oz   23. ■ lb = 64 oz

24. 2 kg = ■ g   25. 4000 g = ■ kg

26. 5 m = ■ cm   27. 7 dm = ■ cm

28. Would it make sense to measure your daily trip to school in centimeters? Why or why not?

Decimals (Chapter 10)

What fraction can you write for 0.6?

Here's A Way!

$\frac{6}{10}$ or 0.6 or six tenths

Another way to write 0.6 is $\frac{6}{10}$.

Use models to write the decimal form of the fraction.

29. $\frac{1}{10}$ = ■   30. $\frac{7}{10}$ = ■   31. $\frac{9}{10}$ = ■

32. $\frac{4}{10}$ = ■   33. $\frac{5}{10}$ = ■   34. $\frac{3}{10}$ = ■

35. Draw a picture to show $\frac{2}{10}$. Label it three ways.

Problem Solving

Problem Solving Process
- ✓ Understand
- ✓ Plan
- ✓ Try It
- ✓ Look Back

Choose a Strategy You Have Learned
- ✓ Act It Out
- ✓ Look for a Pattern
- ✓ Guess and Check
- ✓ Draw a Picture
- ✓ Make a Table
- ✓ Work Backward
- ✓ Make a List
- ✓ Work a Simpler Problem

Solve the problem. Show your work.

36. Two whole numbers add up to 51. One number directly follows the other. What are they?

37. Suppose you have 4 pairs of shoes and 1 pair of boots. The shoes are each 3 inches wide. The boots are each 4 inches wide. A shoe rack is 24 inches across. Can you fit all the shoes and the boots side by side across the rack? Explain.

Craft Festival!

Social Studies Connection   **With Your Group**

Your group is going to plan a craft fair to sell salt-dough ornaments to raise money for your school. First figure out how many ornaments you'll need. Then figure out how long it will take to make them.

1

Plan It

- Read the recipe on the right. Decide how many ornaments your group will make for the fair. You can make the recipe more than once.
- List all the ingredients that you need to make the ornaments.

Salt Dough for about 30 5-inch ornaments

2 c all purpose flour
1 c salt
1/2 teaspoon powdered alum
3/4 c water

Mix all ingredients together with hands. Roll or mold by hand. Shape into ornaments. If you wish to hang them up, use a plastic straw to make a hole at the top. Bake ornaments in 250° oven for 2 hours. Cool on rack. Paint with poster paints. Note: It takes about 30 minutes to mix the dough. Each ornament takes 15–20 minutes to shape.

2

Put it Together

- Figure out how many times you will need to make the recipe in order to make enough dough. How much of each ingredient will you need?
- Use a calculator to find out how long it will take to prepare and bake the ornaments.

3

Wrap it up

- Make a chart showing how much time the cooking will take. Tell the mixing time, shaping time, and baking time. Use hours and minutes.
- Use your chart to plan how you could share the work.

4

Discuss Your Results

- Did you meet all of the goals in Keep In Mind?
- How did different groups share the work?

Internet

> Visit the **Math Center** at **Houghton Mifflin Education Place.** http://www.eduplace.com

Math Power

Use What You Know

- division means separating into equal sets

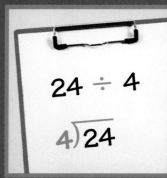

$$24 \div 4$$

$$4\overline{)24}$$

- how to write a division sentence

- divide
- divisor
- dividend
- quotient

- the vocabulary

Dividing By 1-Digit Numbers

Try This!

Use connecting cubes to show the number of students in each team.

What You'll Need

paper, pencil, connecting cubes

1

Suppose there are 24 students. How many teams of 4 can they make? Use your cubes to find out.

2

Explain what happens when you try to make teams of 5 and 7. What can you do so everyone gets to play?

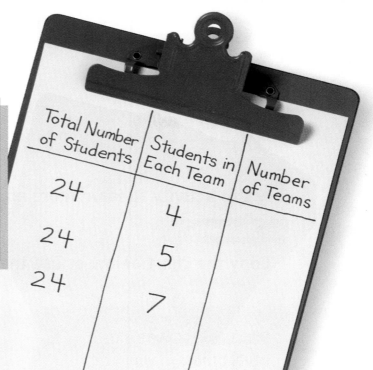

Total Number of Students	Students in Each Team	Number of Teams
24	4	
24	5	
24	7	

3

What other equal teams can you make with 24 students?

Suppose there are 35 students. How many teams of 6 can you make?

Can you always make equal teams? How do you know?

Ready to Go!

Cooperative Learning
Checklist

☐ Work alone.
☑ Work with a partner.
☑ Work with a group.

LESSON 1

Exploring Division

What You'll Need:
▶ 20 counters
▶ recording sheet

Vocabulary:
remainder
Glossary, p. 480

Try this activity to learn more about division.

Activity

• **Copy the chart below or use the recording sheet.**

1 Divide 20 counters into 3 equal groups. If you have counters left over, push them aside. The number left over in division is called the **remainder**.

2 How many counters are in each group? How many are left over? Record the results. Write the division that shows what you did.

6R2
3)20

R means Remainder

3 Push the counters together again. Repeat steps 1 and 2 six more times. Divide the 20 counters into 4, 5, 6, 7, 8, and 9 groups. Record the results.

Number of Counters	Number of Groups	Number in Each Group	Number of Leftovers	Division
20	3	6	2	6 R2 3)20

Show What You Know!

1. Which numbers divided 20 with no remainder?

2. Which numbers divided 20 with a remainder?

Use your counters to finish dividing. How many are in each group? How many are left over? Record what you do.

3.
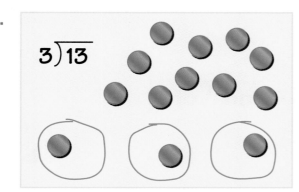

4.
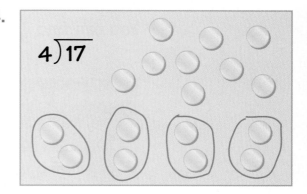

5.
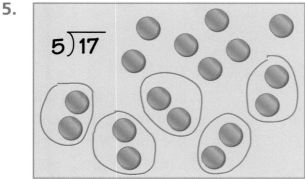

6.
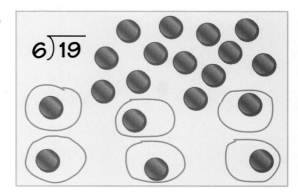

Solve. Use your counters.

7. 2)‾1‾0‾   8. 3)‾1‾0‾   9. 4)‾1‾0‾   10. 5)‾1‾0‾   11. 6)‾1‾0‾

12. 2)‾1‾5‾   13. 3)‾1‾5‾   14. 4)‾1‾5‾   15. 5)‾1‾5‾   16. 6)‾1‾5‾

17. 2)‾1‾8‾   18. 3)‾1‾8‾   19. 4)‾1‾8‾   20. 5)‾1‾8‾   21. 6)‾1‾8‾

22. **Critical Thinking** How can you check your answer to exercise 19 by multiplying and adding?

23. **Create Your Own** Write three division exercises with no remainder. Write three division exercises that have a remainder. Mix up the order. Trade papers with a classmate. Find the answers.

Fractional Parts of a Set

Suppose you have 6 rubber stamps. You are going to give $\frac{1}{3}$ of them to your friend. How many stamps is that?

You can find $\frac{1}{3}$ of 6.

Here's A Way! Find $\frac{1}{3}$ of 6.

1 Divide the stamps into 3 equal groups.

Each group is $\frac{1}{3}$ of 6.

2 Count the stamps in a group.

There are 2 stamps in a group.

3 You found that $\frac{1}{3}$ of 6 is 2. Write a division sentence that means the same thing.

$\frac{1}{3}$ of 6 is 2

$6 \div 3 = 2$

Talk About It! Explain why the picture in Step1 means $\frac{1}{3}$ of 6 and $6 \div 3$.

Other Example

$\frac{1}{4}$ is green

$\frac{1}{4}$ of 8 is 2

$8 \div 4 = 2$

Show What You Know!

Tell how many groups of marbles there are. What fraction is blue? Write the fraction. Then write the number of blue marbles.

1.

2.

3. **Critical Thinking** Explain why $\frac{1}{5}$ of the marbles in exercise 1 is a different amount than $\frac{1}{5}$ of the marbles in exercise 2.

Draw the picture. Shade one group. Write a fraction for the shaded group. Then write how many are in that group.

4. 6 circles in 3 equal groups

5. 10 circles in 2 equal groups

6. Write the division sentence that goes with each picture you drew in exercises 4 and 5.

Work It Out!

Tell how many groups of objects there are. What fraction is green? Write the fraction. Then write the number of green objects.

7.

8.

Draw the picture. Shade one group. Write a fraction for the shaded group. Then write how many are in that group.

9. 6 circles in 2 equal groups

10. 4 circles in 2 equal groups

11. 12 circles in 6 equal groups

12. 12 circles in 3 equal groups

13. Write the division sentence that goes with each picture you drew in exercises 9–12.

14. **Problem Solving** If the rubber stamps in the chart are stored in boxes with two like stamps in each box, how many boxes are needed? What fraction of the boxes is whale stamps?

My Rubber Stamps

Whale	🔨 🔨
Turtle	🔨 🔨 🔨 🔨
Frog	🔨 🔨

Key: 🔨 = 1 rubber stamp

More Practice Set 12.2, p. 476

Division with Remainders

Getting Started

What You'll Need:
▶ counters

Suppose you divide 35 by 4 with counters. You already know how to record the answer. Now find out how to record all the steps you do.

$$4\overline{)35}$$

Here's A Way! Find $4\overline{)35}$.

1. Divide the counters into 4 equal groups. Record the number of counters in each group.

$$\begin{array}{r} 8 \\ 4\overline{)35} \end{array}$$

2. Multiply to record the total number of counters in the 4 groups.

4×8

$$\begin{array}{r} 8 \\ 4\overline{)35} \\ 32 \end{array}$$

3. Subtract to find the remainder.

Remainder

$$\begin{array}{r} 8 \\ 4\overline{)35} \\ -32 \\ \hline 3 \end{array}$$

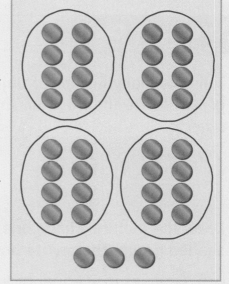

4. Record the remainder next to the quotient.

$$\begin{array}{r} 8\,R3 \\ 4\overline{)35} \\ -32 \\ \hline 3 \end{array}$$

Remainder

Talk About It! Look at the counters. How do they show what you did in Step 3?

Show What You Know!

Look at the counters. Record what was done.

1. 3)17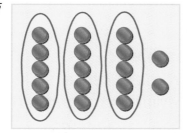

2. 5)23

Use counters to divide. Then record.

3. 5)18	4. 6)43	5. 4)39	6. 3)26	7. 2)13
8. 7)52	9. 8)49	10. 6)56	11. 9)60	12. 5)29

13. **Critical Thinking** If you divide a number by 5, can the remainder ever be 5 or greater? Explain.

14. **Critical Thinking** Sometimes division facts can help you know if a division problem has a remainder. Explain.

Work It Out!

Look at the counters. Record what was done.

15. 4)27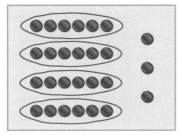

16. 6)32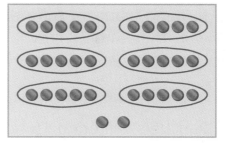

Use counters to divide. Then record.

17. 3)22	18. 5)44	19. 2)15	20. 7)52	21. 9)62
22. 6)49	23. 8)54	24. 4)38	25. 5)24	26. 7)65
27. 2)17	28. 9)59	29. 3)28	30. 6)41	31. 6)33
32. 8)61	33. 5)32	34. 4)19	35. 7)47	36. 3)29

37. Use counters to divide 45 by 7. Then explain to a friend how to record what you did.

More Practice Set 12.3, p. 475

Interpreting Remainders

Suppose you solve a division problem and there is a remainder. Does it make sense to use the remainder in your answer or to ignore it?

Here's A Way! Decide what to do with the remainder.

1 You can include the remainder in the answer.

There are 7 apples for 2 horses. Each horse gets an equal share. How many apples will each horse get?

$$2)\overline{7} \quad 3\ R1$$

Each horse gets 3 apples and $\frac{1}{2}$ of the leftover apple.

2 You can ignore the remainder.

Cowhands at the rodeo are forming teams of 6 for a tug of war. There are 28 cowhands. How many teams can they form?

$$6)\overline{28} \quad 4\ R4$$

They can form 4 teams. The 4 cowhands left over are not enough to form a team.

3 You can round the answer to the next whole number.

Ranchers will bring 16 horses to the rodeo in trailers. They put 3 horses in each trailer. How many trailers will they need?

$$3)\overline{16} \quad 5\ R1$$

They need 6 trailers. One of the trailers will not be full.

Talk About It!

Why did you round to the next whole number to tell how many trailers the ranchers needed?

Show What You Know!

Divide. Tell what you did with the remainder.

1. You want to buy rodeo souvenirs for your friends at home. You have $14.00. How many key chains can you buy?

2. **Critical Thinking** Why did you need to think about the remainder to solve the exercise?

$3.00

Work It Out!

Divide. Decide what to do with the remainder.

3. Clowns at the rodeo will dress up as cows. Each cow costume needs 1 clown for the front legs and 1 clown for the back legs. There are 17 clowns. Will they be able to make 9 cows?

4. Six people can sit at a picnic table. How many picnic tables do you need to seat 32 people? Explain.

5. Suppose there are 28 students in your class. Everyone will be working on a spring project. You form groups of 3. What can you do so no one is left out?

6. You want to frame 17 photographs. Four photos fit in each frame. How many frames do you need?

Use division. Write a story problem about things at the rodeo. Then solve.

7. 29 horses kept in 3 stables

8. 14 cowhands in teams of 4

9. 5 wagon rides, 26 passengers

10. 18 carrots, 4 ponies

More Practice Set 12.4, p. 477

Problem Solving
Is the Answer Reasonable?

Suppose you are inviting 13 friends to a party. The invitations come in packages of 5. How many packages should you buy?

You Decide

- Should you write a division problem to find the answer?

- What are the quotient and the remainder?

- If you buy 2 packages of invitations, how many people can you invite?

Work It Out!

Solve the problem. Explain what you did with the remainder.

1. You want to serve a small can of fruit punch to each of the 14 people at your party. The cans come in packs of 6. How many packs do you need?

2. You have 43 slices of bread. How many sandwiches can you make? Each sandwich has 2 slices of bread.

3. The principal is ordering a workbook for each of 61 third graders. The books come in packages of 8. How many packages must she order?

4. Your teacher puts a photo of each of her 37 students in an album. She puts 8 photos on a page. How many photos will be on the last page she uses?

Share Your Thinking

5. How did you decide what to do with the remainder in problem 4?

Midchapter Review

for Pages 410–420

for Pages 410–420

Problem Solving

Solve using any strategy. Show your work. (pages 414, 416)

1. You plan to buy 12 cans of food for your kitten.

   You want $\frac{1}{2}$ of the cans of catfood to be tuna flavor, $\frac{1}{4}$ of

   the cans to be chicken, and the rest, seafood. How many cans of each kind should you buy?

2. You had a box of 30 dog biscuits. Your brother gave the dog the same number of biscuits each day. After 2 weeks, 2 biscuits are left. How many biscuits did he give the dog each day?

Concepts

Use counters. Decide whether there will be a remainder. If there is a remainder, write it. (page 412)

3. 39 ÷ 6　　　4. 61 ÷ 8　　　5. 27 ÷ 3　　　6. 54 ÷ 9

Tell how many groups there are. Write a fraction for the blue group. Then write how many are in the blue group. (page 414)

7. 　　　8.

9.　　　10.

Skills

Write the quotient and the remainder, if there is one. Check your answer by multiplying, then adding. Show your work. (page 416)

11. 16 ÷ 3　　　12. 48 ÷ 6　　　13. 49 ÷ 6　　　14. 27 ÷ 4

15. 5)32　　　16. 8)68　　　17. 8)64　　　18. 2)13

Math World

Use division to think about sports, time, and thunderstorms. Then, divide a sheet of paper to make a paper windmill.

Sticking with Division

Canada's unofficial national sport is lacrosse (luh kraws). Native Americans made up the game more than 600 years ago. Today, lacrosse is played in schools and clubs throughout the world. Lacrosse games last 60 minutes. They are divided into four 15-minute periods. Think of some other sports. How are the games divided into time periods?

Lacrosse Hall of Fame Museum

Watch Out for Division

About 5000 years ago, the Sumerians divided the day into twelve 2-hour time periods. Today we divide each day into two 12-hour periods. A.M. and P.M. are used to name the two time periods. A.M. and P.M. come from Latin words meaning "before noon" and "after noon." Ships at sea divide the day into 6 time periods called *watches*. How long is each watch?

Lightning in Africa

Try This! PAPER WINDMILLS

Children in China buy paper windmills, or pinwheels, to celebrate the beginning of spring. Try making a paper windmill of your own.

1 Fold a square piece of paper in half to make a triangle. Fold again to make a smaller triangle.

2 Unfold the paper to show the square divided into fourths. Color in the triangles.

3 Punch a hole in the center with a pencil.

4 Cut along the folds, stopping about an inch away from the hole.

5 Make a hole in the left corner of each triangle. Fold these corners down to the middle hole.

6 Push the pin through all of the holes and into the pencil's eraser. Give your pinwheel a try!

Wonder About Thunder?

You can use division to estimate how far away a thunderstorm is. Look for a flash of lightning. Then count the seconds until you hear the thunder. Divide the number of seconds by 5. The quotient tells you about how many miles away the storm is.

Respond

Work with a partner . . .
to find out more about windmills.

 Internet: Houghton Mifflin Education Place Explore the Math Center at http://www.eduplace.com

Estimating Quotients

You and 3 classmates need 115 paper flowers for a spring art project. About how many flowers should each of you make? You can estimate 115 ÷ 4 to find out.

Here's A Way!	**Estimate 115 ÷ 4.**

1 Think of multiplication.

$$115 ÷ 4 = ■$$

⬇

$$4 × ■ = 115$$

2 Find out if the quotient will be less than or greater than 10.

$$4 × ■ = 115$$

$$4 × 10 = 40$$

$$40 < 115$$

The quotient will be greater than **10**. So, it has 2 digits.

3 Use multiples of 10 to get a closer estimate.

$$4 × 10 = 40$$

$$4 × 20 = 80$$

$$4 × 30 = 120$$

120 is close to 115, so the quotient is close to 30.

Each of you will make about 30 flowers.

Talk About It! How do you know that 30 is a close estimate?

Write the letter of the better estimate.

1. 97 ÷ 3
   a. 20
   b. 30

2. 371 ÷ 4
   a. 80
   b. 90

3. 288 ÷ 9
   a. 30
   b. 40

4. **Critical Thinking** For $4\overline{)83}$, will the answer be closer to 20 or to 30? Explain.

Work It Out!

Find a close estimate.

5. 84 ÷ 3

6. 255 ÷ 4

7. 96 ÷ 5

8. 626 ÷ 8

9. 169 ÷ 3

10. 51 ÷ 2

11. 425 ÷ 9

12. 198 ÷ 6

13. 331 ÷ 4

14. 230 ÷ 3

15. 27 ÷ 2

16. 521 ÷ 8

17. 126 ÷ 3

18. 84 ÷ 4

19. 262 ÷ 7

20. 416 ÷ 5

21. **Critical Thinking** For $2\overline{)63}$, will the answer be closer to 30 or to 40? Explain.

Algebraic Reasoning Copy the number sentence. Estimate and compare. Write > or <.

22. 73 ÷ 2 ● 73 ÷ 5

23. 112 ÷ 5 ● 212 ÷ 5

24. 550 ÷ 6 ● 101 ÷ 2

25. **Create Your Own** Write a division problem with a quotient between 30 and 40. Explain how you chose the divisor and the dividend.

Mixed Review

26. 1.8 − 0.5

27. 3.5 + 8.8

28. 4.9 − 2.3

29. 12.8 − 6.9

30. 5.6 + 4.6

31. 2.5 − 1.7

32. 0.7 + 0.9

33. 8.2 + 0.8

More Practice Set 12.6, p. 477

2-Digit Quotients

Your class collects 73 toys for children in 3 hospitals. You want to send the same number of toys to each hospital. How many will go to each? Divide to find out.

| **Here's A Way!** | **Find 73 ÷ 3.** |

1 Estimate first.
Use multiples of 10.

$3 \times \blacksquare = 73$
$3 \times 10 = 30$
$3 \times 20 = 60$

The answer is about 20. Why?

2 Divide the tens. Multiply. Subtract.

Tens Ones

3×2 tens

```
    2
3)73
  -6
   13
```

Regroup 1 ten for 10 ones.

3 Divide the ones. Multiply. Subtract.

Tens Ones

3×4 ones

```
   24
3)73
  -6
   13
  -12
    1
```

4 Write the remainder.

Your class will send 24 toys to each hospital. There will be 1 toy left over.

Tens Ones

```
   24 R1
3)73
  -6
   13
  -12
    1
```

Remainder

| **Talk About It!** | How did estimating help you know to write a 2 in the tens place? |

Estimation Estimate to tell which answer is greater. Write *a* or *b*.

1. a. $2\overline{)89}$ b. $7\overline{)89}$ 2. a. $3\overline{)96}$ b. $4\overline{)96}$

3. **Critical Thinking** In exercise 1, how could you tell which answer would be greater without using multiples of 10? (Hint: Compare the dividends. Then compare the divisors.)

Estimate. Then divide.

4. $3\overline{)65}$ 5. $4\overline{)90}$ 6. $5\overline{)68}$ 7. $2\overline{)25}$ 8. $3\overline{)95}$
                                                       10; 13R3

Work It Out!

Write the quotient. Write the remainder if there is one.

9. $8\overline{)48}$ 10. $8\overline{)96}$ 11. $6\overline{)83}$ 12. $6\overline{)84}$ 13. $7\overline{)78}$

14. $5\overline{)91}$ 15. $2\overline{)77}$ 16. $3\overline{)96}$ 17. $2\overline{)81}$ 18. $3\overline{)68}$

19. $4\overline{)94}$ 20. $5\overline{)85}$ 21. $2\overline{)93}$ 22. $6\overline{)72}$ 23. $2\overline{)69}$

24. $50 \div 2$ 25. $5\overline{)22}$ 26. $75 \div 3$ 27. $6\overline{)80}$

28. **Mental Math** In exercises 9–27, which can you solve with mental math?

Problem Solving

29. A roll of paper wraps 4 toys. How many rolls will you need for 73 toys? (Hint: Think about the remainder.)

30. A sheet of wrapping paper is 17 in. long and 13 in. wide. How would you cut it to make a square?

Mixed Review   Write >, <, or =. Use a number line if you need to.

31. 0.1 ● 1.0   32. 1.0 ● 0.9   33. 5.8 ● 5.5   34. 7 ● 7.0

35. 5247 ● 5369   36. 2001 ● 1989   37. 974 ● 1101   38. 8251 ● 8238

More Practice Set 12.7, p. 478

Dividing Greater Numbers

There are 113 people waiting to ride in a hot air balloon. Only 3 people can ride at a time. How many trips are needed for everyone to get a ride? You can divide 113 by 3 to find out.

Here's A Way! Find 113 ÷ 3.

1 Estimate first.
Use multiples of 10.

$3 \times 30 = 90$
$3 \times 40 = 120$

The quotient is between 30 and 40. Why?

2 Divide the tens.
Multiply. Subtract.

Tens Ones

$$3\overline{)113}$$
quotient 3
-9 ← 3×3 tens
23

Regroup 2 tens for 20 ones.

3 Divide the ones.
Multiply. Subtract.

Tens Ones

$$3\overline{)113}$$
quotient 37
-9
23
-21 ← 3×7 ones
2

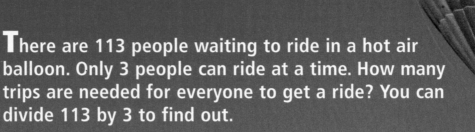

4 Write the remainder.

Make 38 trips. If there were 37 trips, 2 people would be left over.

Tens Ones

$$3\overline{)113}$$
quotient 37 R2
-9
23
-21
2

Remainder

Talk About It! How many ones can you divide evenly in Step 3?

Show What You Know!

Estimate. Then divide.

1. $4\overline{)352}$ 2. $3\overline{)126}$ 3. $5\overline{)456}$ 4. $2\overline{)158}$

5. $200 \div 5$ 6. $201 \div 5$ 7. $202 \div 5$ 8. $320 \div 8$ 9. $321 \div 8$

10. **Patterns** What patterns do you see in exercises 5–7?

Work It Out!

Estimate. If the estimate is greater than 60, then divide.

11. $2\overline{)119}$ 12. $6\overline{)537}$ 13. $4\overline{)305}$ 14. $3\overline{)290}$ 15. $7\overline{)428}$

16. $9\overline{)843}$ 17. $5\overline{)486}$ 18. $8\overline{)724}$ 19. $4\overline{)231}$ 20. $2\overline{)107}$

Divide.

21. $5\overline{)283}$ 22. $4\overline{)264}$ 23. $7\overline{)498}$ 24. $8\overline{)368}$ 25. $3\overline{)257}$

26. $360 \div 4$ 27. $729 \div 9$ 28. $153 \div 3$ 29. $488 \div 8$

30. **Mental Math** Did you use mental math for any of the exercises? Explain.

Problem Solving

31. Suppose a large hot-air balloon holds 4 people. There are 89 people waiting for a ride. How many more people must join the line so that 4 people can ride each time the balloon goes up?

32. Two ballons each carry 3 people. The riders' weights are 103 lb, 210 lb, 60 lb, 185 lb, 140 lb, and 40 lb. Each ballon can carry no more than 375 lb. Which people should ride together?

More Practice Set 12.8, p. 478

Problem Solving
Using Strategies

L·E·S·S·O·N 9

Read more about some sled dogs that saved a town in the pages of *Cricket* magazine.

In 1925, some people in Nome (nohm), Alaska, became very ill. Dog sleds sped across 674 miles of snow to bring medicine. A dog sled race takes place each year in Alaska to honor this event. The race is called the Iditarod (eye DIH tur ahd).

Problem Solving Process
- ✓ Understand
- ✓ Plan
- ✓ Try It
- ✓ Look Back

Choose a Strategy You Have Learned
- ✓ Act It Out
- ✓ Look for a Pattern
- ✓ Guess and Check
- ✓ Draw a Picture
- ✓ Make a Table
- ✓ Work Backward
- ✓ Make a List
- ✓ Work a Simpler Problem

Some racers use teams of 9 dogs. The dogs are arranged in 4 pairs. There is a single lead dog in front of the others. Each dog is about 4 feet long. Each pair of dogs is 2 feet from the next pair. The lead dog is 3 feet in front of the nearest pair. How long is the whole team of dogs?

- What question do you have to answer?

- How are the dogs arranged?

- How long is each dog?

- What is the spacing between the dogs?

- Explain a strategy that can help solve the problem. Then solve it.

Work It Out!

**Use any strategy to solve the problem.
Show your work.**

1. A dog sled racer must put together a team of 7 dogs. He wants 1 lead dog followed by 3 pairs of dogs. Look at his notes. How can he arrange the dogs so they will work well together?

2. A team of sled dogs ran 41 miles without stopping from 11:30 A.M. to 1:30 P.M. They traveled at about the same speed the whole way. About how many miles did they travel each hour?

3. Suppose teams of sled dogs will will take turns carrying supplies 1044 miles across Alaska. Each team will run 36 miles of the distance. How many teams are needed?

4. You are building a wall of snow blocks. A block is 1.5 ft on each side. The shaded parts of the wall are half blocks. If you want your wall to be 9 ft wide and 6 ft tall, how many more whole blocks do you need? How many more half blocks?

5. Suppose 3 racers take turns running a race. They go 90 miles altogether. They each go the same distance. How far did each racer go?

6. A team of sled dogs ran from 10:15 A.M. to 11:55 A.M. Then they rested for 35 minutes and ran again from 12:30 P.M. to 2:50 P.M. How many hours did they run?

Share Your Thinking

7. What strategy did you use to solve problem 6? How did the strategy help you?

8. When a dog team has 1 lead dog followed by pairs of dogs, the number of dogs is always odd. Explain why.

Chapter 12 Test

for Pages 410–431

Test-Taking Tips
Unless you are sure of the answer, read all the choices before answering a multiple-choice question.

Problem Solving

Solve the problem using any strategy. Show your work.
(page 430)

1. Your class is decorating the classroom door with bows. You need 4 feet of ribbon for each bow. How many bows can you make from 10 yards of ribbon? How much ribbon will be left over? (Hint: 1 yard = 3 feet)

2. Suppose you use 2 congruent triangles to form a square. You add 6 more congruent triangles to make a larger square. How many triangles will you add to form a third square?

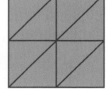

Concepts

Tell whether the division sentence has a remainder. Write the remainder if there is one. (page 412)

3. 72 ÷ 8
4. 43 ÷ 5
5. 15 ÷ 4
6. 24 ÷ 7

Tell how many groups there are. Write a fraction for the blue group. Then write how many are in the blue group. (page 414)

7.

8.

9.

10.

What is the best estimate for the quotient? Write a, b, c, or d. (page 424)

11. 58 ÷ 4   a. 10   b. 20   c. 30   d. 15

12. 319 ÷ 5   a. 70   b. 65   c. 55   d. 60

Solve. Choose the best answer. Write *a*, *b*, or *c*. (pages 416, 426, 428)

13. $9\overline{)82}$ a. 8   b. 9 R1   c. 9 R2

14. $7\overline{)30}$ a. 4 R2   b. 4 R3   c. 5

15. $6\overline{)546}$ a. 90   b. 90 R1   c. 91

16. $508 \div 7$ a. 71 R4   b. 72 R4   c. 73 R4

17. $17 \div 6$ a. 2 R3   b. 2 R4   c. 2 R5

18. $123 \div 4$ a. 30   b. 30 R2   c. 30 R3

Find the answer. Check your answer by multiplying, then adding. Show your work. (pages 416, 426, 428)

19. $40 \div 5$ 20. $52 \div 8$ 21. $300 \div 9$ 22. $240 \div 3$

23. $2\overline{)614}$ 24. $5\overline{)372}$ 25. $8\overline{)185}$ 26. $4\overline{)25}$

 Performance Task

Keep In Mind . . .
Your work will be evaluated on the following:

☑ Correct number sentences

☑ Method for checking

☑ Written explanation about the remainder

☑ Plan for solving

Solve the problem using any strategy. Show your work. (pages 416, 418, 430)

You are making puppets. For each one, you need 3 pieces of felt. You have 11 pieces of felt in all. How many puppets can you make?

• Tell how you found the answer.

• Explain what you did with the remainder and why.

• Change the problem so that there is no leftover part or remainder to think about.

Cumulative Review

Addition (Chapter 3)
Add. Find 318 + 119 + 57 + 42.

Here's A Way!

```
  1 2
  318     Add the ones.
  119     Ask, Do I need to
   57     regroup?
+  42     Add the tens.
  536     Ask, Do I regroup?
          Add the hundreds.
```

Find the sum.

1.	41	2.	86	3.	90
	33		72		66
	170		412		14
	+ 254		+ 110		+ 37

4.	76	5.	290	6.	278
	13		415		525
	+ 88		+ 116		+ 141

7. In exercise 4 what number did you write above the tens place? Why?

Rules for Division (Chapter 6)
Find $389 \div 389$, $60 \div 1$, $0 \div 26$.

Here's A Way!

Any number divided by itself equals 1. **$389 \div 389 = 1$**
Any number divided by 1 equals itself. **$60 \div 1 = 60$**
Zero divided by any number equals zero. **$0 \div 26 = 0$**

Find the quotient. Use division rules.

8. $37 \div 37$ **9.** $0 \div 249$

10. $16 \div 16$ **11.** $72 \div 1$

12. $0 \div 54$ **13.** $180 \div 1$

14. What made it reasonable to use mental math to solve exercises 8–13?

Comparing Fractions (Chapter 8)
Does $\frac{3}{6}$ equal $\frac{4}{8}$?

Here's A Way!

Use models to compare.

Yes, $\frac{3}{6} = \frac{4}{8}$.

Write the fraction for each shaded part. Write > , < , or = between each pair of fractions.

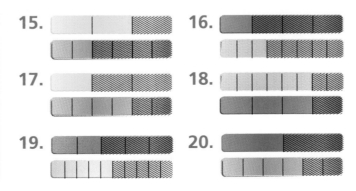

15.   16.

17.   18.

19.   20.

Decimals (Chapter 10)

Write four tenths and seven hundredths as decimals.

Here's A Way!

Ones		Tenths	Hundredths
0	.	4	
0	.	0	7

So, write *0.4* and *0.07*.

Write the decimal form of each number.

21.

Ones		Tenths	Hundredths
0	.	1	3

22. one tenth   23. three tenths

24. twenty-seven hundredths

25. Where did you write a zero in problem 24? Why?

Multiplication (Chapter 11)

Multiply 3 by 12.

Here's A Way!

Use arrays.

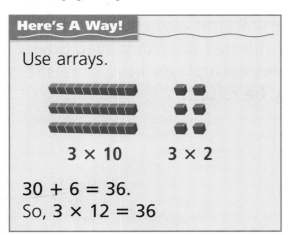

3 × 10   3 × 2

30 + 6 = 36.
So, 3 × 12 = 36

Use the arrays to find the products.

26.

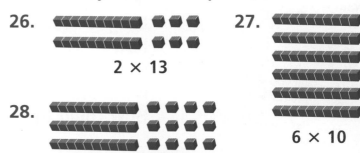

2 × 13

27.

6 × 10

28.

4 × 14

29. Write an addition sentence for exercise 28. Why is the sum the same as the product?

Problem Solving

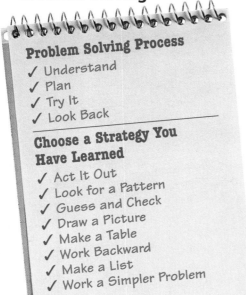

Problem Solving Process
- ✓ Understand
- ✓ Plan
- ✓ Try It
- ✓ Look Back

Choose a Strategy You Have Learned
- ✓ Act It Out
- ✓ Look for a Pattern
- ✓ Guess and Check
- ✓ Draw a Picture
- ✓ Make a Table
- ✓ Work Backward
- ✓ Make a List
- ✓ Work a Simpler Problem

Solve the problem. Show your work.

30. Suppose you lost the combination for your bike lock. You know that the numbers are 17, 38, and 5. You just cannot remember the order. How many possible combinations can you try?

31. You and some friends are making puppets. Plastic eyes cost 15¢ each. You have 6 quarters, but you want to have at least $.50 left after you buy the eyes. How many eyes can you buy?

Go, Team, Go!

Science Connection **With Your Group**

Your group has raised $225 to help sponsor a Little League baseball team in your community. Figure out how much money the uniforms and equipment will cost. Then, figure out the cost for one player. How much more money does each player have to raise? How could the money be raised?

1 Plan It

- Think about what you might wear and use if you played on a baseball team.

2 Put It Together

- Make a chart like the one on the right. Add to the list of items. Find out how much each item costs.
- Write how many items the team will need. There are 9 players on the team. Can the players can share some of the equipment?
- Multiply and write the total cost of each item.

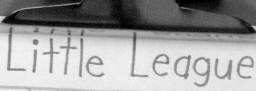

Little League

Item	Price	How Many	Total Cost
hat	$5.00	9	$45.00
shirt	$7.00	9	
glove	$20.00	9	
bat	$15.00	3	
ball	$2.00 each		
Safety Pad	$10.00 per pair		

3 Wrap It Up

- Add to find how much money is needed in all.
- Divide to find the cost for each player.
- Figure out how much money each player already has.
- How much more money does each player need? How could the money be raised?

4 Discuss Your Results

- Did you meet all of the goals in Keep In Mind?
- Was your group's chart for the Little League team like the charts of other groups? Which idea for raising money was the most popular?

 Internet

> Visit the **Math Center** at **Houghton Mifflin Education Place.** http://www.eduplace.com

More Practice

Set 1.2　**Use with pages 4–5.**

Write the missing numbers.

1. ■, 81, 82

2. 28, 29, ■

3. 43, ■, 45

4. 75, 76, ■, ■

5. ■, ■, ■, 93, 94

6. ■, ■, ■, 12, 13

Write the missing number.

7. 25 26   ■

8. ■   66 67

9. ■   11 12

10. 47 48   ■

Set 1.5　**Use with pages 10–11.**

Write the sum.

1.   8
  + 8
	2. 6
	  + 5
		3. 8
		  + 9

4.   8
  + 7
	5. 7
	  +7
		6. 7
		  + 6

7.   6
  + 6
	8. 4
	  + 5
		9. 10
		  + 9

10.   6
  + 7
	11. 10
	  + 10
		12. 11
		  + 12

13.   9
  + 9
	14. 9
	  + 10
		15. 5
		  + 5

16.   5
  + 6
	17. 7
	  + 8
		18. 4
		  + 4

19. 4 + 5

20. 6 + 6

21. 9 + 8

22. 10 + 10

23. 7 + 8

24. 5 + 4

25. 3 + 3

26. 10 + 11

Write the sum.

1. 7 + 5	2. 4 + 8	3. 6 + 4	4. 9 + 5	5. 8 + 6	6. 7 + 8
7. 6 + 7	8. 4 + 6	9. 9 + 4	10. 4 + 7	11. 8 + 2	12. 9 + 7
13. 9 + 4	14. 7 + 7	15. 5 + 5	16. 9 + 3	17. 6 + 9	18. 7 + 3

19. 8 + 3   20. 7 + 4   21. 7 + 9   22. 3 + 6

23. 4 + 5   24. 9 + 2   25. 5 + 7   26. 6 + 5

1. 8 1 + 2	2. 7 5 + 3	3. 3 9 + 8	4. 3 10 + 4	5. 4 4 + 4	6. 1 3 + 4
7. 6 6 + 7	8. 5 2 + 8	9. 7 1 + 6	10. 9 4 + 6	11. 5 3 + 7	12. 1 6 + 7
13. 6 6 + 6	14. 7 3 + 1	15. 9 0 + 1	16. 8 9 + 2	17. 7 7 + 2	18. 4 9 + 1

19. 10 + 2 + 1   20. 4 + 2 + 6   21. 8 + 9 + 3

22. 5 + 6 + 5   23. 5 + 4 + 10   24. 6 + 6 + 2

Write the difference.

1. 13
   − 4

2. 11
   − 3

3. 12
   − 2

4. 18
   − 9

5. 15
   − 0

6. 11
   − 7

7. 10
   − 2

8. 7
   − 7

9. 13
   − 9

10. 5
    − 5

11. 6
    − 0

12. 7
    − 4

13. 15
    − 9

14. 16
    − 9

15. 14
    − 7

16. 20
    − 9

17. 12
    − 4

18. 10
    − 9

19. 10 − 8

20. 9 − 9

21. 14 − 2

22. 15 − 6

23. 12 − 3

24. 13 − 3

25. 14 − 5

26. 15 − 7

Copy and complete the number sentence.

1. 8 + ■ = 17

2. ■ + 7 = 15

3. ■ + 9 = 14

4. ■ + 7 = 16

5. 8 + ■ = 16

6. 6 + ■ = 14

7. ■ + 8 = 15

8. 9 + ■ = 18

9. 5 + ■ = 13

10. ■ + 9 = 13

11. 7 + ■ = 13

12. 10 + ■ = 16

13. 5 + ■ = 11

14. 13 = ■ + 6

15. ■ + 8 = 8

16. 9 = ■ + 7

Solve.

17. You have 15 spelling words to learn by Friday.
    By Wednesday you know 8 spelling words.
    How many spelling words do you still need to learn?

18. Your class made 9 model snakes in the afternoon.
    You made only 4 model snakes. Your friend made the rest.
    How many model snakes did your friend make?

Write the answer.

1. You want to invite 14 children to a party. You have sent out 8 invitations. How many invitations do you need to send?

2. You went looking for sea glass at the beach. You found 16 pieces of clear glass and 8 colored pieces. How many more clear pieces than colored pieces did you find?

3. A girl got $10 from her aunt. She wants to buy a dog collar that costs $8. Will she have enough money left over to buy a poster for $3?

4. A baker needs 15 candles for a birthday cake. He has 7 candles. How many more candles does he need?

5. Suppose you made $9 mowing lawns. You want to buy a new bike seat that costs $12. How much more money do you need?

Write the answer. Use mental math when you can.

1. $9 + 3$	2. $17 - 9$	3. $6 + 9$	4. $11 - 9$	5. $13 - 9$	6. $7 + 9$
7. $9 + 9$	8. $16 - 6$	9. $12 - 9$	10. $8 + 9$	11. $9 + 4$	12. $15 - 5$

13. $9 + 3$ 14. $13 - 9$ 15. $15 - 9$ 16. $10 - 9$

17. $8 + 9$ 18. $9 + 9$ 19. $10 + 9$ 20. $11 + 9$

Copy and complete the number sentences.

21. $2 + \blacksquare = 11$ 22. $16 - \blacksquare = 9$

23. $9 + \blacksquare = 11$ 24. $\blacksquare + 9 = 17$

25. $16 - \blacksquare = 7$ 26. $9 + \blacksquare = 14$

27. $10 + \blacksquare = 18$ 28. $9 + \blacksquare = 18$

Set 1.14 Use with pages 30–31. ••••••••••••••••••••••••••••••••

Write the number sentence that is missing from the fact family.

1. 4 + 5 = 9
5 + 4 = 9
9 − 4 = 5

2. 15 − 8 = 7
15 − 7 = 8
7 + 8 = 15

3. 6 + 6 = 12

4. 5 + 8 = 13
13 − 8 = 5
8 + 5 = 13

5. 0 + 9 = 9
9 − 0 = 9
9 − 9 = 0

6. 10 − 5 = 5

Write a family of facts for these numbers.

7. 5, 7, 12

8. 8, 8, 16

9. 8, 7, 15

10. 0, 4, 4

11. 13, 6, 7

12. 6, 14, 8

13. 3, 8, 11

14. 9, 9, 18

15. 1, 7, 6

16. 10, 3, 7

Set 2.1 Use with pages 42–43. ••••••••••••••••••••••••••••••••••

Write the number of tens and ones. Then, write the number.

1.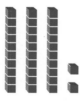

2.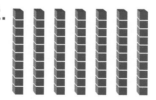

3.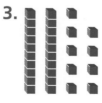

4.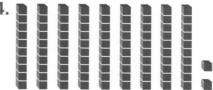

Copy and complete the number sentence.

5. 13 = ▤ ten + ▤ ones

6. 79 = ▤ tens + ▤ ones

7. 48 = ▤ tens + ▤ ones

8. 84 = ▤ tens + ▤ ones

9. 25 = ▤ tens + ▤ ones

10. 60 = ▤ tens + ▤ ones

Set 2.2 **Use with pages 44–45.**

Write how many hundreds, tens, and ones. Then, write the number.

1.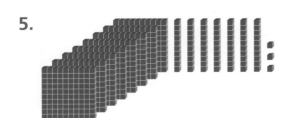

2.

3.

4.

5.

6.

Set 2.3 **Use with pages 46–47.**

Write the number in standard form.

1. six hundred eighteen

2. 400 + 7

3. two hundred thirty

4. 400 + 60 + 1

5. one hundred sixty

6. nine hundred nine

7. 8 hundreds + 2 tens + 3 ones

8. 6 hundreds + 7 tens

9. nine hundreds + six tens + eight ones

10. four hundreds + zero tens + three ones

Write the value of the colored digit.

11. 654   12. 137   13. 867   14. 520   15. 196

16. 602   17. 476   18. 398   19. 516   20. 753

Use with pages 50–51. ·····································

Write the number in standard form.

1. one thousand fifteen

2. five thousand six hundred eleven

3. nine thousand eight hundred

4. six thousand nine hundred forty

5. two thousand seven

6. eight thousand one hundred fifty-six

7. 9000 + 400 + 20

8. 4000 + 300 + 1

9. 8000 + 500 + 10 + 2

Write the value of the colored digit.

10. 2431	11. 8056	12. 690	13. 2435	14. 6209
15. 129	16. 3790	17. 3014	18. 2641	19. 25

Set 2.7 **Use with pages 56–57.** ·····································

Write the answer.

1. 60	2. 400	3. 30	4. 8000	5. 15,000
+ 30	+ 600	+ 20	− 2000	− 7000

6. 40	7. 5000	8. 16,000	9. 700	10. 100
+ 90	+ 5000	− 8000	− 300	− 80

11. 700	12. 1000	13. 600	14. 12,000	15. 1600
+ 400	+ 9000	− 300	− 5000	− 900

16. 2000 + 3000   17. 40 + 90

18. 900 − 300   19. 500 + 400 + 100

20. 30 + 40 + 50   21. 1000 + 5000 + 2000

Use with pages 60–61. •••••••••••••••••••••••••••••••••

Copy and complete. Write < or >.

1. 98 ● 99

2. 634 ● 643

3. 2643 ● 2638

4. 3136 ● 7982

5. 7413 ● 7143

6. 3784 ● 3874

7. 1040 ● 1050

8. 287 ● 278

9. 3880 ● 3008

10. 4205 ● 4250

11. 3809 ● 3890

12. 3125 ● 3152

Order from least to greatest.

13. 96, 69, 71

14. 123, 119, 132

15. 471, 741, 417

16. 1312, 1684, 1296

17. 752, 546, 216

18. 1560, 1078, 1643

19. 461, 68, 276

20. 2932, 2039, 2392

21. 8422, 5478, 2634

Use with pages 64–65. ••••••••••••••••••••••••••••••

Write the value of the coins.

1. 1 dime and 3 nickels

2. 1 quarter and 2 dimes

3. 1 half-dollar and 1 penny

4. 2 quarters and 2 dimes

5. 8 nickels and 2 pennies

6. 3 quarters, 3 nickels, and 3 pennies

Write each answer.

7. You have 1 quarter, 2 dimes, and 7 pennies. How much money do you have? Can you buy a pencil that costs 42¢?

8. A notebook costs 89¢. You have 3 quarters and 3 nickels. Do you have enough money to buy the notebook?

Write the amount. Use a dollar sign and decimal point.

1. two dollars and thirty-two cents

2. eighty-five cents

3. twelve dollars

4. eight dollars and ten cents

5. 5 dollars and 3 cents

6. 11 dollars and 15 cents

7. 75 cents

8. 1 dollar and 3 cents

9. two dimes

10. 6 nickels

Write each answer.

11. You have 1 five-dollar bill, 1 half-dollar, 2 dimes, and 5 pennies. How much money do you have? Can you buy a book that costs $5.69?

Has the store clerk given the correct change? Write too much, too little, or correct.

1. You paid 30¢. The pencil costs 27¢. Change: 3 pennies

2. You paid $2.00. The notebook costs $1.79. Change: 1 penny, 3 dimes

3. You paid $1.75. The juice costs $1.55. Change: 3 nickels

4. You paid $2.00. The model plane costs $1.86. Change: 4 pennies, 1 dime

5. You paid $1.00. The popcorn costs $.62. Change: 3 pennies, 1 nickel, 1 dime, 1 quarter

Which clock shows the same time? Write *a* or *b*.

1.

$$12:55$$

a.   b.

2.

$$5:15$$

a.   b.

Write the time.

3.   4.   5.   6.

For each exercise, write *A.M.* or *P.M.*

1. The sun rises at 6:15.

2. The scout meeting begins at 3:30.

3. The mall opens at 10:00.

4. The late-night movie ends at 12:15.

Solve. Be sure to write *A.M.* or *P.M.*

5. The parade started at 10:30 A.M. It lasted for 2 hours. What time did it end?

6. Two doctors came on duty at 11:00 P.M. They stayed at the hospital 10 hours. When did they leave the hospital?

Use with pages 88–89. ••••••••••••••••••••••••••••••••••

Write the sum.

1.	30 + 36	2.	69 + 18	3.	41 + 89

4. 35
   + 71

5. 67
   + 92

6. 12
   + 19

7. 74
   + 88

8. 42
   + 56

9. 25 feet
   + 26 feet

10. 82
    + 91

11. 76
    + 48

12. 73
    + 59

13. 65 miles
    + 88 miles

14. 45
    + 95

15. 54
    + 7

16. 31 + 70   17. 26 + 53   18. 87 + 68   19. 95 + 78

20. 40 + 27   21. 42 + 62   22. 55 + 45   23. 95 + 77

Use with pages 90–91. ••••••••••••••••••••••••••••••••

Write the answer.

1. 425
   + 528

2. 771
   + 269

3. 594
   + 332

4. 262
   + 35

5. 931
   + 78

6. 653
   + 29

7. 529
   + 274

8. 100
   + 847

9. 735
   + 628

10. 385
    + 15

11. 623
    + 48

12. 351
    + 399

13. 545
    + 225

14. 439
    + 38

15. 209
    + 369

16. 700 + 189   17. 674 + 35

18. 730 + 805   19. 459 + 786

20. $400 + $300   21. 139 + 47

22. 184 + 229   23. 500 + 25

Use with pages 92–93. ·······························

Estimate. Use the front-end digits or round.

1. 356 + 282	2. 728 + 149	3. 597 + 354	4. 304 + 249	5. 567 + 298
6. 492 + 352	7. 428 + 216	8. 511 + 476	9. 369 + 432	10. 569 + 318

Estimate. Which two numbers in the box have a sum of:

125	360	412	180

11. about 300   12. about 800

13. about 500   14. about 600

Use with pages 94–95. ·······························

Write the sum.

1. 386 52 + 342	2. 57 43 + 80	3. 28 35 + 91	4. 193 18 + 322	5. 45 10 + 77
6. 359 374 + 253	7. 124 312 163 + 98	8. 319 447 + 231	9. 253 106 + 58	10. 350 204 38 + 246

Write the sum.

11. 708 miles + 66 miles + 37 miles

12. 536 + 52 + 55

13. 460 + 50 + 64 + 30

14. $84 + $355 + $880 +$85

15. 633 + 418 + 185 + 876

16. 210 + 143 + 631 + 104

Write the difference.

1. 81 − 50	2. 53 − 29	3. 94 yards − 58 yards
4. $81 − 69	5. 78 − 12	6. 91 − 87
7. $61 − 28	8. 93 − 46	9. 66 − 47
10. $95 − 51	11. 75 − 36	12. 90 − 35
13. 72 − 66	14. $53 − 47	15. 75 − 9

16. $34 − $25   17. 72 − 7

18. 67 − 12   19. $75 − $25

20. 50 meters − 17 meters   21. 99 − 10

Write the difference.

1. 359 − 45	2. $717 − 56	3. 637 − 44	4. 347 − 175	5. 612 − 467
6. $781 − 692	7. 854 − 66	8. 323 − 277	9. 495 − 10	10. $469 − 292
11. 832 − 662	12. $893 − 799	13. 645 − 287	14. 365 − 87	15. 592 − 138

16. 366 − 171   17. 523 − 235

18. 243 feet − 76 feet   19. 732 − 300

20. 279 − 79   21. 634 meters − 76 meters

Set 3.11   **Use with pages 108–109.** •••••••••••••••••••••••••••••••••••

Write the letter of the closest estimate.

1. 826
   − 483
       a. 100   b. 400   c. 700

2. $733
   − 352
       a. $400   b. $600   c. $1000

3. 345
   − 262
       a. 10   b. 100   c. 1000

4. 852
   − 609
       a. 200   b. 400   c. 600

Write *a*, *b*, *c*, or *d*. Which exercise has a difference of:

5. about 200   6. about 20   7. about 50   8. about 500

  a.   588   b.   92   c.   71   d.   984
    − 398   − 45   − 53   − 490

Set 3.12   **Use with pages 110–111.** •••••••••••••••••••••••••••••••

Write the difference.

1. 580   2. 550   3. 807   4. 304   5. $900
   − 163   − 30   − 22   − 246   −   33

6. 703   7. 508   8. 130   9. 902   10. 930
   − 57   − 413   − 77   − 747   − 56

11. $250   12. $490   13. 306   14. 500   15. $300
   − 162   − 64   − 85   − 98   − 215

16. 800 − 592   17. 790 − 482   18. 600 feet − 91 feet

19. 403 − 181   20. 300 − 42   21. $730 − $145

22. 670 − 70   23. 500 − 200   24. $805 − $206

Use the pictograph to solve each problem.

Muffins Sold at Your School Bake Sale	
Banana Muffins	🧁 🧁 🧁
Blueberry Muffins	🧁 🧁 🧁 🧁 🧁 🧁 🧁
Bran Muffins	🧁 🧁
Corn Muffins	🧁 🧁 🧁
Raisin Nut Muffins	🧁 🧁 🧁 🧁 🧁

Key 🧁 = 5 muffins

1. How many kinds of muffins were sold at the bake sale?

2. How many corn muffins were sold?

3. Which muffins were the most popular?

4. How many muffins were sold in all?

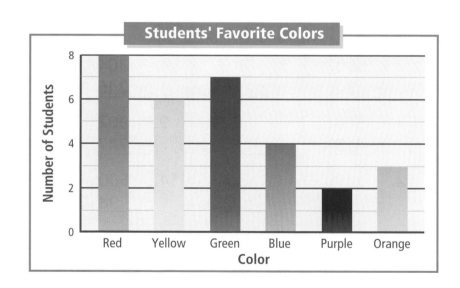

Students' Favorite Colors

Use the bar graph on page 452 to solve each problem.

1. How many students named green as their favorite color?

2. Which color was chosen most?

3. Which color was chosen least?

4. Which colors were chosen by more than four students?

5. How many more students chose red than chose orange?

Set 4.6   Use with pages 134–135. ··································

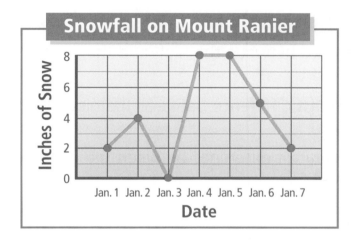

Use the line graph to solve each problem.

1. Which day had the least amount of snowfall?

2. On which two days did the same amount of snow fall?

3. On which days did less than 5 inches of snow fall?

4. How many more inches of snow fell on January 6 than on January 2?

Daily High and Low Temperatures for Week in June							
	Mon.	Tues.	Wed.	Thur.	Fri.	Sat.	Sun.
High	67°	78°	82°	79°	84°	85°	91°
Low	57°	58°	72°	65°	70°	70°	72°

Use the information from the table to answer each question.

1. What was the highest temperature?

2. What was the lowest temperature?

3. What was the difference between the high and the low on Wednesday?

4. Which days had the least difference between the high and low temperatures?

5. Which day had the greatest difference between the high and low temperatures?

Write the product.

1. 5×2 2. 2×3 3. 4×2 4. 1×2

5. 3×2 6. 2×1 7. 2×2 8. 2×5

Write a multiplication sentence for the addition sentence.

9. $3 + 3$ 10. $1 + 1$ 11. $4 + 4$ 12. $5 + 5$

Use with pages 166–167. ••••••••••••••••••••••••••••••

Write the quotient.

1. 6 ÷ 2   2. 8 ÷ 2   3. 10 ÷ 2   4. 4 ÷ 2

Write a division sentence. Draw a picture if you like.

5. 8 mittens put into pairs

6. 10 bananas put into 2 bunches

7. 6 dimes shared equally between 2 people

8. 4 wheels shared equally between 2 bicycles

Set 5.7   **Use with pages 172–173.** ••••••••••••••••••••••••••••

Write the answer.

1. 3	2. 5	3. 3	4. 4
× 2	× 3	× 1	× 3

5. 3 × 5   6. 3 × 3   7. 15 ÷ 3   8. 6 ÷ 3

9. 3 × 4   10. 12 ÷ 3   11. 2 × 3   12. 9 ÷ 3

Set 5.8   **Use with pages 174–175.** ••••••••••••••••••••••••••••

Write the answer.

1. 3	2. 1	3. 4	4. 4	5. 4
× 4	× 4	× 5	× 2	× 4

6. 2 × 4   7. 16 ÷ 4   8. 4 × 5   9. 20 ÷ 4   10. 12 ÷ 4

11. 12 ÷ 3   12. 5 × 4   13. 15 ÷ 3   14. 8 ÷ 4   15. 4 × 4

Write the answer.

1. 5
    $\times\,3$

2. 4
    $\times\,5$

3. 1
    $\times\,5$

4. 5
    $\times\,2$

5. 5
    $\times\,5$

6. 15 ÷ 5

7. 4 × 5

8. 5 × 1

9. 25 ÷ 5

10. 5 × 5

11. 3 × 5

12. 20 ÷ 5

13. 10 ÷ 5

Write a multiplication sentence and a related division sentence for the numbers.

14. 20, 4, 5

15. 12, 3, 4

16. 2, 5, 10

17. 2, 6, 3

Write the missing factor.

1. 3 × ▧ = 15

2. ▧ × 2 = 8

3. 4 × ▧ = 16

4. ▧ × 4 = 12

5. ▧ × 3 = 9

6. 2 × ▧ = 10

7. 3 × ▧ = 6

8. ▧ × 5 = 25

9. ▧ × 4 = 20

10. 4 × ▧ = 8

11. ▧ × 2 = 4

12. ▧ × 5 = 20

Write a related multiplication sentence.

13. 15 ÷ 3 = ▧

14. 20 ÷ 4 = ▧

15. 16 ÷ 4 = ▧

16. 6 ÷ 3 = ▧

17. 12 ÷ 2 = ▧

18. 9 ÷ 3 = ▧

Write a related division sentence.

19. 4 × ▧ = 20

20. 4 × ▧ = 16

21. ▧ × 3 = 9

22. 3 × ▧ = 12

23. ▧ × 2 = 6

24. ▧ × 5 = 25

Use with pages 200–201. •••••••••••••••••••••••••••••••

Write the answer.

1. 3	2. 6	3. 6	4. 9
$\times\ 6$	$\times\ 5$	$\times\ 6$	$\times\ 6$

5. 6	6. 2	7. 0	8. 7
$\times\ 1$	$\times\ 6$	$\times\ 6$	$\times\ 6$

9. $6 \div 6$ 10. $48 \div 6$ 11. $18 \div 6$ 12. $30 \div 6$

13. 6×2 14. 6×8 15. 4×6 16. 6×7

17. $12 \div 6$ 18. $24 \div 6$ 19. $36 \div 6$ 20. $42 \div 6$

21. 6×9 22. 6×1 23. 5×6 24. 0×6

Use with pages 202–203. •••••••••••••••••••••••••••••••

Write the answer.

1. 7	2. 4	3. 7	4. 9
$\times\ 7$	$\times\ 7$	$\times\ 1$	$\times\ 7$

5. $7\overline{)63}$ 6. $7\overline{)56}$ 7. $7\overline{)49}$ 8. $7\overline{)7}$

9. 2×7 10. 7×8 11. 7×5 12. 3×7

13. $42 \div 7$ 14. $14 \div 7$ 15. $21 \div 7$ 16. $28 \div 7$

17. $56 \div 7$ 18. $35 \div 7$ 19. $0 \div 7$ 20. $7 \div 1$

21. 7×9 22. 4×7 23. 7×7 24. 3×7

Use with page 204. ••••••••••••••••••••••••••••••••••

Write the answer. Write whether you used a calculator or mental math.

1. 250 + 200

2. 50 ÷ 5

3. 80 × 4

4. 652 − 99

5. 308 + 502

6. 28 ÷ 2

7. 301 − 2

8. 125 × 2

9. Suppose you work 5 days a week delivering papers. You worked 4 weeks last month. How many days did you work?

10. A boy buys some treats for his pets. He spends $1 for hamster treats, $3 for dog treats, and $2 for fish food. How much does he spend?

Set 6.8 **Use with pages 208–209.** •••••••••••••••••••••••••••••

Write the answer.

1.
$$\begin{array}{r} 5 \\ \times\ 8 \\ \hline \end{array}$$

2.
$$\begin{array}{r} 9 \\ \times\ 8 \\ \hline \end{array}$$

3.
$$\begin{array}{r} 4 \\ \times\ 8 \\ \hline \end{array}$$

4.
$$\begin{array}{r} 8 \\ \times\ 1 \\ \hline \end{array}$$

5. $8\overline{)48}$

6. $8\overline{)64}$

7. $8\overline{)72}$

8. $8\overline{)8}$

9. 8 × 8

10. 8 × 2

11. 7 × 8

12. 3 × 8

13. 32 ÷ 8

14. 56 ÷ 8

15. 16 ÷ 8

16. 24 ÷ 8

17. 40 ÷ 8

18. 8 × 6

19. 8 ÷ 8

20. 8 × 0

21. 9 × 8

22. 0 ÷ 8

23. 4 × 8

24. 48 ÷ 8

Write the answer.

1. $\begin{array}{r} 4 \\ \times\ 9 \\ \hline \end{array}$ 2. $\begin{array}{r} 7 \\ \times\ 9 \\ \hline \end{array}$ 3. $\begin{array}{r} 9 \\ \times\ 3 \\ \hline \end{array}$ 4. $\begin{array}{r} 9 \\ \times\ 2 \\ \hline \end{array}$

5. $9\overline{)36}$ 6. $9\overline{)9}$ 7. $9\overline{)54}$ 8. $9\overline{)63}$

9. 8×9 10. 9×0 11. 9×9 12. 5×9

13. $72 \div 9$ 14. $45 \div 9$ 15. $81 \div 9$ 16. $27 \div 9$

17. $9 \div 1$ 18. 9×6 19. $18 \div 9$ 20. 9×1

1. During a basketball game, you made some field goals worth 2 points each and some foul shots worth one point each. You made 3 more field goals than foul shots. If you got 12 points, how many field goals did you make?

2. Two numbers added together give a sum of 30. One number is 2 more than the other number. What are the numbers?

3. At the store, an apple costs 55¢ and a pack of gum costs 45¢. You bought 4 items and received a dime in change from $2. What did you buy?

4. It takes three times as long for you to walk to your friend's house as it does for you to ride your bike. How much time will you save by riding your bike if it takes 18 minutes to walk?

1. Write the letters of the angles in order from the smallest angle to the largest.

a.   b.  c.   d.

Tell whether each angle is less than a right angle, greater than a right angle, or equal to a right angle.

2.   **3.**  **4.**   **5.**

Look at the figures and answer each question.

a. b. c. d.

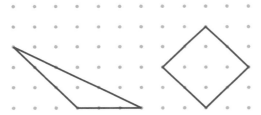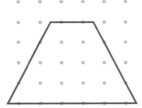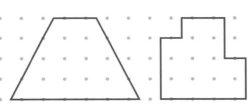

6. How many right angles does figure b have?

7. Which figure has the most angles of any kind?

8. Which figure has the largest angle?

9. Which figure has the smallest angle?

10. Which figure has the fewest angles?

11. Does figure b or c have more right angles?

Tell which pairs of figures are the same size and shape.

1.
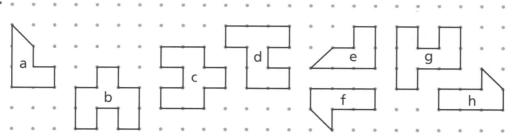

Copy each figure onto square dot paper. Next to each, draw another figure that is the same size and shape. The figures can show a slide, flip, or turn.

2.   3.   4.   5.

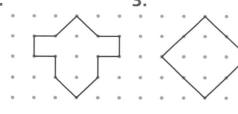 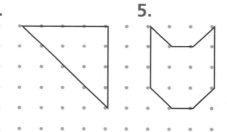

Write the answer. Write whether you used mental math or a calculator to find the answer.

1.   78
      93
   + 42

2.   10
   + 51

3.   500
   − 198

4. $32 \div 4$

5. $56 \div 7$

6. $350 + 150$

7. 25×2

8. $325 + 110$

9. 4×20

10. $615 + 318$

11. $46 + 13 + 2$

12. $500 - 293$

Write the answer. Write whether you used mental math or paper and pencil to find the answer.

13. A librarian worked part time at the library. On Monday he worked 2 hours, on Tuesday he worked 3 hours, on Wednesday he worked 3 hours, and on Saturday he worked 6 hours. How many hours did the librarian work?

Set 7.13 Use with pages 254–255. ·····························

Use the grid to solve each problem.

1. What is located at (1, 1)?

2. What is located at (3, 2)?

3. Where is the picnic table located?

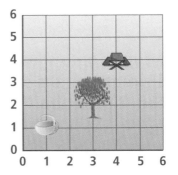

Use the grid to solve each problem.

4. Where is the circle located?

5. Which shape is closest to the circle? Where is it located?

6. What is located at (7, 1)?

7. Where is the rectangle located?

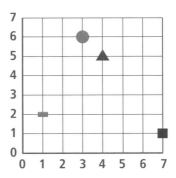

Write a fraction for the shaded part of the figure. Then, write a fraction for the unshaded part.

1.

2.

3.

4.

5.

6.

7.

8.

Write the answer. Write whether you used a calculator or mental math.

1. 9
  × 7

2. 402
  ×   3

3. $1.29
   2.98
  + 1.11

4. 625
  − 126

5. 550 ÷ 5

6. 225 + 375

7. 402 × 2

8. 398 + 110

9. 800 − 518

10. 615 ÷ 3

11. 112 × 8

12. 500 − 293

13. A video game costs $49.35 plus $2.47 tax. How much will it cost to buy the video game?

Use with pages 284–285. •

Estimate. About how much of the strip is shaded?

Write $\frac{1}{4}$, $\frac{1}{2}$ or $\frac{3}{4}$.

1.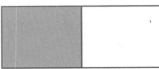

2.

3.

4.

5.

6.

Use with pages 290–291. •

Write a mixed number for the shaded part.

1.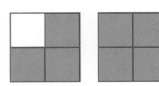

2.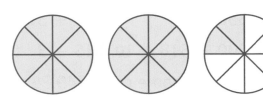

3.

4.

5.

6.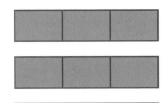

1. You and your friend ate $\frac{2}{3}$ of a pizza that was cut into 9 pieces. How many pieces are left?

2. To make a bag of popcorn you need $\frac{1}{4}$ cup of popcorn kernels. How many bags of popcorn can you make with 1 cup of kernels?

3. Your dog eats 2 cans of dog food a day. If dog food costs $1 per can, how much will it cost to feed the dog each week?

4. It is 8:15 A.M. Your class leaves on a field trip at 8:45 A.M. What part of an hour will you wait before you can leave?

Set 9.1   Use with pages 304–305.

Use paper clips to estimate the length of each line segment. Write the estimate in inches.

1. •————————————•   2. •————————•

3. •————————————————•

4. •——————————————•

Use a ruler. Write the length of each object to the nearest inch.

5.

6.

Use with pages 306–307.

Measure each line segment to the nearest inch. Then measure to the nearest half inch. Write the lengths.

1. •————————•

2. •————————————————————•

3. •————————————————•

4. •————————————————•

Use a ruler to draw the line segments.

5. 2 in.

6. 11 in.

7. 8 in.

8. $10\frac{1}{2}$ in.

9. $3\frac{1}{2}$ in.

10. $9\frac{1}{2}$ in.

11. 6 in.

12. $4\frac{1}{2}$ in.

13. 5 in.

14. $7\frac{1}{2}$ in.

15. 3 in.

16. $2\frac{1}{2}$ in.

Use with pages 308–309.

Write the perimeter of the figure.

1.
8 in. 8 in.
7 in.

2.
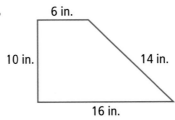
6 in.
10 in. 14 in.
16 in.

3.
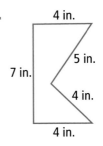
4 in.
5 in.
7 in.
4 in.
4 in.

4.
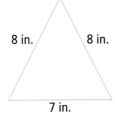
5 in. 4 in.
4 in. 4 in.
7 in.

5.
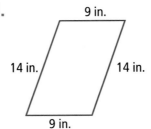
9 in.
14 in. 14 in.
9 in.

6.
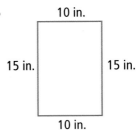
10 in.
15 in. 15 in.
10 in.

466

Choose the better estimate. Write *a* or *b*.

1. distance across Texas   a. 771 yd   b. 771 mi
2. length of a book   a. 9 in.   b. 9 yd
3. perimeter of a bedroom   a. 44 in.   b. 44 ft
4. length of a soccer field   a. 100 yd   b. 100 mi
5. length of a spoon   a. 5 in.   b. 50 in.
6. height of a man   a. 6 ft.   b. 2 ft.

Complete. Write <, >, or =. You can use the table on page 310.

7. 12 in ● 2 ft   8. $4\frac{1}{2}$ ft ● 1 yd   9. 5280 ft ● 1 mi

10. 36 in ● 1 yd   11. 8 ft ● 8 in.   12. 28 in. ● 2 ft

Does the object hold more than or less than a gallon? Write *more than* or *less than*.

1. spoon   2. washing machine   3. well
4. cereal bowl   5. juice glass   6. duck pond

Choose the better unit of measure. Write *a* or *b*.

7. milk in cereal bowl   a. quart   b. cup
8. soup in a can   a. gallon   b. pint
9. juice in a baby bottle   a. cup   b. quart
10. large can of paint for a house a. quart   b. gallon

Which unit would you use to measure these objects? Write *ounce* or *pound*.

1. a VCR
2. a video tape
3. a chair
4. 10 flashlights
5. 10 pencils
6. a gerbil
7. a watermelon
8. an orange
9. a gallon of milk
10. a baby
11. a letter
12. 10 math books
13. a calculator
14. 5 potato chips
15. 25 potatoes
16. a bicycle
17. a pair of gloves
18. a bowling ball

Use a ruler to measure the length of each line segment. Write the length in centimeters.

1. ————
2. ——————————
3. ——————————————————
4. ————————————————
5. ——————
6. ————

Use a ruler to draw the line segments.

7. 6 cm
8. 11 cm
9. 15 cm
10. 10 cm
11. 25 cm
12. 1 cm
13. 3 cm
14. 7 cm
15. 9 cm
16. 4 cm
17. 2 cm
18. 19 cm

Use with pages 320–321. ·······················

Choose the better estimate. Write *a* or *b*.

1. distance across town	a. 15 km	b. 15 m
2. height of a glass	a. 10 m	b. 10 cm
3. length of a boat	a. 5 m	b. 5 km
4. length of a finger	a. 7 cm	b. 7 m
5. height of a child	a. 14 cm	b. 123 cm
6. length of a desk	a. 14 cm	b. 1 m
7. length of a race	a. 500 m	b. 500 cm
8. thickness of a math book	a. 2 km	b. 2 cm

Copy and complete. Write < or >. You can use the table on page 320.

9. 5000 m ● 4 km

10. 32 cm ● 1 m

11. 1 km ● 500 m

12. 75 cm ● 7 m

13. 2 km ● 2500 cm

14. 48 m ● 48 cm

Use with pages 324–325. ·······················

Does the object hold more than or less than a liter? Write *more than* or *less than*.

1. paper cup	2. shoe	3. bathroom sink
4. wheelbarrow	5. straw	6. soap dish
7. fish tank	8. baby bottle	9. garbage can

Choose the better estimate. Write *a* or *b*.

10. bottle of shampoo	a. 450 mL	b. 4 mL
11. bottle of bleach	a. 100 mL	b. 4 L
12. a spoonful of water	a. 2000 mL	b. 5 mL
13. a large bucket of water	a. 2 L	b. 20 L

Use with page 326.

Which unit would you use to measure how heavy the object is?
Write *gram* or *kilogram*.

1. a TV set

2. a music tape

3. a table

4. a toothbrush

5. a box of crayons

6. a hamster

7. a large pumpkin

8. a bottle of bleach

9. a gallon of milk

10. a baby

11. a letter

12. 10 paperclips

13. a calculator

14. 5 potato chips

15. 25 potatoes

16. a bicycle

17. a beachball

18. a bowling ball

Use with pages 330–331.

Write the temperature each thermometer shows.

1.

2.

3.

Answer each question. You can use the thermometer at the top of page 330.

4. The outside temperature is 25°C. Can you build a snowman?

5. Your family is going away for the weekend. It is 50°F where you are going. Are you more likely to go swimming or play football?

Write the time.

1.

2.

3.

4.

5.

6.

7.

8.

9.

Write how much time has passed.

1.

2.

3.

4.

Use with pages 352–353. •••••••••••••••••••••••••••••

Write the decimal.

1.

2.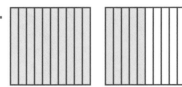

3.

4.
Ones		Tenths
0	•	8

5.

6.

7.
Ones		Tenths
0	•	4

8.
Ones		Tenths
3	•	7

9.
Ones		Tenths
6	•	2

10. $\frac{1}{10}$

11. $2\frac{3}{10}$

12. $6\frac{2}{10}$

13. 5 and 7 tenths

14. 2 and 4 tenths

15. 1 and 9 tenths

Use with pages 356–357. •••••••••••••••••••••••••••••

Write the decimals from least to greatest.

1. 3.4, 3.1, 3.5.

2. 0.6, 1.3, 0.3

3. 0.8, 0.5, 1.4

4. 0.7, 0.6, 0.4

5. 4.8, 3.7, 6.2

6. 12.4, 1.2, 2.4

7. 1.0, 0.1, 5.0

8. 7.6, 8.7, 6.8

9. 0.4, 5.0, 0.6

10. 7.7, 6.7, 7.6

11. 3.0, 0.3, 3.3

12. 4.5, 4.4, 4.6

Set 10.6 — Use with pages 358–359. •••••••••••••••••••••••••••••••••

Write the decimals from least to greatest.

1. 0.92, 0.96, 0.94
2. 0.73, 0.79, 0.71
3. 0.16, 0.61, 0.06
4. 0.23, 0.46, 0.19
5. 0.65, 0.56, 0.06
6. 0.10, 0.01, 0.11
7. 0.83, 0.57, 0.21
8. 0.03, 0.30, 0.13
9. 0.34, 0.92, 0.78
10. 0.99, 0.90, 0.09
11. 0.79, 0.98, 0.56
12. 0.63, 0.87, 0.29

Set 10.9 — Use with pages 366–367. •••••••••••••••••••••••••••••••••

Write the sum.

1. 0.2
    $+\ 0.6$

2. 1.0
    $+\ 0.6$

3. 5.3
    $+\ 2.1$

4. 4.8
    $+\ 0.5$

5. 5.7
    $+\ 3.8$

6. 4.3
    $+\ 3.9$

7. 6.4
    $+\ 2.8$

8. 3.2
    $+\ 0.9$

9. 0.8 cm + 0.8 cm
10. 0.3 + 0.7
11. 2.1 + 0.7

Write the difference.

12. 8.2
    $-\ 1.0$

13. 0.9
    $-\ 0.3$

14. $9.0\ \text{m}$
    $-\ 0.5\ \text{m}$

15. 4.2
    $-\ 3.9$

16. 8.2
    $-\ 4.8$

17. 3.9
    $-\ 1.8$

18. 5.3
    $-\ 0.7$

19. 8.2
    $-\ 6.0$

20. 8.6 − 8.2
21. 0.7 − 0.6
22. 5.3 cm − 0.6 cm
23. 9.2 − 6.4

Estimate the product.

1. 52 $\times\ 3$	**2.** $2.72 $\times\ \ \ 4$	**3.** 62 $\times\ 3$	**4.** 91 $\times\ 8$
5. 398 $\times\ 6$	**6.** 806 $\times\ 8$	**7.** 543 $\times\ 6$	**8.** 375 $\times\ 6$

9. 2 × 118   **10.** 6 × 49   **11.** 5 × 398   **12.** 8 × 65

13. 3 × $9.15   **14.** 7 × $1.89   **15.** 4 × 31   **16.** 2 × 453

17. A book of stamps costs $5.60. Can you buy 3 books with $20.00? Estimate and explain.

Write the product. You can use the array.

1. 19
$\times\ 5$
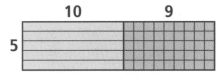

2. 23
$\times\ 8$
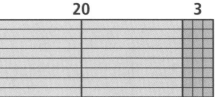

3. 9 × 12
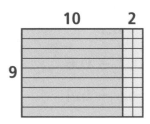

4. 7 × 24
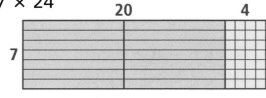

Write the product. Draw an array when it helps.

5. 2 × 29   **6.** 3 × 18   **7.** 5 × 22

8. 4 × 17   **9.** 6 × 27   **10.** 9 × 19

Use with pages 388–389. ••••••••••••••••••••••••••••••••••••••

Write the product.

1. 94 $\times$ 5	2. 54 $\times$ 3	3. 18 $\times$ 4	4. 47 $\times$ 6	5. 72 $\times$ 9
6. 97 $\times$ 2	7. 85 $\times$ 7	8. 32 $\times$ 6	9. 48 $\times$ 8	10. 17 $\times$ 2

11. 7×12 12. 3×72 13. 3×22

14. $7 \times 2 \times 5$ 15. $6 \times 4 \times 9$ 16. $9 \times 5 \times 4$

17. $5 \times 5 \times 4$ 18. $2 \times 7 \times 4$ 19. $3 \times 9 \times 3$

20. $2 \times 6 \times 8$ 21. $3 \times 5 \times 5$ 22. $8 \times 6 \times 6$

Use with pages 394–395. ••••••••••••••••••••••••••••••••••••

Write the product.

1. 322 $\times$ 4	2. 418 $\times$ 2	3. 745 $\times$ 5	4. 316 $\times$ 3	5. 475 $\times$ 4
6. 621 $\times$ 8	7. 129 $\times$ 8	8. 454 $\times$ 2	9. 924 $\times$ 5	10. 117 $\times$ 7
11. 785 $\times$ 4	12. 434 $\times$ 8	13. 897 $\times$ 9	14. 452 $\times$ 1	15. 889 $\times$ 6

16. 2×942 17. 8×447 18. 4×227

19. 3×933 20. 9×199 21. 7×516

22. 5×716 23. 4×475 24. 9×967

Write the product.

1. $9.83
   ×   6

2. $1.06
   ×   7

3. $7.54
   ×   7

4. $3.22
   ×   4

5. $9.94
   ×   9

6. $3.66
   ×   6

7. $1.86
   ×   3

8. $9.83
   ×   8

9. $9.03
   ×   4

10. $1.17
   ×   3

11. $6.87
   ×   5

12. $8.85
   ×   4

13. $4.68
   ×   4

14. $8.53
   ×   9

15. $5.58
   ×   8

16. 9 × $6.33

17. 6 × $2.85

18. 2 × $7.26

19. 9 × $4.08

20. 4 × $1.44

21. 7 × $1.93

**Write a fraction for each shaded group of objects. Then write
how many objects are in that group.**

1.

2.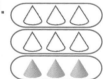

3.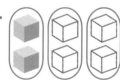

4.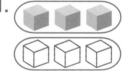

5.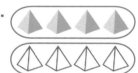

6.

**Write the answer. Use objects or pictures if you like.
Remember: 1 dozen = 12.**

7. How many are in $\frac{1}{3}$ dozen?

8. How many are in $\frac{1}{4}$ dozen?

9. How many are in $\frac{2}{3}$ dozen?

10. How many are in $\frac{3}{4}$ dozen?

Write the quotient and the remainder.

1. 4)25   2. 6)35   3. 7)34

4. 4)19   5. 2)15   6. 5)36

7. 9)33   8. 6)56   9. 3)28

10. 4)15   11. 3)14   12. 6)21

13. 8)21   14. 7)69   15. 4)37

16. 26 ÷ 5   17. 10 ÷ 6   18. 47 ÷ 7

19. 15 ÷ 7   20. 35 ÷ 6   21. 53 ÷ 8

22. 27 ÷ 5   23. 15 ÷ 2   24. 52 ÷ 7

25. 17 ÷ 7   26. 60 ÷ 8   27. 38 ÷ 9

28. 39 ÷ 6   29. 29 ÷ 4   30. 44 ÷ 5

**Look at the colored numbers. Write the two numbers the quotient
is between.**

1. 4)87   2. 5)96   3. 7)75
   4 × 10 = 40   5 × 1 = 5   7 × 1 = 7
   4 × 20 = 80   5 × 10 = 50   7 × 10 = 70
   4 × 30 = 120   5 × 20 = 100   7 × 20 = 140

4. 2)108   5. 8)723   6. 9)962
   2 × 40 = 80   8 × 80 = 640   9 × 90 = 810
   2 × 50 = 100   8 × 90 = 720   9 × 100 = 900
   2 × 60 = 120   8 × 100 = 800   9 × 110 = 990

Which is the better estimate? Write a or b.

7. 136 ÷ 4   Estimate between: a. 20 and 30   b. 30 and 40

8. 525 ÷ 6   Estimate between: a. 60 and 70   b. 80 and 90

9. 443 ÷ 9   Estimate between   a. 40 and 50   b. 50 and 60

Use with pages 426–427. ·····································

Write the quotient and any remainder. Check your answer.

1. 4)57
2. 5)86
3. 7)95
4. 6)24
5. 8)74
6. 2)76
7. 3)63
8. 5)87
9. 6)36
10. 7)92
11. 5)76
12. 2)67
13. 8)38
14. 2)77
15. 5)77
16. 83 ÷ 2
17. 44 ÷ 8
18. 66 ÷ 2
19. 57 ÷ 6
20. 70 ÷ 6
21. 45 ÷ 9
22. 48 ÷ 5
23. 90 ÷ 7
24. 81 ÷ 6
25. 60 ÷ 7
26. 66 ÷ 5
27. 50 ÷ 2

Use with pages 428–429. ·····································

Divide. Check your answer.

1. 2)108
2. 8)183
3. 9)862
4. 2)165
5. 4)365
6. 7)559
7. 6)525
8. 4)118
9. 9)436
10. 9)853
11. 2)149
12. 2)155
13. 5)333
14. 7)292
15. 6)381
16. 594 ÷ 6
17. 668 ÷ 9
18. 375 ÷ 5
19. 330 ÷ 4
20. 663 ÷ 7
21. 258 ÷ 6
22. 134 ÷ 8
23. 441 ÷ 9
24. 485 ÷ 9
25. 329 ÷ 6
26. 573 ÷ 8
27. 313 ÷ 5

Table of Measures

This table shows some common measures. If you need more information about a measure, look in the glossary or index.

Customary Measures

Length

1 foot (ft) = 12 inches (in.)
1 yard (yd) = 3 feet
1 yard = 36 inches
1 mile (mi) = 5280 feet

Liquid

1 pint (pt) = 2 cups (c)
1 quart (qt) = 2 pints
1 gallon (gal) = 4 quarts

Weight

1 pound (lb) = 16 ounces (oz)

Metric Measures

Length

1 meter (m) = 100 centimeters (cm)
1 decimeter (dm) = 10 centimeters
1 kilometer (km) = 1000 meters

Liquid

1 liter (L) = 1000 milliliters (mL)

Mass

1 kilogram (kg) = 1000 grams (g)

Time

Time

1 minute (min) = 60 seconds (s)
1 hour (h) = 60 minutes
1 day (d) = 24 hours
1 week (wk) = 7 days
1 year (yr) = 12 months (mo)
1 year = 52 weeks

addend A number that is added to another number. Example: 5 + 9 = 14

addend

addition properties

- grouping property No matter how addends are grouped, the sum is always the same. Example: Add the colored numbers first.
  5 + 1 + 3 = 9
  5 + 1 + 3 = 9

- order property Changing the order of addends does not change the sum. Example: 5 + 3 = 8
  3 + 5 = 8

- zero property If 0 is added to a number, the sum equals that number. Example: 4 + 0 = 4
  0 + 26 = 26

A.M. The hours from 12:00 midnight to 12:00 noon.

angle A corner that can be of different sizes.

area The number of square units needed to cover a figure.

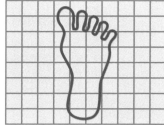

array A model of rows of cubes.

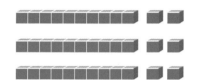

bar graph A graph that uses bars to show data.

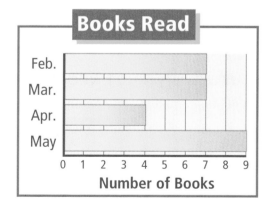

capacity The amount of liquid a container can hold.

center The middle of a circle.

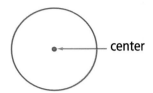

centimeter (cm) A metric unit of length. 100 centimeters equals 1 meter.

centimeter ruler A ruler marked in centimeters.

centimeter

cone A solid that has a circular base and comes to a point.

congruent figures Figures that are the same size and shape.

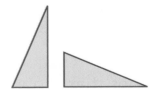

cube A solid having six square faces the same size.

cup (c) A customary unit of capacity. 2 cups equal 1 pint.

customary system The measurement system that uses foot, quart, pound, and degree Fahrenheit.

cylinder A solid having circles of equal size at each end.

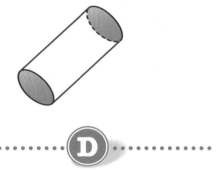

•••••••••••**D**•••••••••••

data Information, facts.

day A unit of time. 1 day equals 24 hours.
Example: Tuesday is the third day of the week.

decimal A number with one or more digits to the right of a decimal point.
Example: 0.9 and 1.08 are decimals.

decimal point A symbol used to separate dollars and cents in money amounts. A symbol used to separate ones and tenths in decimals.
Example: $1.50 1.3

decimal point

decimeter (dm) A metric unit of length. 1 decimeter equals 10 centimeters.

degree A unit for measuring temperature.

degree Celsius (°C) The metric unit for measuring temperature.

degree Fahrenheit (°F) The customary unit for measuring temperature.

denominator The number written below the bar in a fraction.
Example:

$\frac{1}{4}$ ◀ denominator

diameter A line that passes through the center of a circle.

difference The answer in a subtraction problem.
Example: $7 - 3 = 4$

difference

digit Any of the symbols 0, 1, 2, 3, 4, 5, 6, 7, 8, or 9 used to write numbers.

dividend The number that is divided in a division problem.
Example: $12 \div 4 = 3$

dividend

divisor The number to divide by in a division problem.
Example: $36 \div 9 = 4$

divisor

dollar sign A symbol written to show dollars in money amounts.
Example: $1.50

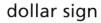

dollar sign

E

edge Where two faces of a solid meet.

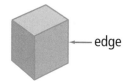

edge

endpoint The point at an end of a line segment.
Example:

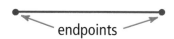

endpoints

equivalent fractions Fractions that show the same amount.
Example:

$\frac{6}{8}$

$\frac{3}{4}$

estimate A number close to an exact amount. An estimate tells *about* how much.

even number A whole number ending in 0, 2, 4, 6, or 8.
Example: 12   56   704

expanded form A way to write a number to show the value of each digit.
Example: The way to expand 3962 is
3000 + 900 + 60 + 2.

face A flat surface of a solid.

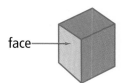

fact family A group of facts that are related.
Example:

5 + 4 = 9	6 × 3 = 18
4 + 5 = 9	3 × 6 = 18
9 − 4 = 5	18 ÷ 6 = 3
9 − 5 = 4	18 ÷ 3 = 6

factor A number that is multiplied in a multiplication problem.
Example: 2 × 9 = 18

factor

flip A move that makes a figure face in the opposite direction.

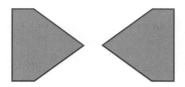

foot (ft) A customary unit of length. 1 foot equals 12 inches.

fraction A number that names a part of a whole or a part of a set.

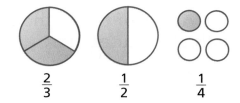

$\frac{2}{3}$ $\frac{1}{2}$ $\frac{1}{4}$

front-end estimation Using the digits with the greatest place value to find *about* how much.
Example:

230	200
+ 325	+ 300
	500

gallon (gal) A customary unit of capacity. 1 gallon equals 4 quarts.

gram (g) A metric unit of mass, or heaviness. 1 gram equals 1000 milligrams.

graph A picture that shows information by using bars, lines, or symbols.

half turn A turn that causes a figure to point in a different direction.

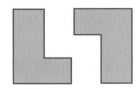

The second figure is a half-turn image of the first.

hour A unit of time. 1 hour equals 60 minutes.

inch (in.) A customary unit of length. 12 inches equal 1 foot.

inch ruler A ruler marked in inches.

key Tells what each picture stands for in a pictograph. Example:

Key: = 6 butterflies

kilogram (kg) A metric unit of mass, or heaviness. 1 kilogram equals 1000 grams.

kilometer (km) A metric unit of length. 1 kilometer equals 1000 meters.

line A straight path that goes on forever in two directions.

line graph A graph that uses line segments to show changes over time.

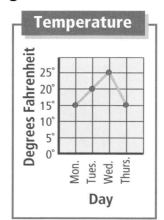

line of symmetry A line along which you could fold a figure so that both halves match.

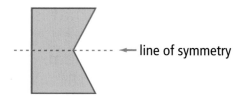

line segment Part of a line having two endpoints.

liter (L) The metric unit of capacity. 1 liter equals 1000 milliliters.

mass The heaviness of an object. Often measured with grams or kilograms.

meter (m) A metric unit of length. 1 meter equals 100 centimeters.

metric system The measurement system that uses units such as meter, liter, gram, and degree Celsius.

mile (mi) A customary unit of length. 1 mile equals 5280 feet.

milliliter (mL) A metric unit of capacity. 1000 milliliters equal 1 liter.

minute A unit of time. 1 minute equals 60 seconds.

missing addend An addend that is missing in an addition sentence.
Example: 5 + ■ = 9

missing addend

missing factor A factor that is missing in a multiplication sentence.

Example: 5 × ■ = 45

missing factor

mixed numbers Numbers that have a whole number and a fraction part.
Example: $3\frac{1}{2}$

multiplication properties

- **order property** Changing the order of factors does not change the product.
  Example: 6 × 4 = 24
  4 × 6 = 24

- **property of one** If 1 is a factor, the product always equals the other factor.
  Example: 6 × 1 = 6
  1 × 51 = 51

- **zero property** If 0 is a factor, the product is always 0.
  Example: 8 × 0 = 0
  0 × 17 = 0

number line A line showing numbers equally spaced and in counting order.

0 1 2 3 4 5 6 7 8 9 10

numerator The number written above the bar in a fraction.
Example:  numerator

· · · · · · · · · · · **O** · · · · · · · · · ·

odd number A whole number ending in 1, 3, 5, 7, or 9.
Example: 13　67　429

ordered pair The numbers used to name a point on a grid.

ounce (oz) A customary measure of weight. 16 ounces equal 1 pound.

· · · · · · · · · · · **P** · · · · · · · · · ·

parallel lines Lines that are always the same distance apart.

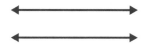

perimeter The distance around a figure. The perimeter of the rectangle below is 12 cm.

pictograph A graph that shows data with pictures.

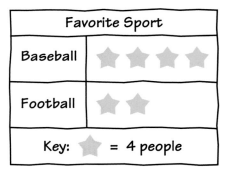

pint (pt) A customary unit of capacity. 2 pints equal 1 quart.

place value The value of each place in a number.
Example: In 7943, the digit 7 is in the thousands place.

Thousands	Hundreds	Tens	Ones
7	9	4	3

P.M. The hours from 12:00 noon to 12:00 midnight.

point An exact place or position, marked by a dot.

pound (lb) A customary unit of weight. 1 pound equals 16 ounces.

prediction What someone thinks may happen.

prism A solid having 2 bases of equal size and shape at each end. The faces are all rectangles or a related shape.

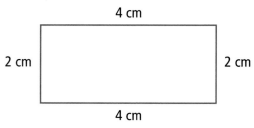

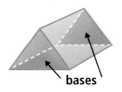

probability The chance that an event will happen.

product The answer in a multiplication problem. Example: $5 \times 3 = 15$

product

property A rule for addition, multiplication, or another operation.

pyramid A solid having 1 base that varies in shape. The faces are triangles and meet at a point.

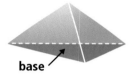

base

quart (qt) A customary unit of capacity. 4 quarts equal 1 gallon.

quarter Another name for a fourth, 25¢, or $\frac{1}{4}$.

quotient The answer in a division problem. Example: $54 \div 9 = 6$

quotient

rectangle A figure having 4 sides and 4 square corners. A square is a kind of rectangle.

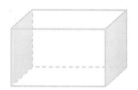

rectangular prism A prism with 2 rectangular bases and 4 rectangular faces.

remainder The number leftover when one number does not exactly divide another.
Example:

$$9\overline{)38} \quad 4\ R2$$

2 is the remainder

right angle A square corner.

round To find the ten or the hundred nearest to an exact number.
Example: 436 rounded to the nearest hundred is 400.

second A unit of time. 60 seconds equal 1 minute.

side A line forming part of a figure.

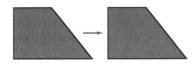
side

slide A move of a figure along a line.

The second figure is a slide image of the first.

sphere A solid having the shape of a ball.

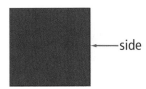

square A figure with 4 square corners and 4 equal sides.

square corner A right angle.

square pyramid A pyramid with a square base.

standard form The usual way of writing a number, using digits.
Example: The standard form of twenty-seven is 27.

sum The answer in an addition problem.
Example: $5 + 4 = 9$

sum

survey A way to collect data by asking people questions.

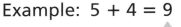

table A chart showing data.

Favorite Ways to Travel		
Students	Planes	Trains
Boys	12	15
Girls	8	20

tally A count made using tally marks.
Example:

The tally is 10.

temperature The measurement of how warm or cold something is.

tenth One of ten equal parts of a whole.

thermometer An instrument that measures temperature.

ton (t) A customary unit of weight. 1 ton equals 2000 pounds.

triangle A figure with three sides and three corners.

triangular prism A prism with 2 triangular bases and 3 rectangular faces.

triangular pyramid A pyramid with a triangular base.

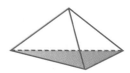

value The amount that a digit stands for in a number. Example: In 324, the 2 stands for 2 tens. Its value is 20.

Hundreds	Tens	Ones
3	2	4

yard (yd) A customary unit of length. 1 yard equals 3 feet.

yardstick A ruler, marked in inches and feet, that is 1 yard long.

Index

meaning of, 158–159
missing factor, 192–193
money, 400–401
patterns of, 214–215
product, 160–161
regrouping
    with, 388–389
    without, 394–395
related to addition, 158–159,
    180–181
related to division, 172–173,
    174–175, 176–177,
    192–193, 200–201,
    208–209, 210–211
tables (grid), 196–197
three factors, 388–389
whole numbers, 158–189,
    160–161, 172–173,
    174–175, 176–177,
    180–181, 192–193,
    200–201, 202–203,
    208–209, 210–211,
    214–215, 261
    1-digit multipliers, 380–381,
      386–387, 388–389,
      394–395, 398–399, 426
    2-digit multipliers, 388–389
    3-digit multipliers, 394–395

Number cubes, 30–31, 43–44,
    86–87, 100–101, 146–147
Number line
count back, 20–21
count on, 4–5
count up, 20–21
decimals, 356–357, 364–365
halfway points, 58–59
using, 4–5, 58–59, 356–357
whole numbers, 4–5, 58–59
Number sense, 5, 19, 25, 45,
    51, 65, 95, 96, 101, 109,
    143, 159, 161, 209, 285,
    305, 351, 355, 371, 389
Numeration and Number
    Theory
African number words and
    hand signals, 15, 55
ancient numerals, 14, 171, 362
even numbers, 109, 161
factor, 160–161
ordinal numbers, 4
Roman numerals, 316–317

square number arrays,
    158–159, 172–173

Ordered pairs, 254–255
Ordering
decimals, 358–359
fractions, 276–277
whole numbers, 4–5, 60–61

Parallel lines, 252–253
Pattern blocks, 272–273
Patterns
finding, 62–63, 64–65, 73, 103,
    144–145
geometric, 138, 234–235, 259
numerical, 57, 103, 214–215,
    216–217, 237, 335, 353,
    355
predicting from, 40–41,
    142–143, 239, 305,
    328–329, 333, 413, 415
Perimeter, 94–95, 308–309
Pictograph, 130–131, 290
Place value
chart, 46–47, 50–51
decimals, 352–353, 359,
    366–367
expanded form, 46–47, 50–51
model, 46–47, 50–51
standard form, 46–47, 50–51
whole numbers, 46–47, 50–51
word form, 50–51
Place-value blocks, 43–44,
    46–47, 50–51, 56, 61, 86–87,
    88–89, 100–101, 102–103,
    214–215, 216–217, 380–381,
    386–387, 388–389, 416–417
Predicting outcomes, 146–147
Prism, 248–249
Probability
comparing
    results of experiments,
      142–143, 144–145
    results of predictions,
      142–143, 144–145,
      146–147

experiments, 142–143,
    144–145
predictions, 146–147
recording results, 144–145
Problem formulation (Create
    Your Own), 3, 31, 33, 49,
    57, 69, 71, 89, 115, 129,
    133, 135, 137, 138, 143,
    145, 167, 197, 204, 211,
    229, 233, 241, 253, 255,
    257, 261, 275, 280, 287,
    321, 387, 390, 397, 413,
    425, 427
Problem solving process, 6,
    48, 106, 126, 162, 198, 234,
    288, 322, 354, 384
Problem solving strategies
decisions
    does answer fit the
      problem, 327
    finding needed
      information, 244, 360
    logical reasoning, 52, 61,
      75, 101, 138, 203, 243,
      168
    not enough information,
      12, 390
    using data, 17, 70–71, 105,
      111, 143, 167, 201,
      250, 280, 315, 420
    using math sense, 76, 96,
      204
strategies
    Act It Out, 6–7, 24–25
    Draw a Picture, 65,
      126–127, 128–129,
      288–289, 292–293
    Guess and Check, 106–107,
      112–113, 115,
      198–199, 212–213
    Look for a Pattern, 48–49,
      62–63, 138, 234–235,
      256–257
    Make a List, 162–163,
      354–355, 368–369
    Make a Table, 162–163,
      178–179
    Work a Simpler Problem,
      384–385, 396–397
    Work Backward, 322–323,
      336–337
    using, 32–33, 114–115,
      148–149, 182–183,
      218–219, 262–263,
      294–295, 338–339,

Acknowledgments

For each of the selections listed below, grateful acknowledgment is made for permission to reprint copyrighted material as follows:

Cover of *Appalachian Mountain Club* magazine, March 1996 issue. Courtesy of AMC Outdoors, the magazine of the Appalachian Mountain Club.

Cover of *Children's Digest* magazine, December 1993 issue. Reprinted by permission of Children's Better Health Institute.

Cover of *Cobblestone* magazine, January 1996 issue: *A Historical Look at Washington, D.C.,* ©1996, published by Cobblestone Publishing Company, 7 School St., Peterborough, NH 03458.

Cover of *Cricket* magazine. Reprinted by permission of *Cricket* magazine, January 1996. Vol. 23, #5, ©1996 by Friso Henstra.

Cover of *Junior League Baseball* magazine, March 1997 issue. Reprinted by permission of 2D Publishing.

Cover of *Kids Discover: Flight* magazine, November 1991 issue. Reprinted by permission of Kids Discover.

Cover of *Kids Discover: Vikings* magazine, 1996 issue. Reprinted by permission of Kids Discover.

Cover of *National Geographic* magazine, October 1996 issue. Reprinted by permission of National Geographic Society.

Cover of *Newsweek* magazine, May 29, 1995 issue. ©1995, Newsweek, Inc. All rights reserved. Reprinted by permission.

Cover of *Ranger Rick* magazine. Reprinted from the July 1996 issue of *Ranger Rick* magazine, with the permission of the publisher, National Wildlife Federation. Copyright 1996 by NWF.

Cover of *Weatherwise* magazine, June/July 1996 issue. Reprinted by permission of Weatherwise.

Cover of *Zillions* magazine. Copyright 1996 by Consumers Union of U.S., Inc., Yonkers, NY 10703-1057. Referenced by permission from *Zillions*, September/October 1996.

Decimal Squares, Fraction Bars, and *Tower of Bars* were created by Professor Albert C. Bennett, Jr. and are registered trademarks of Scott Resources. They are used by permission of Scott Resources. All rights reserved.

Photo Credits

Cover: Scuba Diver © Stuart Westmorland/Tony Stone Images; iii: Steve Grubman(l); vii: Phil Schermeister/Corbis (t); ©1996 PhotoDisc, Inc. (b); xi: Stephen Frisch/Stock Boston/PNI (l); Alon Reininger/Contact Press/PNI (r); 4–5: Alex Priest/Panoramic Images; 4: Galen Rowell/Corbis; 6: Colter Bay Indian Arts Musuem, Grand Tetons National Park, Wyoming, David T. Vernon Collection; 10: ©1996 PhotoDisc,Inc. (l,m); Steve Grubman (r); 11: ©1996 PhotoDisc, Inc.; 14: Bodleian Library, Oxford University (t); Mary Van de Ven/Pacific Stock (b); 16: Steve Grubman; 17: Norbert Wu/Tony Stone Images (l); Art Wolfe/Tony Stone Images (lm); Carl Roessler/Tony Stone Images (rm); Hal Beral/Photo Network/PNI (r); 18: Tony Freeman/PhotoEdit; 24: William R. Sallaz/Duomo; 32: Johnny Johnson/Animals Animals; ©1996 PhotoDisc, Inc. (inset); 33: Pat and Tom Leeson/Photo Researchers (t); Wolfgang Bayer/Bruce Coleman, Inc./PNI (b); 48: Rosanne Olson/Allstock/PNI; 50–51: Gordon Joffrion/Stock South/PNI; 50: Michael Newman/PhotoEdit; 54: Corbis/Bettmann; 60: ©1996 PhotoDisc,Inc.; David Young Wolf/PhotoEdit (t); 62: Richard Nowitz/PhotoTake/PNI; 64–65: Mark Wyatt/Inside Track; 64: Gail Mooney/Corbis; 66: David Young Wolf/PhotoEdit; 67: ©1996 PhotoDisc, Inc.; 68: J.D. Schwalm/Stock South/PNI; 70: John White/Blackstar (bkgd); Craig Laughlin Collection; 75: Michael Matson/Allstock/PNI (l); Michael Newman/PhotoEdit/PNI (m); Lawrence Migdale/Stock Boston/PNI (r); 76: Phil Schermeister/Corbis; 90–91: Library of Congress/Corbis; 90: Corbis/Bettmann; 98: C M Dixon (t); Scala/Art Resource (l); Science and Society Picture Library (m,r); 99: Science and Society Picture Library (l); 102–03: Chris Harvey/Tony Stone Images; 102: Manoj Shah/Tony Stone Images (t); Chris Harvey/Tony Stone Images (b); 104–05: NASA; 106: ©1996 PhotoDisc, Inc.(t); Lee Foster/Words & Pictures/PNI (b); 112: Bob Daemmrich/Tony Stone Images; 114: Stuart Westmoreland/Tony Stone Images; 115: Art Wolfe/Tony Stone Images; 125: Nik Wheeler/Corbis ; 128: Tom Bean/Corbis (bkgd); Colter Bay Indian Arts Musuem, Grand Tetons National Park, Wyoming, David T. Vernon Collection; 129: Colter Bay Indian Arts Musuem, Grand Tetons National Park, Wyoming, David T. Vernon Collection; 130–31: Alon Reininger/Contact Press/PNI; 134–35: Tim Ribar/Stock South/PNI; 134: ©1996 PhotoDisc, Inc.; 135: ©1996 PhotoDisc, Inc.; 136–37: Mark Segal/Panoramic Images; 136: David Stover/Stock South/PNI; 138: Jose Azel/Aurora/PNI; 140: Brown Brothers (l); Owen Franken/Stock Boston (r); 148: Telegraph Colour Library/FPG; 149: ©1996 PhotoDisc, Inc.; 160: Stephen Frisch/Stock Boston/PNI; 162–63: Merlin D. Tuttle/BCI; 162: Merlin D. Tuttle/BCI; 166: Casey B. Gibson; 168: ©1996 PhotoDisc, Inc.; 170: Corbis/Bettmann; 172: Greg Ryan/Allstock/PNI; 174: Darwin Wiggett/Westlight; 176: George Disario/The Stock Market; 178: Richard Pasley/Stock Boston/PNI; 182: Lester Sloan/Gamma Liaison; 200–01: A. Keuning/Panoramic Images; 202: Stanley M. Jay, Mandolin Bros., Inc.; 204: Jason Laure; 206: C M Dixon (l); 208–09: Kit Kittle/Corbis; 208: Kevin and Cat Sweeney/Tony Stone Images; 210–11: Paul Souders/Tony Stone Images; 210: Ned Gillette/Stock Market; 212: Mug Shots/The Stock Market; 217: ©1996 PhotoDisc, Inc.; 218: John Dunn; 219: John Dunn; 228: Joel Rogers/Corbis; 236: Peter Timmermans/Allstock/PNI; 247: Bowl with repeated feather motif, Courtesy of the Michael C. Carlos Museum, Emory University, Acc. No. 1994.6.2; Owen Franken/Stock Boston/PNI (b); 254–55: Richard Nowitz/Phototake/PNI; 256: Lawrence Migdale; 260–61: David Muench/Corbis; 260: John Boykin; 262: ©1996 PhotoDisc, Inc. (bkgd); National Archives; 263: National Archives; 274–75: Adam Woolfitt/Corbis; 274: Kevin R. Morris/Corbis; 280: Gwyn M. Kibbe/Stock Boston; 284: Kevin Schafer/Allstock/PNI (t); ©1996 PhotoDisc, Inc. (l); 285: ©1996 PhotoDisc, Inc.; 286: Ellsworth Kelly. Blue, Green, Yellow, Orange, Red. 1966, Acrylic on canvas, each of five panels 5 x 4'. Solomon R. Guggenheim Museum, New York.; 290: Triolo Burke/Foodpix/PNI; 292: Miro Vintoniv/Stock Boston/PNI; 293: Chris Brown/Stock Boston/PNI; 294: Randa Bishop/Uniphoto; 316: Arthur Beck/The Stock Market (t); Dallas & John Heaton/Westlight; 320: Woodward Payne/Photo 20–20/PNI; 327: Jim Pickerell/Westlight (t); © 1996 PhotoDisc, Inc. (b); 332: Greg L. Ryan/Allstock/PNI; 334–35: Bob Daemmrich/Stock Boston/PNI; 336: Tom McCarthy/PhotoEdit; 337: Tom McCarthy/PhotoEdit; 338: Brian Bahr/Allsport; 352–53: Dennis Kunkel/CNRI/Phototake/PNI; 352: Scott Camazine/Photo Researchers; 356: Kathi Lamm/Allstock/PNI (r); ©1996 PhotoDisc, Inc. (l); 357: ©1996 PhotoDisc, Inc.; 358: Peter Harholdt/Corbis (l); Buddy Mays/Corbis (r); 359: Roman Soumar/Corbis; 360: Courtesy of Pima Air & Space Museum, Tucson, Arizona (t,b); Roger/Tidman (m); 366–67: Charles Krebs/Tony Stone Images/PNI; 366: Gay Bumgarner/Allstock/PNI; 368: S.D. Butcher Collection, Nebraska State Historical Society, neg#B983–1231; 369: Archive Photos/American Stock Photography/PNI; 370: Scott Halleran/Allsport; 382: Frank Siteman/PhotoEdit; 384: Photograph by Thomas A Heinz, © Copyright Thomas A. Heinz; 386: ©1996 PhotoDisc, Inc.; 387: ©1996 PhotoDisc, Inc.; 390: Fredrik D. Bodin/Stock Boston/PNI (t); Johnny Johnson/Allstock/PNI (b); 393: C M Dixon; 394–95 Art Wolfe/Tony Stone Images; 394: Kevin Schafer/Tony Stone Images; 396: Bob Daemmrich/Stock Boston/PNI; 398–99: Paul Harris/Allstock/PNI; 398: e.t. archive/Bibliotheque National, Paris; 402: Howard Bluestein/Photo Researchers; 403: Jeffry Myers/Stock Boston; 419–20: K. Penovac/Sovfoto/Eastfoto/PNI; 422–23: Superstock (b); 422: Larry Sherer/High Impact Photography (l); 428–29: Andrea Booher/Tony Stone Images; 430: Paul Souders/Tony Stone Images/PNI

Assignment Photo Credits

170 (l) Karen AHola; pg. 238 (t), 246 (l), 268, 312, 328, 362, 376,392, 436, 437, 412 Petrisse Briel; pg. 304 (t), 424, 425, Dave Desroches; pg.308, 268 Fayfoto; pg. 1 (b), 2-3, 15, 22, 29, 38, 39 (t), 41 (b), 55, 82, 85 (b), 98 (mr), 99 (m), 120, 121, 122, 122, 154, 155, 224 Allan Landau; pg 2, 22, 100, 124, 126 (t) 230, 244 (t),256, 320 (t), 320 (m), 322, 324, 326, 328 (b), 354, 364, 380 Parker / Boon Productions; pg. 83 (b), 122 (tl, ml),123 (bl), 140 (b),141, 156 (tl, ml),157 (bl), 171 (l), 189, 190 (tl), 191 (bl) 206 (bl), 207, 224 (t), 225, 227 (bl), 238 (ml), 246 (br), 247 (tl), 254 (b, m), 269, 270 (tl, ml), 271 (bl), 282 (l), 300, 303 (bl), 361 (bl), 393(bl), 425(bl), 450, Tony Scarpetta; pg.83(t), 224, 283, 316(l), 317, 376, 377 Tracey Wheeler